Lecture Notes in Computer Science 10155

Commenced Publication in 1973
Founding and Former Series Editors:
Gerhard Goos, Juris Hartmanis, and Jan van Leeuwen

More information about this series at http://www.springer.com/series/7410

Gerhard P. Hancke
Konstantinos Markantonakis (Eds.)

Radio Frequency Identification and IoT Security

12th International Workshop, RFIDSec 2016
Hong Kong, China, November 30 – December 2, 2016
Revised Selected Papers

Springer

Editors
Gerhard P. Hancke
City University of Hong Kong
Hong Kong
China

Konstantinos Markantonakis
University of London
Egham
UK

ISSN 0302-9743   ISSN 1611-3349 (electronic)
Lecture Notes in Computer Science
ISBN 978-3-319-62023-7   ISBN 978-3-319-62024-4   (eBook)
DOI 10.1007/978-3-319-62024-4

Library of Congress Control Number: 2017944356

LNCS Sublibrary: SL4 – Security and Cryptology

Printed on acid-free paper

This Springer imprint is published by Springer Nature
The registered company is Springer International Publishing AG
The registered company address is: Gewerbestrasse 11, 6330 Cham, Switzerland

Preface

Welcome to the proceedings of the 12th edition of RFIDSec. Since 2005, RFIDsec has become the premier venue devoted to security and privacy of radiofrequency identification (RFID). This year RFIDsec broadened its scope to security and privacy in all application areas related to any constrained devices, with the event being renamed the Workshop on RFID and IoT Security (previously Workshop on RFID Security and Privacy). This reflects the fact that the nature of radio-enabled item identification and automatic data capture has significantly changed over the years, driven by the interest in overarching applications such as the Internet of Things and cyber-physical systems. This year also marked the first occasion of RFIDSec being held outside of Europe and the USA. We were excited to host RFIDSec in Asia's World City.

RFIDsec 2016 assembled five technical sessions with exciting results in RFID and IoT security. Eleven regular papers and three short paper were selected after a rigorous review process of 30 submissions. The review procedure included a review phase, with each paper receiving at least three reviews, followed by discussion between the Program Committee members and the program chairs. The program also included three invited talks and one tutorial. In the first invited talk "Secure Proximity Verification and Localization: Challenges and Solutions." Aanjhan Ranganathan of ETH Zurich spoke about attacks on proximity and location systems, and presented some work on countermeasures for GPS spoofing attacks. In the second invited talk "IT+OT=IoT? On Security for Industrial Control Systems," Nils Tippenhauer of the Singapore University of Technology and Design talked about industrial IoT and presented practical examples of security issues within deployed industrial control systems. In the third talk, the audience were given a industry perspective on IoT security by Duncan Wong of the Hong Kong Applied Science and Technology Research Institute (ASTRI). Finally, David Cox of the University of Birmingham presented a tutorial on the Chameleon, an RFID emulater and reader platform developed by Kasper & Oswald GmbH.

We thank all authors and participants who contributed to make this event a great success, the Technical Program Committee members and additional reviewers who worked on the program, and the volunteers who did much organization behind the scenes. We greatly appreciate the input of the RFIDSec Steering Committee, whose help and advice was invaluable, and we would like to thank the Department of Computer Science at City University of Hong Kong for supporting for this event and providing assistance with general arrangements.

December 2016

Gerhard P. Hancke
Konstantinos Markantonakis

Organization

General Chair

Gerhard Hancke — City University of Hong Kong, Hong Kong, SAR China

Program Chairs

Gerhard Hancke — City University of Hong Kong, Hong Kong, SAR China
Konstantinos Markantonakis — Royal Holloway University of London, UK

Local Organizers

Yunhui Zhuang — City University of Hong Kong, Hong Kong, SAR China
Anjia Yang — Jinan University, PR China·

Steering Committee

Lejla Batina — RU Nijmegen, The Netherlands
Srdjan Capkun — ETH Zurich, Switzerland
Yingjiu Li — Singapore Management University, Singapore
Andrew Martin — University of Oxford, UK
Ivan Martinovic — University of Oxford, UK
Christof Paar — Ruhr University Bochum, Germany
Bart Preneel — KU Leuven, Belgium
Ahmad-Reza Sadeghi — Technische Universität Darmstadt, Germany
Nitesh Saxena — University of Alabama at Birmingham, USA
Patrick Schaumont — Virginia Tech, USA

Program Committee

Raja Naeem Akram — Royal Holloway University of London,UK
Frederik Armknecht — Universität Mannheim, Germany
Gildas Avoine — INSA Rennes France and UCL, Belgium
Lejla Batina — Radboud University Nijmegen, The Netherlands
Mike Burmester — Florida State University, USA
Rajat Subhra Chakraborty — IIT Kharagpur, India
Sherman Chow — Chinese University of Hong Kong, Hong Kong, SAR China
Thomas Eisenbarth — WPI, Austria
Martin Feldhofer — NXP Semiconductors, Austria

Contents

Proximity

Communication

Protocols

Security Analysis of Niu *et al.* Authentication and Ownership Management Protocol

Masoumeh Safkhani[1], Hoda Jannati[2], and Nasour Bagheri[2,3(✉)]

[1] Computer Engineering Department,
Shahid Rajaee Teacher Training University, Tehran, Iran
Safkhani@srttu.edu
[2] School of Computer Science,
Institute for Research in Fundamental Sciences (IPM), Tehran, Iran
hodajannati@ipm.ir
[3] Electrical Engineering Department,
Shahid Rajaee Teacher Training University, Tehran, Iran
Nbagheri@srttu.edu

Abstract. Over the past decade, besides authentication, ownership management protocols have been suggested to transfer or delegate the ownership of RFID tagged items. Recently, Niu *et al.* have proposed an authentication and ownership management protocol based on 16-bit pseudo random number generators and exclusive-or operations which both can be easily implemented on low-cost RFID passive tags in EPC global Class-1 Generation-2 standard. They claim that their protocol offers location and data privacy and also resists against desynchronization attack. In this paper, we analyze the security of their proposed authentication and ownership management protocol and show that the protocol is vulnerable to secret disclosure and desynchronization attacks. The complexity of most of the attacks is only two runs of the protocol and the success probability of the attacks is almost 1. We also proposed an improved version of the protocol which is secure against the attacks presented in this paper.

Keywords: RFID · Ownership transfer · Secret disclosure attack · Desynchronization attack

1 Introduction

Radio Frequency IDentifiction (RFID) is a wireless identification technology which contains tags, readers and servers and works using radio waves. Tag is a microchip which connects to the objects and the reader can read or modify the information of tags. Complex operations can be done in the servers and also more information about tags and readers are stored in them [14].

Electronic Product Code Class-1 Generation-2 (or in brief EPC-C1G2) [8] is one of the important standards related to passive tags which supports only

© Springer International Publishing AG 2017
G.P. Hancke and K. Markantonakis (Eds.): RFIDSec 2016, LNCS 10155, pp. 3–16, 2017.
DOI: 10.1007/978-3-319-62024-4_1

Cyclic Redundancy Check (CRC) functions, Pseudo Random Number Generator (PRNG) functions and lightweight operations such as AND, OR, XOR and etc. Due to the widespread use of passive tags, many EPC-C1G2 complaint protocols such as authentication [15], ownership transfer [11], tag search [20], distance bounding protocols [12], grouping proof [17] and etc. have been designed. There also are many reports on vulnerabilities of these protocols against different attacks [3,4,13]. All of these efforts show that designing a secure protocol in the framework of EPC-C1G2 is not a straight forward task and we still need secure protocols in this area. Recently, in response to this need, in [16], Niu *et al.* presented a mutual authentication and ownership management protocol including ownership transfer and ownership delegation in order to provide location and data privacy in EPC-C1G2 passive tags. Their protocol relies only on pseudo random number generators and exclusive-or operations for execution. Both operations are easily implemented on low-cost RFID passive tags that comply with EPC-C1G2 standard. Niu *et al.* claim that their protocol provides location privacy, backward privacy, forward privacy and also suitable security against replay attack, desynchronization attack and windowing.

In this paper, we analyze the security of the authentication and ownership management protocol proposed by Niu *et al.* and show that unfortunately their security claims do not hold. In particular, their protocol is vulnerable against secret disclosure and desynchronization attacks. In fact, this paper shows that this need is still unmet.

The rest of this paper is arranged as follows: In Sect. 2, we review authentication and ownership management protocol proposed by Niu *et al.* Secret disclosure and desynchronization attacks against the protocol are presented in Sects. 3 and 4 respectively and finally Sect. 7 concludes the paper.

2 Review of Niu *et al.* Authentication and Ownership Management Protocol

There are four types of players in the protocol proposed by Niu *et al.* [16]: (1) A trusted third party TTP, (2) An RFID tag T, (3) An old owner (reader R_{ID1}) and (4) A new owner (reader R_{ID2}). It must be noted that Niu *et al.* have assumed all the protocol parameters are 96 bits to preserve compatibility to EPC standard and all 96-bit parameters are broken into six 16-bit words because of convenience of the protocol implementation [16]. To prevent desynchronization attack, they also have assumed that the reader and the tag both should maintain their old and current pseudonyms and keys.

In the following, we begin with an overview of the system notations, then their protocol is described in three phases. EPC is the unique and static electronic product code of the tag T and IDS is the pseudonym of the tag T. R_{ID_i} denotes the identifier of ith reader. K is a secret key which is shared between the tag T and its owner, K_M is a master key which is shared between the tag T and its owner (the owner of the tag T with K_M is able to modify the key K) and K_{TTP} is a secret key which is shared between the tag

T and TTP. $W(i)$ denotes i^{th} 16-bit of W and $PRNG(.)$ denotes a 16-bit pseudo random number generator. $Per(X, Y)$ also denotes the permutation of $X = x_1 x_2 \ldots x_n$ according to $Y = y_1 y_2 \ldots y_n$ $(x_i, y_i \in \{0, 1\},$ for $0 \leq i \leq n)$ as $Per(X, Y) = x_{k_1} x_{k_2} \ldots x_{k_m} x_{k_n} x_{k_{n-1}} \ldots x_{k_{m+2}} x_{k_{m+1}}$ where m $(0 \leq m \leq n)$ is the hamming weight of Y, so that $y_{k_1} = y_{k_2} = \ldots = y_{k_m} = 1$ and $y_{k_{m+1}} = y_{k_{m+2}} = \ldots = y_{k_m} = 0$ for $1 \leq k_1 < k_2 < \ldots < k_m \leq n$ and $1 \leq k_{m+1} < k_{m+2} < \ldots < k_n \leq n$.

Mutual Authentication Phase

In the mutual authentication phase of Niu *et al.* protocol the reader R_{ID1} (the old owner of the tag T) authenticates the tag T before the reader R_{ID1} delegates the ownership of the tag T to the reader R_{ID2}. This phase of the protocol is described below:

1. To start this phase of the protocol, the reader R_{ID1} (the old owner of the tag T) generates two random numbers rnd_1 and rnd_2. Then, it computes $A(i) = rnd_1(i) \oplus PRNG(K(i) \oplus R_{ID1}(i)) \oplus PRNG(K(i) \oplus R_{ID2}(i))$, $B(i) = rnd_2(i) \oplus PRNG(rnd_1(i) \oplus K(i))$ and $C(i) = PRNG(rnd_1(i) \oplus R_{ID1}(i)) \oplus PRNG(rnd_2(i) \oplus R_{ID2}(i))$ for $i = 1, \ldots, 6$.
2. The reader R_{ID1} sends A, B and C to the tag T.
3. After receiving the messages A, B and C from the reader R_{ID1}, the tag T computes $rnd_1(i) = A(i) \oplus PRNG(K(i) \oplus R_{ID1}(i)) \oplus PRNG(K(i) \oplus R_{ID2}(i))$, $rnd_2(i) = B(i) \oplus PRNG(rnd_1(i) \oplus K(i))$ and $C'(i) = PRNG(rnd_1(i) \oplus R_{ID1}(i)) \oplus PRNG(rnd_2(i) \oplus R_{ID2}(i))$ for $i = 1, \ldots, 6$. Then, the tag T verifies whether $C' \overset{?}{=} C$ is or not. In the case of equality, the tag T authenticates the reader R_{ID1}, updates $K(i)$ and $IDS(i)$ as $K^*(i) = Per(rnd_1(i), K(i)) \oplus K((i+1) \bmod 6)$ and $IDS^*(i) = Per(rnd_2(i), K(i)) \oplus K(i)$ respectively, and computes $D(i) = PRNG(K^*(i) \oplus IDS^*(i))$ for $i = 1, \ldots, 6$.
4. The tag T sends D to the reader R_{ID1}.
5. After receiving the message D from the tag T, the reader R_{ID1} computes $K^*(i) = Per(rnd_1(i), K(i)) \oplus K((i+1) \bmod 6)$, $IDS^*(i) = Per(rnd_2(i), K(i)) \oplus K(i)$ and $D'(i) = PRNG(K^*(i) \oplus IDS^*(i))$ for $i = 1, \ldots, 6$. Then, it verifies whether $D' \overset{?}{=} D$ is or not. In the case of equality, it authorizes the tag T and updates K and IDS as K^* and IDS^* respectively.

Ownership Delegation Phase

In ownership delegation phase of the protocol, the reader R_{ID1} (which is the old owner of the tag T) wants to delegate all its rights over the tag T to the reader R_{ID2} by using the parameter called *ticket*. The old owner R_{ID1} and the tag T both compute $ticket = K_M \oplus EPC \oplus rnd_1 \oplus rnd_2$. Then, the reader R_{ID1} sends *ticket*, EPC, IDS and K through a secure channel to the reader R_{ID2} (the new owner R_{ID2} of the tag T). Ownership delegation steps are as follows:

1. The reader R_{ID2} sends its identification R_{ID2} and a *Query* command to the tag T.
2. The tag T sends its IDS to the reader R_{ID2}.

3. The reader R_{ID2} generates one random number rnd_3, computes $E(i) = rnd_3(i) \oplus PRNG(K(i) \oplus R_{ID2}(i)) \oplus PRNG(K(i))$ and $F(i) = PRNG(ticket(i) \oplus rnd_3(i))$ for $i = 1, \ldots, 6$.
4. The reader R_{ID2} sends E and F to the tag T.
5. After receiving the messages E and F from the reader R_{ID2}, the tag T computes $rnd_3(i) = E(i) \oplus PRNG(K(i) \oplus R_{ID2}(i)) \oplus PRNG(K(i))$ and $F'(i) = PRNG(ticket(i) \oplus rnd_3(i))$ for $i = 1, \ldots, 6$. Then, the tag T verifies whether $F' \overset{?}{=} F$. In the case of equality, the tag T authenticates the new owner R_{ID2} and updates $K(i)$ and $IDS(i)$ as $K^*(i) = Per(rnd_3(i), K(i)) \oplus K((i + 1) \bmod 6)$ and $IDS^*(i) = Per(rnd_3(i), K(i)) \oplus K(i)$ respectively as well as computing $G(i) = PRNG(K^*(i) \oplus IDS^*(i))$ for $i = 1, \ldots, 6$.
6. The tag T sends G to the reader R_{ID2}.
7. After receiving the message G from the tag T, the reader R_{ID2} computes $K^*(i) = Per(rnd_3(i), K(i)) \oplus K((i + 1) \bmod 6)$ and $IDS^*(i) = Per(rnd_3(i), K(i)) \oplus K(i)$ and $G'(i) = PRNG(K^*(i) \oplus IDS^*(i))$ for $i = 1, \ldots, 6$. Then, it verifies whether $G' \overset{?}{=} G$ is or not. In the case of equality, it authorizes the tag T and updates K and IDS as K^* and IDS^* respectively.

Complete Ownership Transfer Phase

Since the old owner R_{ID1} holds the same values shared between the new owner R_{ID2} and the tag T, the above mentioned ownership delegation transfer does not provide backward privacy. In order to address this pitfall, Niu *et al.* have proposed the complete ownership phase by using TTP in which all its rights over the tag T are transferred to the reader R_{ID2} as a new owner. This phase is described below:

1. TTP generates a random number rnd_4, calculates $H(i) = rnd_4(i) \oplus PRNG(K_{TTP}(i))$, $L(i) = PRNG(K_M(i) \oplus rnd_4(i))$ and $K_M^*(i) = PRNG(Per(K_M, rnd_4(i))$ for $i = 1, \ldots, 6$. Then, TTP updates K_M as K_M^*.
2. TTP sends K_M^* to the reader R_{ID2} (the new owner). It also sends H and L to the tag T.
3. Once the tag T received the messages H and L, it retrieves $rnd_4(i)$ as $H(i) \oplus PRNG(K_{TTP}(i))$ and computes $L'(i) = PRNG(K_M(i) \oplus rnd_4(i))$ for $i = 1, \ldots, 6$. Then, the tag T verifies whether $L' \overset{?}{=} L$. In the case of equality, it updates $K_M(i)$ as $K_M^*(i) = PRNG(Per(K_M(i), rnd_4(i)))$ for $i = 1, \ldots, 6$.
4. New owner R_{ID2} and the tag T go to mutual authentication phase. If mutual authentication succeeds, the ownership transfer has successfully been done.

3 Secret Disclosure Attack on Niu *et al.* Authentication and Management Protocol

In this section, we show that it is possible to disclose secret parameters in Niu *et al.* authentication and management protocol efficiently. The main observation is that in this protocol the 96-bit parameters are divided into 16-bit strings and messages are generated using a 16-bit PRNG. On the other hand, several related works have shown that it is hard to achieve high security using small components [19]. Based on this observation, we present an attack to disclose secret parameters in this protocol.

In an off-line phase of the attack, the adversary creates a table TB and for $0 \leq x < 2^{16}$ stores $(x, PRNG(x))$ in TB. Hence, given TB and $PRNG(x)$, it is possible to determine possible values of x. We use $(A, B, C)_{r_1^j, r_2^j}^{K^j}$ to show the messages based on the secret key $K = K^j$ and random values $rnd_1 = r_1^j$ and $rnd_2 = r_2^j$. The secret disclosure attack works as follows:

1. Assume that the current state of the tag T and the reader R_{ID1} is (K^0, IDS^0, K^1, IDS^1) where K^0 and IDS^0 are the old key and pseudonym as well as K^1 and IDS^1 are the current key and pseudonym of T. The adversary also has a table TB include $(x, PRNG(x))$ for $0 \leq x < 2^{16}$.
2. In the mutual authentication phase, the reader R_{ID1} (old owner of the tag T) sends $(A, B, C)_{r_1^1, r_2^1}^{K^1}$ to the tag T.
3. The tag T updates its state to (K^1, IDS^1, K^2, IDS^2) and sends $D(i) = PRNG(K^2(i) \oplus IDS^2(i))$ to the reader R_{ID1} for $i = 1, \ldots, 6$.
4. The adversary eavesdrops $(A, B, C)_{r_1^1, r_2^1}^{K^1}$ and D. The adversary also determines possible values of $K^2(i) \oplus IDS^2(i)$, for $i = 1, \ldots, 6$, using TB and D.
5. In the ownership delegation phase, the reader R_{ID2} (new owner of the tag T) sends its identification R_{ID2} and a *Query* command to the tag T.
6. The tag T sends its IDS^2 to the reader R_{ID2}.
7. The adversary eavesdrops IDS^2 and determines possible values of K^2, given the result of step 4.
8. The reader R_{ID2} generates a random number r_3^2 and computes $E(i) = r_3^2(i) \oplus PRNG(K^2(i) \oplus R_{ID2}(i)) \oplus PRNG(K^2(i))$ and $F(i) = PRNG(ticket(i) \oplus r_3^2(i))$ for $i = 1, \ldots, 6$ and sends E and F to the tag T, where $ticket = K_M \oplus EPC \oplus r_1^1 \oplus r_2^1$.
9. The adversary eavesdrops E and F and determines possible values of r_3^2 and $ticket$ using TB.
10. Once the tag T received the messages E and F, it authenticates the new owner R_{ID2} and updates $K(i)$ as $K^3(i) = Per(r_3^2(i), K^2(i)) \oplus K^2((i + 1) \bmod 6)$ and $IDS(i)$ as $IDS^3(i) = Per(r_3^2(i), K^2(i)) \oplus K^2(i)$.
11. The tag T computes $G_i = PRNG(K^3(i) \oplus IDS^3(i))$ for $i = 1, \ldots, 6$ and sends it to R_{ID2}.
12. The adversary eavesdrops G and uses TB to determine possible values of $K^3(i) \oplus IDS^3(i)$ for $i = 1, \ldots, 6$.

Given information extracted in steps 7 and 9, the adversary has some possible values of $K^2(i)$ and $r_3^2(i)$ for $i = 1, \ldots, 6$. On the other hand, given $K^2(i)$, $K^2((i+1) \bmod 6)$ and $r_3^2(i)$, it is possible to determine $K^3(i)$ and $IDS^3(i)$. Hence, given the extracted information from step 12 of the attack, it is possible for the adversary to filter the wrong guesses for the extracted $K^2(i)$ and $r_3^2(i)$. Following the given attack, the adversary can extract the tag's secret parameters, i.e., K^2, IDS^2, K^3 and IDS^3. The major complexity of the attack is eavesdropping one run of the protocol and doing 216 calls to a $PRNG$ function in an off-line mode and the success probability is almost 1.

Moreover, each tag has a secrete parameter K_{TTP} which is shared between the tag and the TTP. This parameter is expected to be known only by the tag and the TTP, even not a legitimate owner. Now, we present an attack to retrieve this parameter by a legitimate old owner. In this attack, the old owner at the first generates the table TB and for $0 \leq x < 2^{16}$ stores $(x, PRNG(x))$ in TB. Next, assume that the current secret shared between the tag T and the owner is K_M^1 and the TTP wants that all rights over the tag T are transferred to the reader R_{ID2} from the reader R_{ID1}. The attack procedure which is performed by the reader R_{ID1} is as follows:

1. In the complete ownership transfer phase of the protocol, the TTP generates a random number r_4^1 and updates $K_M^1(i)$ as $K_M^2(i) = PRNG(Per(K_M^1(i), r_4^1(i))$ for $i = 1, \ldots, 6$.
2. The TTP calculates $H^1(i) = r_4^1(i) \oplus PRNG(K_{TTP}(i))$ and $L^1(i) = PRNG(K_M^1(i) \oplus r_4^1(i))$ for $i = 1, \ldots, 6$ and sends K_M^2 to R_{ID2} (the new owner of the tag T) and H^1 and L^1 to the tag T.
3. The old owner R_{ID1}, as the adversary, eavesdrops H^1 and L^1.
4. Given the eavesdropped H^1 and L^1 and the table TB, the old owner R_{ID1} does as follows for all $i = 1, \ldots, 6$:
   - Computes $r_4^1(i) = PRNG^{-1}(L^1(i)) \oplus K_M^1(i)$;
   - Assigns $H^1(i) \oplus r_4^1(i)$ to $PRNG(K_{TTP}(i))$ and calculates $K_{TTP}(i)$ by looking up at TB.

Following the above passive attack, the old owner retrieves $r_4^1(i)$ and $K_{TTP}(i)$ for $i = 1, \ldots, 6$. Since K_{TTP} is the value that is needed as the permanent parameter to access the tag T, the old owner R_{ID1} finds a permanent control like TTP on the tag T in this attack. On the other hand, the old owner R_{ID1} knows K_M^1 and it can calculate $K_M^2(i) = PRNG(Per(K_M^1(i), r_4^1(i)))$ which is the secret parameter shared between the tag T and the new owner R_{ID2}. This information compromises the new owner privacy. The complexity of the given attack is eavesdropping a sessions between the target tag and the new owner and the success probability is almost 1.

Now we present another attack that an adversary can follow to extract K_M and $PRNG(K_{TTP})$. Similarly, as the off-line phase of the attack, the adversary generates the table TB and for $0 \leq x < 2^{16}$ stores $(x, PRNG(x))$ in TB. Then, the adversary does as follows:

1. In complete ownership transfer phase of the protocol, the TTP generates a random number r_4^1 and updates $K_M^1(i)$ as $K_M^2(i) = PRNG(Per(K_M(i), r_4^1(i))$ for $i = 1, \ldots, 6$.
2. The TTP calculates $H^1(i) = r_4^1(i) \oplus PRNG(K_{TTP}(i))$ and $L^1(i) = PRNG(K_M^1(i) \oplus r_4^1(i))$ for $i = 1, \ldots, 6$ and sends K_M^2 to R_{ID2} (the new owner of the tag T) and H^1 and L^1 to the tag.
3. The adversary eavesdrops and blocks H^1 and L^1.

4. The tag T will not authenticate the new owner R_{ID2} and the TTP generates another random number r_4^2 and updates $K_M^1(i)$ as $K_M^3(i) = PRNG(Per(K_M^1(i), r_4^2(i)))$.
5. The TTP calculates $H^2(i) = r_4^2(i) \oplus PRNG(K_{TTP}(i))$ and $L^2(i) = PRNG(K_M^1(i) \oplus r_4^2(i))$ for $i = 1, \ldots, 6$ and sends K_M^3 to the new owner R_{ID2} and H^2 and L^2 to the tag T.
6. The adversary eavesdrops H^2 and L^2 and does as follows for all $i = 1, \ldots, 6$:
   (a) For $j = 1, \ldots, 2^{16}$ does as follows:
       - $r_4^1(i) \longleftarrow j$;
       - $PRNG(K_{TTP}(i)) \longleftarrow H^1(i) \oplus r_4^1(i)$;
       - $K_M^1(i) \longleftarrow PRNG^{-1}(L^1(i)) \oplus r_4^1(i)$;
       - $r_4^2(i) \longleftarrow PRNG^{-1}(L^2(i)) \oplus K_M^1(i)$;
       - If $H^2(i) = r_4^2(i) \oplus PRNG(K_{TTP}(i))$, return $K_M^1(i)$ and $PRNG^{-1}(PRNG(K_{TTP}(i)))$

Following the above attack, the adversary retrieves $r_4^1(i)$, $r_4^2(i)$, $K_M^1(i)$ and $K_{TTP}(i)$ for $i = 1, \ldots, 6$. Since K_{TTP} is the value that is needed as the permanent parameter to access the tag T, the adversary R_{ID1} finds a permanent control like TTP on the tag T in this attack. On the other hand, the adversary extracted K_M^1 and r_4^2 and she can calculate $K_M^3(i) = PRNG(Per(K_M^1(i), r_4^2(i))$ which is the secret parameter shared between the tag T and the new owner R_{ID2}. This information compromises the new owner privacy. The complexity of the given attack is eavesdropping two sessions between the target tag and the new owner and blocking one session and the success probability is almost 1.

4 Desynchronization Attacks on Niu *et al.* Authentication and Management Protocol

In this section, we explain two different desynchronization attacks against Niu *et al.* authentication and management protocol on mutual authentication phase and ownership delegation phase.

4.1 Desynchronization Attack on Mutual Authentication Phase

As explained in Sect. 2, in the mutual authentication phase of the Niu *et al.* protocol, the reader R_{ID1} generates two random numbers rnd_1 and rnd_2 and sends A, B and C to the tag T. Once the tag T received the messages A, B and C, it verifies the received values, updates K and IDS to K^* and IDS^* respectively and sends D to the reader. In addition, the designers stated that [16, p. 4, Sect. II. B] *"both the reader and the tag should maintain a copy of the old key and IDS to avoid desynchronization problems"*. Now we present a desynchronization attack which works even with this assumption.

We use $(A, B, C)_{r_1^j, r_2^j}^{K^l}$ and $(D)_{r_1^j, r_2^j}^{K^l}$ to show the messages based on the secret key $K = K^l$ and random values $rnd_1 = r_1^j$ and $rnd_2 = r_2^j$. The procedure of the proposed attack is as follows:

1. Assume that the current state of the tag T and the reader R_{ID1} is (K^0, IDS^0, K^1, IDS^1) where K^0 and IDS^0 are the old key and pseudonym as well as K^1 and IDS^1 are the current key and pseudonym of the tag T.
2. In the next mutual authentication phase, the reader R_{ID1} sends $(A,B,C)_{r_1^1,r_2^1}^{K^1}$ to the tag T.
3. The tag T updates its state to (K^1, IDS^1, K^2, IDS^2) and sends $(D)_{r_1^1,r_2^1}^{K^2}$ to the reader R_{ID1}.
4. The adversary blocks $(D)_{r_1^1,r_2^1}^{K^2}$.
5. Since the reader R_{ID1} does not receive the tag's feedback, it will assume that the tag T does not recognize K^1 and sends $(A,B,C)_{r_1^2,r_2^2}^{K^0}$ to the tag T.
6. However, the tag T has no record of K^0 and will not authenticate the reader R_{ID1} anymore and the tag T and the reader R_{ID1} has been desynchronized.

One may argue that the reader R_{ID1} will try with K^1 once again. In this case, the adversary does as follows:

1. Assume that the current secrets of the tag T and the reader R_{ID1} is (K^0, IDS^0, K^1, IDS^1).
2. In the next mutual authentication phase, the reader R_{ID1} sends $(A,B,C)_{r_1^1,r_2^1}^{K^1}$ to the tag T.
3. The tag T updates its states to (K^1, IDS^1, K^2, IDS^2) and sends $(D)_{r_1^1,r_2^1}^{K^2}$ to the reader R_{ID1}.
4. The adversary stores $(A,B,C)_{r_1^1,r_2^1}^{K^1}$.
5. The reader R_{ID1} also updates its state to (K^1, IDS^1, K^2, IDS^2).
6. Since the designers stated that [16, p. 3, Sect. II. A] *"before either delegation or complete ownership transfer take place, mutual authentication is needed to verify the authority of all parties involved"*. So, the adversary blocks all the messages of the phase after authentication which can be delegation phase or complete ownership transfer phase so. Once again the mutual authentication phase starts.
7. In the next mutual authentication phase, the reader R_{ID1} sends $(A,B,C)_{r_1^2,r_2^2}^{K^2}$ to the tag T.
8. The adversary stores $(A,B,C)_{r_1^2,r_2^2}^{K^2}$ and prevents the tag T to receive them.
9. Since the reader R_{ID1} does not receive the tag's feedback, it will assume that the tag T does not recognize K^2. So, the reader R_{ID1} sends $(A,B,C)_{r_1^3,r_2^2}^{K^1}$ to the tag T.
10. The tag T updates its state to (K^1, IDS^1, K^3, IDS^3) and sends $(D)_{r_1^3,r_2^2}^{K^3}$ to the reader R_{ID1}.
11. The reader R_{ID1} also updates its state to (K^1, IDS^1, K^3, IDS^3).
12. The adversary sends $(A,B,C)_{r_1^1,r_2^1}^{K^1}$ to the tag T.
13. The tag T sends $(D)_{r_1^1,r_2^1}^{K^2}$ to the expected reader and updates its state to (K^1, IDS^1, K^2, IDS^2).
14. The adversary prevents the reader R_{ID1} to receive $(D)_{r_1^1,r_2^1}^{K^2}$.

15. The adversary sends $(A, B, C)^{K^2}_{r_1^2, r_2^2}$ to the tag T.

16. The tag T sends $(D)^{K^4}_{r_1^1, r_2^1}$ to the expected reader and updates its state to (K^2, IDS^2, K^4, IDS^4).

17. The adversary prevents the reader R_{ID1} to receive $(D)^{K^4}_{r_1^1, r_2^1}$.

After the above attack, the reader has K^1, IDS^1, K^3, IDS^3 as its records of secret parameters while the tag T has K^2, IDS^2, K^4 and IDS^4. It is clear that, after the given attack neither of the tag's records for secret parameters matches the reader's records for secret parameters. Hence, the tag and the reader have been desynchronized. Although it may be possible to contact the trusted third party(TTP) to re-synchronize the tag, but this attack shows that the given protocol does not satisfy the designers expectation. The complexity of the attack is a few runs of the protocol while the success probability is almost 1.

4.2   Desynchronization Attack on Ownership Delegation Phase

In the ownership delegation phase of the protocol, the old owner R_{ID1} sends *ticket*, EPC, IDS and K through a secure channel to the new owner (the reader R_{ID2}). The reader R_{ID2} generates a random number rnd_3 and computes E and F using K and rnd_3. Then, the reader R_{ID2} sends E and F to the tag T. Once the tag T received the messages E and F, it verifies the received values and updates K and IDS to K^* and IDS^* using rnd_3. Then, the tag computes G using K^* and IDS^* and sends it to the reader R_{ID2}. In the protocol, the parameter $G(i)$ for $i = 1, \cdots, 6$ is not dependent on $K^*(i)$, $IDS^*(i)$ and the random number $rnd_3(i)$ selected by the new owner R_{ID2}. It is computed only using the secret key $K(i)$ as shown as follows:

$$
\begin{aligned}
G(i) &= PRNG(\ K^*(i) \oplus IDS^*(i) \ ) \\
&= PRNG(\ Per(rnd_3(i), K(i)) \ \oplus \ K((i+1) \ mod \ 6) \oplus Per(rnd_3(i), K(i)) \ \oplus \ K(i) \ ) \\
&= PRNG(\ K((i+1) \ mod \ 6) \ \oplus \ K(i) \ );
\end{aligned}
$$

In other words, the response of E and F which are computed by rnd_3 and K, i.e., G, is computed by K not K^* and rnd_3. Now, we show that this property can be used by the attacker to perform desynchronization attack in the ownership delegation phase of the protocol. We use $(E, F)^{K^j}_{r_3^j}$ and $(G)^{K^j}$ to show the messages based on the secret key K^j and the random value $rnd_3 = r_3^j$. We assume that both parties are synchronized in state (K^1, IDS^1). The procedure of the proposed attack is as follows:

1. To update the tag T by the new owner (the reader R_{ID2}) for the first time, the new owner sends $(E, F)^{K^1}_{r_3^1}$ to the tag T.

2. The tag T updates its state to (K^2, IDS^2) where $K^2(i) = Per(r_3^1(i), K^1(i)) \oplus K^1((i+1) \ mod \ 6)$ and $IDS^2(i) = Per(r_3^1(i), K^1(i)) \oplus K^1(i)$. Then, the tag T sends $(G)^{K^1}$ to the reader R_{ID2}.

3. The adversary prevents the reader R_{ID2} to receive $(G)^{K^1}$ and stores it.

4. Since the reader R_{ID2} does not receive the tag's feedback, it will assume that the tag T does not receive $(E, F)^{K^1}_{r_3^1}$. Therefore, R_{ID2} chooses another random number r_3^2 and sends $(E, F)^{K^1}_{r_3^2}$ to the tag T again.

5. The adversary prevents the tag T to receive $(E, F)^{K^1}_{r_3^2}$ and sends $(G)^{K^1}$ (which is stored by the adversary in step 3) to the reader R_{ID2}.

6. Note that according to the property G which is not dependent on the random number selected by the reader, the reader R_{ID2} detects the validity of $(G)^{K^1}$. So, the reader R_{ID2} updates its state to (K^3, IDS^3) where $K^3(i) = Per(r_3^2(i), K^1(i)) \oplus K^1((i+1) \bmod 6)$ and $IDS^3(i) = Per(r_3^2(i), K^1(i)) \oplus K^1(i)$.

After the above attack, the reader R_{ID2} has K^2 and IDS^2 as its records of secret parameters while the tag T has K^3 and IDS^3. It is clear that, these two states are not the same and the adversary succeeds in performing desynchronization attack between the tag T and the new owner R_{ID2}. Although it may be possible to contact the old owner R_{ID1} to re-synchronize the tag, but this attack shows that the given protocol does not satisfy the designers expectation. The complexity of the attack is only three runs of the protocol and the probability of a successful de-synchronization attack is equal to 1.

5   Improved Protocol

This paper and similar articles in the field of cryptanalysis of RFID security protocols such as [1–5,9,10,18] demonstrated that designing a secure protocol without using a secure cryptographic element has not been achieved. So in this section, to improve the Niu *et al.*'s protocols we propose to use recent available lightweight block ciphers such as SIMON [6], SIMECK [21] and PRESENT [7] that are very lightweight and can be used in constrain environments such as RFID passive tags. Therefore, we use a lightweight block cipher denoted by $\mathcal{E}$ instead of $PRNG$ in the messages of the protocol.

Improved Mutual Authentication Phase

In the improved mutual authentication phase of protocol the reader R_{ID1} (the old owner of the tag T) authenticates the tag T before the reader R_{ID1} delegates the ownership of the tag T to the reader R_{ID2}. This phase of the protocol is described below:

1. To start this phase of the protocol, the reader R_{ID1} (the old owner of the tag T) generates two random numbers rnd_1 and rnd_2. Then, it computes $A = rnd_1 \oplus \mathcal{E}_K(R_{ID1}) \oplus \mathcal{E}_K(R_{ID2})$, $B = rnd_2 \oplus \mathcal{E}_K(rnd_1)$ and $C = \mathcal{E}_{rnd_1}(R_{ID1}) \oplus \mathcal{E}_{rnd_2}(R_{ID2})$.

2. The reader R_{ID1} sends A, B and C to the tag T.

3. After receiving the messages A, B and C from the reader R_{ID1}, the tag T computes $rnd_1 = A \oplus \mathcal{E}_K(R_{ID1}) \oplus \mathcal{E}_K(R_{ID2})$, $rnd_2 = B \oplus \mathcal{E}_K(rnd_1)$ and $C' =$

$\mathcal{E}_{rnd_1}(R_{ID1}) \oplus \mathcal{E}_{rnd_2}(R_{ID2})$. Then, the tag T verifies whether $C' \overset{?}{=} C$ is or not. In the case of equality, the tag T authenticates the reader R_{ID1}, updates K and IDS as $K^* = Per(rnd_1, K) \oplus K$ and $IDS^* = Per(rnd_2, K) \oplus K$ respectively, and computes $D = \mathcal{E}_{K^*}(IDS^*)$.

4. The tag T sends D to the reader R_{ID1}.

5. After receiving the message D from the tag T, the reader R_{ID1} computes $K^* = Per(rnd_1, K) \oplus K$, $IDS^* = Per(rnd_2, K) \oplus K$ and $D' = \mathcal{E}_{K^*}(IDS^*)$. Then, it verifies whether $D' \overset{?}{=} D$ is or not. In the case of equality, it authorizes the tag T and updates K and IDS as K^* and IDS^* respectively.

Ownership Delegation Phase

In ownership delegation phase of the proposed protocol, the reader R_{ID1} (which is the old owner of the tag T) wants to delegate all its rights over the tag T to the reader R_{ID2} by using the parameter called *ticket*. The old owner R_{ID1} and the tag T both compute $ticket = K_M \oplus EPC \oplus rnd_1 \oplus rnd_2$. Then, the reader R_{ID1} sends *ticket*, EPC, IDS and K through a secure channel to the reader R_{ID2} (the new owner R_{ID2} of the tag T). Improved ownership delegation steps are as follows:

1. The reader R_{ID2} sends its identification R_{ID2} and a *Query* command to the tag T.

2. The tag T sends its IDS to the reader R_{ID2}.

3. The reader R_{ID2} generates one random number rnd_3, computes $E = rnd_3 \oplus \mathcal{E}_K(R_{ID2}) \oplus \mathcal{E}_K(ticket)$ and $F = \mathcal{E}_{ticket}(rnd_3)$.

4. The reader R_{ID2} sends E and F to the tag T.

5. After receiving the messages E and F from the reader R_{ID2}, the tag T computes $rnd_3 = E \oplus \mathcal{E}_K(R_{ID2}) \oplus \mathcal{E}_K(ticket)$ and $F' = \mathcal{E}_{ticket}(rnd_3)$. Then, the tag T verifies whether $F' \overset{?}{=} F$. In the case of equality, the tag T authenticates the new owner R_{ID2} and updates K and IDS as $K^* = Per(rnd_3, K) \oplus K$ and $IDS^* = Per(rnd_3, K) \oplus K$ respectively as well as computing $G = \mathcal{E}_{K^*}(IDS^* \| rnd_3)$.

6. The tag T sends G to the reader R_{ID2}.

7. After receiving the message G from the tag T, the reader R_{ID2} computes $K^* = Per(rnd_3, K) \oplus K$ and $IDS^* = Per(rnd_3, K) \oplus K$ and $G' = \mathcal{E}_{K^*}(IDS^* \| rnd_3)$. Then, it verifies whether $G' \overset{?}{=} G$ is or not. In the case of equality, it authorizes the tag T and updates K and IDS as K^* and IDS^* respectively.

Improved Complete Ownership Transfer Phase

The above mentioned improved ownership delegation transfer has not the property of the backward privacy since the old owner R_{ID1} holds the same values shared between the new owner R_{ID2} and the tag T. In order to address this pitfall, same as Niu *et al.*'s protocol we propose the improved complete ownership phase by using TTP in which all its rights over the tag T are transferred to the reader R_{ID2} as a new owner. This phase is described below:

1. TTP generates a random number rnd_4, calculates $H = rnd_4 \oplus \mathcal{E}_{K_{TTP}}(K_{TTP})$, $L = E_{rnd_4}(K_M)$ and $K_M^* = \mathcal{E}_{rnd_4}(Per(K_M, rnd_4))$. Then, TTP updates K_M as K_M^*.
2. TTP sends K_M^* to the reader R_{ID2} (the new owner). It also sends H and L to the tag T.
3. Once the tag T received the messages H and L, it retrieves rnd_4 as $H \oplus \mathcal{E}_{K_{TTP}}(K_{TTP})$ and computes $L' = \mathcal{E}_{rnd_4}(K_M)$. Then, the tag T verifies whether $L' \overset{?}{=} L$. In the case of equality, it updates K_M as $K_M^* = \mathcal{E}_{rnd_4}(Per(K_M, rnd_4))$.
4. New owner R_{ID2} and the tag T go to mutual authentication phase. If mutual authentication succeeds, the ownership transfer has successfully been done.

6   Security Analysis of the Improved Protocol

Since the improved protocol is based on Niu *et al.*'s protocol, so its resistance against other attacks except secret disclosure attack and desynchronization attacks is same as Niu *et al.*'s protocol security. The improved protocol also resists against the mentioned attacks in this paper as follows.

6.1   Resistance Against Secret Disclosure Attack

Because of using a lightweight block cipher instead of $PRNG$, in the improved protocol, the adversary cannot do offline evaluations of block cipher and so the mentioned disclosure attack in the Sect. 3 is not applicable on the improved protocol, assuming that the key size matches the desired security level, e.g. 64 bits.

6.2   Resistance Against Desynchronization Attack

To resistance against desynchronization attack, in the improved protocol we assume that the tag saves both old and new keys and IDS and the reader saves only the recent used key and IDS. Also in the protocol messages all tag responses i.e. $D = \mathcal{E}_{K^*}(IDS^*) = \mathcal{E}_{Per(rnd_1,K) \oplus K}(Per(rnd_2, K) \oplus K)$ and $G = \mathcal{E}_{K^*}(IDS^* \| rnd_3) = \mathcal{E}_{Per(rnd_3,K) \oplus K}((Per(rnd_3, K) \oplus K) \| rnd_3)$ are dependent to random numbers which are generated by the reader. So the improved protocol is not vulnerable against desynchronization attack which was described in Sect. 4.

7   Conclusion

In this paper, we scrutinized the security of the mutual authentication and ownership transfer management protocol proposed by Niu *et al.* Precisely, we present secret disclosure and desynchronization attacks against the protocol with the complexity of a few runs of the protocol and the success probability of almost

1. Finally, we improved the protocol's vulnerabilities by using lightweight block ciphers in the protocol's messages and proved its resistance against the attacks presented in this paper and the other passive and active attacks.

This paper shows that the need to secure EPC-C1G2 complaint protocols is still unmet and the new secure protocols must be designed.

References

1. Ahmadian, Z., Salmasizadeh, M., Aref, M.R.: Desynchronization attack on RAPP ultralightweight authentication protocol. Inf. Process. Lett. **113**(7), 205–209 (2013)
2. Ahmadian, Z., Salmasizadeh, M., Aref, M.R.: Recursive linear and differential cryptanalysis of ultralightweight authentication protocols. IEEE Transactions on Information Forensics and Security **8**(7), 1140–1151 (2013)
3. Avoine, G., Carpent, X.: Yet another ultralightweight authentication protocol that is broken. In: Hoepman, J.-H., Verbauwhede, I. (eds.) RFIDSec 2012. LNCS, vol. 7739, pp. 20–30. Springer, Heidelberg (2013). doi:10.1007/978-3-642-36140-1_2
4. Avoine, G., Carpent, X., Martin, B.: Privacy-friendly synchronized ultralightweight authentication protocols in the storm. J. Netw. Comput. Appl. **35**(2), 826–843 (2012)
5. Bagheri, N., Safkhani, M., Peris-Lopez, P., Tapiador, J.E.: Weaknesses in a new ultralightweight RFID authentication protocol with permutation - RAPP. Secur. Commun. Netw. **7**(6), 945–949 (2014)
6. Beaulieu, R., Shors, D., Smith, J., Treatman-Clark, S., Weeks, B., Wingers, L.: The SIMON and SPECK lightweight block ciphers. In Proceedings of the 52nd Annual Design Automation Conference, San Francisco, CA, USA, June 7–11, 2015, p. 175. ACM (2015)
7. Bogdanov, A., Knudsen, L.R., Leander, G., Paar, C., Poschmann, A., Robshaw, M.J.B., Seurin, Y., Vikkelsoe, C.: PRESENT: an ultra-lightweight block cipher. In: Paillier, P., Verbauwhede, I. (eds.) CHES 2007. LNCS, vol. 4727, pp. 450–466. Springer, Heidelberg (2007). doi:10.1007/978-3-540-74735-2_31
8. Class-1 generation 2 UHF air interface protocol standard version 1.2.0, Gen 2 (2008). http://www.epcglobalinc.org/standards/
9. D'Arco, P., Santis, A.: Weaknesses in a recent ultra-lightweight RFID authentication protocol. In: Vaudenay, S. (ed.) AFRICACRYPT 2008. LNCS, vol. 5023, pp. 27–39. Springer, Heidelberg (2008). doi:10.1007/978-3-540-68164-9_3
10. D'Arco, P., Santis, A.D.: On ultralightweight RFID authentication protocols. IEEE Trans. Dependable Sec. Comput. **8**(4), 548–563 (2011)
11. Doss, R., Zhou, W., Yu, S.: Secure RFID tag ownership transfer based on quadratic residues. IEEE Trans. Inf. Foren. Secur. **8**(2), 390–401 (2013)
12. Falahati, A., Jannati, H.: All-or-nothing approach to protect a distance bounding protocol against terrorist fraud attack for low-cost devices. Electron. Commer. Res. **15**(1), 75–95 (2015)
13. Jannati, H., Falahati, A.: Cryptanalysis and enhancement of a secure group ownership transfer protocol for RFID tags. In: Georgiadis, C.K., Jahankhani, H., Pimenidis, E., Bashroush, R., Al-Nemrat, A. (eds.) ICGS3/e-Democracy 2011. LNICST, vol. 99, pp. 186–193. Springer, Berlin, Heidelberg (2011). doi:10.1007/978-3-642-33448-1_26
14. Miles, S.B., Sarma, S.E., Williams, J.R.: RFID Technology and Applications. Cambridge University Press, New York (2011)

15. Niu, B., Zhu, X., Chi, H., Li, H.: Privacy and authentication protocol for mobile RFID systems. Wirel. Pers. Commun. **77**(3), 1713–1731 (2014)
16. Niu, H., Taqieddin, E., Jagannathan, S.: EPC gen2v2 RFID standard authentication and ownership management protocol. IEEE Trans. Mob. Comput. **15**(1), 137–149 (2016)
17. Peris-Lopez, P., Orfila, A., Mitrokotsa, A., van der Lubbe, J.C.A.: A comprehensive RFID solution to enhance inpatient medication safety. I. J. Med. Inf. **80**(1), 13–24 (2011)
18. Phan, R.C.-W.: Cryptanalysis of a new ultralightweight RFID authentication protocol - SASI. IEEE Trans. Dependable Secure Comput. **6**(4), 316–320 (2009)
19. Safkhani, M., Bagheri, N., Naderi, M.: A note on the security of IS-RFID, an inpatient medication safety. I. J. Med. Inf. **83**(1), 82–85 (2014)
20. Sundaresan, S., Doss, R., Piramuthu, S., Zhou, W.: Secure tag search in RFID systems using mobile readers. IEEE Trans. Dependable Sec. Comput. **12**(2), 230–242 (2015)
21. Yang, G., Zhu, B., Suder, V., Aagaard, M.D., Gong, G.: The Simeck family of lightweight block ciphers. In: Güneysu, T., Handschuh, H. (eds.) CHES 2015. LNCS, vol. 9293, pp. 307–329. Springer, Heidelberg (2015). doi:10.1007/978-3-662-48324-4_16

PTSLP: Position Tracking Based Source Location Privacy for Wireless Sensor Networks

Hao Wang[1], Guangjie Han[1(✉)], Chunsheng Zhu[2], and Sammy Chan[3]

[1] Department of Information and Communication Systems,
Hohai University, Changzhou 213022, China
wanghaohhu@outlook.com, hanguangjie@gmail.com
[2] Department of Electrical and Computer Engineering,
The University of British Columbia, Vancouver, BC V6T 1Z4, Canada
cszhu@ece.ubc.ca
[3] Department of Electronic Engineering,
City University of Hong Kong, Kowloon Tong, Hong Kong
eeschan@cityu.edu.hk

Abstract. Abundant experiments have shown that phantom source nodes cannot leave far away from the real source node. In this paper, we propose a novel position tracking based source location privacy (PTSLP) protection scheme for wireless sensor networks (WSNs). First, we construct a phantom area in order to make phantom source nodes being far from the real source node. Secondly, we combine shortest path routing and random routing to forward packets to sink node rather than deviating from sink node. Then, we make every packet pass through a special area called trace cost area which consists of many sensor nodes with different weights in different areas and finally reach the ring around sink node. Compared with SLP-E, which fails to take overlapping path into consideration, our proposed scheme can reduce overlapping path. Simulation results show that PTSLP can increase safety time and enhance source location privacy in WSNs.

Keywords: Wireless sensor networks · Source location privacy · Trace cost

1 Introduction

As an important part of the Internet of Things [1], wireless sensor networks (WSNs) [2–7] have played a vital role in military, healthcare, industry and many other fields to help people acquiring accurate and reliable information in any place any time, such as environment monitoring, disaster warning and traffic management. However, due to some common features of WSNs such as limited resources and simplified communication protocol, it is very easy for adversary to launch cyber attacks such as that which causes serious location privacy leakage problem [8]. For example, in animal-monitoring application, adversary can catch

© Springer International Publishing AG 2017
G.P. Hancke and K. Markantonakis (Eds.): RFIDSec 2016, LNCS 10155, pp. 17–29, 2017.
DOI: 10.1007/978-3-319-62024-4_2

animals' locations by monitoring traffic path [8]; in intelligent transportation, adversary can get users' privacy by analyzing users' trace and habit [9].

Nowadays, with the development of WSNs, source location privacy becomes a hot issue and raises a lot of attention. So far, privacy in WSNs can be categorized as data privacy and context privacy [10]. Data privacy aims to protect sensitive data collected by sensor nodes. For examples, methods like anonymous and recombination are used to protect data privacy. For context privacy, it mainly focuses on source location privacy (SLP) and sink location privacy. The main protections behind the context privacy (e.g., geographic routing [11], random walk [12], phantom source nodes [13], fake source nodes [14], etc.) are to prohibit adversaries from reaching the source node by analyzing data traffic and tracing back. In the classic Panda-Hunter model [8], when a sensor node detects the panda, it becomes the source node and sends message to the sink node periodically. Hunters can listen to the messages and trace back to the source node. In this model, location privacy is to prevent the adversary from finding panda while messages can be sent to sink node. As a solution, deploying phantom nodes can protect SLP to some extent. However, the scheme has a leakage that the adversary may find source node easily.

Considering the problems of phantom source node, in this paper, we propose a position tracking based source location privacy (PTSLP) protection mechanism for WSNs to prevent adversaries from reaching the source node and resist angle attack. We propose a new concept, trace cost, to formalize the difficulty that the adversary faces. Packets in a trace cost area are transmitted with random routing and thereby the safety time of the whole network is increased. In our scheme, steps can be summarized as follows.

- Establish a phantom area which is to decrease the probability of acquiring the real source node.
- Combine two routing strategies (i.e., shortest path routing and random routing) to make sure the packets can be transmitted to the sink node rather than deviating from sink node.
- Construct a trace cost area to further enhance SLP.
- Form a ring around the sink node to resist angle attack.

With these four steps, SLP is maintained and the safety time of network can be improved. In the first step, the phantom area is divided into several parts and all the phantom nodes are deployed in different parts. When a packet leaves the source node, it first starts a h-hop random walk to the phantom source node and is then routed to the sink node. In this way, the phantom source node can be far from the real source node. In the second step, by combining the shortest path routing and random routing, we make sure that the packet is routed toward the sink node rather than deviating from it. If we only use the random routing strategy, the packet has the probability that it cannot reach the sink node. In the third step, packets are routed with random routing in the trace cost area. For examples, the route may pass through mountains, plains or forests, which can slow down the adversary's tracking speed. In the fourth step, packets will be routed in a ring for several hops with different directions, either in clockwise or anticlockwise, which can resist angle attack to some extent. Simulation results will show that PTSLP can increase safety time and improve source location privacy in WSNs, compared with SLP-E [15]. Even though SLP-E can make packets transmit in all directions, but it does not consider the situation that a phantom node can be selected as the source node's next hop for many times, which increases the energy consumption of nodes and overlapping degree of transmission path. When the overlapping degree of transmission path increases, the source location privacy decreases.

The rest of this paper is organized as follows. Section 2 presents the related work. Section 3 outlines the network model. Section 4 introduces the proposed PTSLP scheme. Section 5 shows the simulation results. Finally, Sect. 6 makes the conclusion.

2   Related Work

So far, many location privacy protection protocols have been proposed. Li *et al.* [10] summarized the traditional panda-hunter model. When a node detects the panda, it becomes a source node and sends packets to sink node periodically. He *et al.* [16] used flooding to send packets. However, this method sends packets to all the neighbor nodes and source location privacy mainly depends on the number of nodes between the source node and sink node. Moreover, flooding consumes too much energy and may not be suitable for large networks.

For the purpose of decreasing the negative effects of flooding, Lu *et al.* [17] presented a method using phantom source nodes to protect source location privacy. Each packet will first start a *h*-hop random walk. After the random walk finishes, the last node of the random walk becomes a phantom source node and then this phantom source node transmits packets to sink node by the shortest path routing or flooding. However, these phantom nodes cannot leave far away from the real source node. Thus, this approach may not provide enough privacy protection.

Yao *et al.* [18] used *h*-directed hop random walk to make phantom nodes far away from the real source node. In *h*-directed hop random walk, each packet is given a direction and neighbors of a node are divided into either the far or close list. Next hop is chosen in the far list which makes phantom source nodes far away from the real source node. However, these phantom nodes often gather close to each other.

In [15,19] Chen *et al.* proposed a limited flooding protocol. First, the source node starts a limited flooding for *h* hops. After limited flooding finishes, a phantom area is formed and nodes within the phantom area become phantom source nodes. Second, each packet is transmitted in all directions to phantom source nodes. This method also takes visible area into consideration, which provides good source location privacy. But in each transmission, the real source node has to perform a limited flooding repeatedly, therefore consuming too much energy.

Moreover, in order to make phantom nodes to be deployed more uniformly and decrease overlapping transmitting paths, Zhao *et al.* [20] presented a protocol named RAPFPR based on angle and probability. First, a phantom area is divided into several parts and packets are transmitted into different parts. Second, from a phantom source node to the sink node, RAPFPR takes probabilistic forwarding strategy that only some of the nodes take part in each transmission, which decreases overlapping paths. In [21] Zhang *et al.* presented EPURA and further addressed angle problem in phantom area. In [22] Liu *et al.* improved the energy consumption problem by choosing nodes with the minimum energy cost as next hop.

Wang *et al.* [23] presented a protocol named PRLA to protect source location privacy. In PRLA, a visible area is taken into consideration and a phantom area is formed by phantom nodes. First, when a packet leaves the source node, it will start a random walk for h hops and the last hop of the random walk becomes a phantom source node. Phantom source nodes work similarly as the real source node to confuse adversaries. After that, packets are routed from a phantom source node to sink node by the shortest path routing strategy.

3   Network Model

3.1   Scenario

We consider a scenario that all the sensor nodes are randomly deployed. Figure 1 shows our network model which is based on the model proposed in [15]. In our model, there are four kinds of nodes in the network: source node, sink node, ring nodes and common nodes. Once a sensor node detects the event, it becomes a source node. The source node will then generate encrypted event packets and send them to sink node periodically. However, an adversary, who tries to localize the source node, should be prevented from acquiring this kind of information. They usually try to locate the source node by hop by hop back tracking from the sink node. The purpose of our scheme is to protect the location of source node and increase the time that adversary takes to find the source.

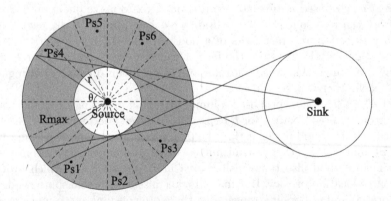

Fig. 1. Network model

3.2 Node Capability

We assume that nodes have the same capability of computing, communicating and storing. Each node only can have direct link with its one-hop neighbors. Moreover, all the sensor nodes in WSN are homogeneous, which means all the sensor nodes have the same initial energy levels and communication ranges. Each node is assigned a unique ID and a pair of public/private keys for encrypting and decrypting packets. Each node keeps a list of its neighbors which stores their IDs and communication information.

3.3 Adversary Model

Our adversary model is human, e.g., hunters. So, the adversary has to trace back on his own feet. The reason why we choose this restrictive model is that in the wild environment, the aim of hunters is to capture animals like panda, then hunters kill them or sell them. The more advanced equipment they use, the higher probability they will be found, because there are many monitoring systems in these rare animals shelter. In view of this, this adversary model is realistic. Commonly, an adversary has sufficient energy and enough memory for data storage, as well as equipment to monitor packets. The monitoring range of an adversary is equal to the communication radius of common nodes and the speed of an adversary can refer to speed of human. Moreover, in order not to be detected, the adversary only performs passive attacks such as traffic analysis and hop by hop back tracking.

4 Source Location Privacy Protection Based on Trace Cost

The proposed PTSLP is described in this section. Firstly, the sink node initializes the whole network by periodically broadcasting beacon messages. After the network initialization, every sensor node in the network knows their neighbors and parents. When a sensor node detects the event, it becomes a source node.

First, the source node will perform a h-hop random walk and thereby common nodes in h-hop random walk will get their distance to source node. Then, the source node will send packets for h-directed hops to phantom nodes. After a packet is routed to a phantom node, it will be routed to the sink node with the combined shortest path routing and random routing, then the packet will pass a sophisticated area which will increase the adversarys trace time. Finally, the packet will be routed to a ring node and then be routed to the sink node through the shortest path routing, which can resist angle attack to some extent. Detailed notations in our scheme are summarized in Table 1.

4.1 Network Initialization

The sink node broadcasts beacon messages periodically. When a node gets the broadcasted message, it first gets the hop information from the message and

Table 1. Parameter introduction

Parameter	Definition
h	The hop of random walk
H	The hop between source node and sink node
r	The radius of visible area
R	The communication radius of nodes
R_{max}	The max range of phantom area
r_s	The radius of ring around the sink node
α	The system constant
λ	The density of ring node
P_s	The Phantom source node
N	The number of sensor nodes

rebroadcasts the new message to its neighbors. Other nodes use the same method to get information about their hope distance to sink node. After all the nodes in network get the message, they will have the information of the hop counts to sink node. When a node detects an activity, it becomes the source node and then sends packets to sink node timely.

4.2 Phantom Area

When the network has been initialized, the source node will first calculate the range of the phantom area. As shown in Fig. 1, the shaded area is the phantom area and nodes such as Ps1, Ps2 are phantom source nodes. The phantom area is assumed to be a circle even though it is an uneven geographical environment. Nodes in phantom area will have a certain distance to source node. The distance to source node is obtained in the same way as the network initialization. The source node broadcasts beacon message periodically. When a node gets the message, it only records the minimum hop count. After these nodes get the hop counts to the source node, the phantom area is formed and is divided into several equal sectors. Each sector spans an angle θ, thereby we have $2\pi/\theta$ sectors.

Then the nodes in the visible area have to be removed. Because if nodes in these areas are chosen to be the next hop of the message, it is very easy for an adversary to trace back and finally catch source node since these nodes are extremely close to source node, and the adversary may monitor the communication among nodes and capture the packet, then reaches source node by tracing back hop by hop. So, in our scheme, we not only take visible area into consideration, but also expand the range of invalid region. By creating two tangents between visible area and the ring around sink node, then the overlapping area in phantom area is removed.

4.3   Combination of Two Routing Strategies

After a packet is routed to a phantom source node, then it will be transmitted to the ring nodes. Different from traditional routing strategy which uses only one routing method, in our scheme, we mix two routing strategies together: the shortest path routing and the random routing. Hence, when a node receives a packet, it will decide which routing strategy should be used.

In our scheme, we use a random number to make the two routing strategies work together. We first draw a random number between 0 and 1. If the number is larger than 0.7, the shortest path routing is selected, otherwise the random routing is selected.

The mixed routing strategy will work for a certain period. When choosing the next hop, our scheme first narrows the candidate region by using two tangents which is drawn from ring around the sink node to visible area. As shown in Fig. 2, the dotted lines between Ps1 and sink node are two tangents. Each node first draws two tangents and then next hop is selected in tangent area to make sure packets will be routed to the sink node instead of getting far away from sink node. Other sensor nodes work likewise.

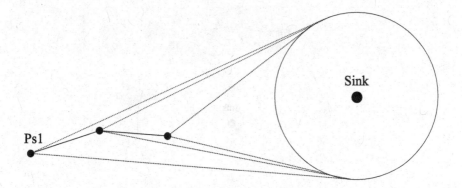

Fig. 2. Combination of two routing strategies

In the tangent area, our scheme increases the angle of invalid region of the phantom area. As shown in Fig. 1, for common visible area, the angle of invalid area can be calculated by the following equation:

$$\theta = \frac{arcsin(\frac{r}{R_{max}}) + arcsin(\frac{r}{H})}{\pi} \tag{1}$$

where H is the distance between the real source node and the sink node, r is the radius of the visible area, R_{max} is the radius of the phantom area.

When we take account of two tangents, this angle will get bigger. After combination of two routing strategy, packets will be transformed into the trace cost area and ring around the sink node. The trace cost area is a special area in which packets are routed by random routing and nodes in this area are mainly deployed in mountains, plains, and forests, which conforms to real environment.

4.4   Ring Routing Around Sink Node

Ring around the sink node is shown in Fig. 3. After a packet passes the trace cost area, it will be relayed to nodes in the ring around the sink node. In order to form the ring, some parts of the network are divided into small grids and several nodes will be placed in each grid. Ring nodes are randomly chosen from the nearby grid according to the residual energy of nodes, which means a node that has more residual energy has a higher likelihood to be arranged as a ring node.

Ring nodes will consume huge energy after several turns since all the packets are transmitted to ring nodes. Hence, ring nodes can be replaced by nodes in the corresponding grids. When a packet arrives at a ring node, it creates a random hop. This hop represents how long the packet can be transmitted. During each transmission, this random hop has two opposite directions: clockwise and anticlockwise. Transmitting in this way can prevent adversary from deducing the location of the source node by reverse extension cord of each packet. By the end of random hop, packets will be routed to sink node by shortest path routing.

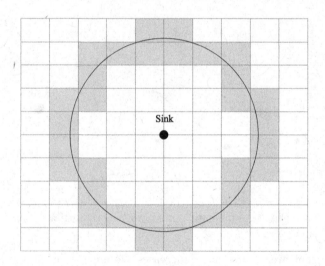

Fig. 3. Ring routing around the sink node

For reducing the energy consumption, we adapt the formula in [24] to calculate the radius of the ring around the sink node. We first set the sink node as center to establish axis and partition the ring into 8 parts. Energy consumption is proportional to the square of distance as the following equation:

$$\epsilon_{total} = 8\alpha\lambda \int_0^{\frac{\pi}{4}} \int_0^{\frac{s}{cos\theta}} (r-e)^2 r \, dr \, d\theta \qquad (2)$$

After derivation, we can evaluate the suitable ring radius.

5 Performance Evaluation

In this section, we evaluate our scheme through extensive simulations. We mainly consider two metrics: safety time and energy cost. Energy cost is the average energy consumed by nodes during one round data transmission. We use the number of hops to represent safety time and safety time is the number of packets that have been sent to sink node before the source node is captured by the adversary.

5.1 Simulation Environment

We have implemented the proposed PTSLP with MATLAB. In our simulation, 1000 nodes are deployed in a 600 m * 600 m square area. The communication radius of a node is 30 m. The radius of the ring and the visible area are 75 m and 50 m respectively and the maximum range of the phantom area is 150 m. For each transmission in network, there only exists a source node and a sink node. The simulation is performed for 400 times.

The performance of the PTSLP simulation is evaluated by two parameters, safety time and energy cost. We analyze the two parameters by varying the random walk hops from 2 to 10 and the hops between source node and sink node from 12 to 20. Then, safety time and energy cost of PTSLP and SLP-E [15] are compared.

5.2 Simulation Results of Safety Time

We evaluate the performance of our scheme by varying the hops of the random walk between 2 and 10 and the hops between source node and sink node from 12 to 20. The simulation results are shown in Figs. 4 and 5.

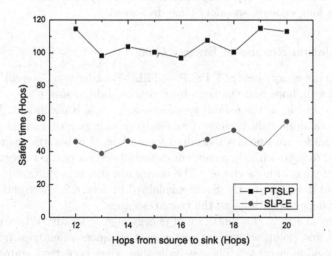

Fig. 4. Safety time under hops from source to sink

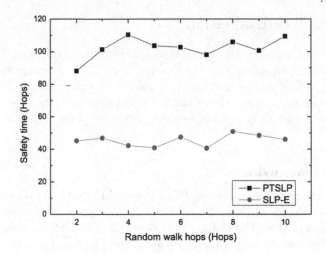

Fig. 5. Safety time under random walk hops

As presented in Fig. 4, safety time fluctuates when hops from source to sink varies. The reason that safety time is not linear is that each packet has to pass the trace cost area, and in this area, packets are routed in the random routing strategy. So the main determination of safety time depends on hops in the trace cost area while hops from source to sink play an auxiliary function in safety time. But when the number of hops increase, the safety time tends to increase and the safety time of our scheme is acceptable.

As shown in Fig. 5, when hops of the random walk varies, the overall performance of safety time is rising even though with some fluctuation. The reason is that these nodes are closer to sink node compared with other nodes at 4 to 6 random hops. Moreover, the transmission path of these nodes in the trace cost area are not long enough, so safety time decreases.

5.3   Simulation Results of Energy Cost

We compare the energy cost of PTSLP and SLP-E under two different variables: the random walk hops and the hops from source node to sink node.

As shown in Fig. 6, the overall trend of energy cost is ascendant. When the hops of the random walk increase progressively, energy cost increases steadily even in the middle of line chart declines for a little. It is because energy cost is proportional to hops while hops are composed of several parts. Energy cost will change when parts of hops change. The maximum energy cost stays in the trace cost area and it varies greatly. So, as explained in Sect. 4.2, the trend of energy cost mainly depends on hops in the trace cost area.

As shown in Fig. 7, the tendency of energy cost is steady. When we do not consider the first point, we can see energy cost enhances when hops from source node to sink node increases. The reason is that when hops from source node to sink node increase, each packet needs more hops to be relayed. The increased hops account for why energy cost grows.

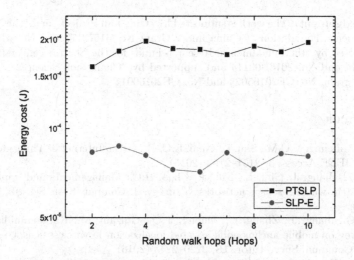

Fig. 6. Energy cost under random walk hops

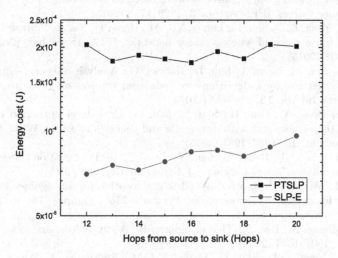

Fig. 7. Energy cost under hops from source to sink

6   Conclusion

In this paper, we have proposed the PTSLP protection mechanism for WSNs. Particularly, by utilizing the phantom source nodes and two routing strategies, source location privacy in WSNs can be maintained. In addition, the ring around the sink node can prevent the adversary from the angle attack in WSNs. Simulation results have shown that the proposed PTSLP mechanism is able to improve the safety time for WSNs, compared with SLP-E.

Acknowledgement. The work is supported by "Qing Lan Project" and "the National Natural Science Foundation of China under Grant No. 61572172 and No. 61602152" and supported by "the Fundamental Research Funds for the Central Universities, No. 2016B10714 and No. 2016B03114 and supported by "Changzhou Sciences and Technology Program, No. CE20165023 and No. CE20160014".

References

1. Zhu, C., Leung, V.C.M., Shu, L., Ngai, E.C.-H.: Green Internet of Things for smart world. IEEE Access. **3**, 2151–2162 (2015)
2. Han, G., Jiang, J., Shu, L., Niu, J., Chao, H.C.: Managements and applications of trust in wireless sensor networks: a survey. J. Comput. Syst. Sci. **80**, 602–617 (2014)
3. Han, G., Jiang, J., Zhang, C., Duong, T.Q., Guizani, M., Karagiannidis, G.K.: A survey on mobile anchor node assisted localization in wireless sensor networks. IEEE Commun. Surv. Tutor. **18**, 2220–2243 (2016)
4. Wan, L., Han, G., Shu, L., Feng, N., Zhu, C., Lloret, J.: Distributed parameter estimation for mobile wireless sensor network based on cloud computing in battlefield surveillance system. IEEE Access. **3**, 1729–1739 (2015)
5. Zhu, C., Yang, L.T., Shu, L., Leung, V.C.M., Hara, T., Nishio, S.: Insights of top-k query in duty-cycled wireless sensor networks. IEEE Trans. Ind. Electron. **62**, 1317–1328 (2015)
6. Han, G., Liu, L., Jiang, J., Shu, L., Hancke, G.: Analysis of energy-efficient connected target coverage algorithms for industrial wireless sensor networks. IEEE Trans. Ind. Inform. **13**, 135–143 (2015)
7. Han, G., Dong, Y., Guo, H., Shu, L., Wu, D.: Cross-layer optimized routing in wireless sensor networks with duty-cycle and energy harvesting. Wirel. Commun. Mob. Comput. **15**, 1957–1981 (2015)
8. Peng, H., Chen, H., Hang, X., Fan, Y., Li, C.P., Li, D.: Location privacy preservation in wireless sensor networks. J. Softw. **26**, 617–639 (2015)
9. Chen, H., Wei, L.: On protecting end-to-end location privacy against local eavesdropper in wireless sensor networks. Pervasive Mob. Comput. **16**, 36–50 (2014). Elsevier B.V
10. Li, N., Zhang, N., Das, S., Thuraisingham, B.: A state-of-the-art survey. Ad Hoc Netw. **7**, 1501–1514 (2009)
11. Zhu, C., Yang, L.T., Shu, L., Leung, V.C.M., Rodrigues, J., Wang, L.: Sleep scheduling for geographic routing in duty-cycled mobile sensor networks. IEEE Trans. Ind. Electron. **61**, 6346–6355 (2014)
12. Jia, D., Chi, Y.: REAL: a reciprocal protocol for location privacy in wireless sensor networks. IEEE Trans. Dependable Secur. Comput. **12**, 458–471 (2015)
13. Conti, M., Willemsen, J., Crispo, B.: Providing source location privacy in wireless sensor networks: a survey. IEEE Commun. Surv. Tutor. **15**, 1238–1280 (2013)
14. Jhumka, A., Bradbury, M., Leeke, M.: Fake source-based source location privacy in wireless sensor networks. Concurr. Comput. Pract. Exp. **27**, 189–203 (2014)
15. Chen, J., Lin, Z., Hu, Y., Wang, B.: Hiding the source based on limited flooding for sensor networks. Sensors **15**, 29129–29148 (2015)
16. He, W., Liu, X., Nguyen, H., Nahrstedt, K.: A cluster-based protocol to enforce integrity and preserve privacy in data aggregation. In: 29th IEEE International Conference on Distributed Computing Systems Workshops (ICDCS Workshops 2009), pp. 14–19. IEEE, Los Alamitos. IEEE Computer Society (2009)

17. Lu, M., Zhao, Z., Tang, X., Zhou, J.: Research on phantom routing to provide source-location privacy in wireless sensor network. Inf. Technol. **10**, 72–79 (2012)
18. Yao, J., Hao, X., Wen, G.: Location privacy protecting in wireless sensor networks. Chin. J. Sens. Actuators **21**, 1437–1441 (2008)
19. Chen, J., Fang, B., Yin, L., Su, S.: A source-location privacy preservation protocol in wireless sensor networks using source-based restricted flooding. Chin. J. Comput. **33**, 1736–1749 (2010)
20. Zhao, Z., Liu, Y., Zhang, F., Zhou, J., Zhang, P.: Research on source location privacy routing based on angle and probability in wireless sensor networks. J. Shandong Univ. (Nat. Sci.) **48**, 1–9 (2013)
21. Zhang, Y., Xu, Y., Wu, X.: Enhanced source-location privacy preservation protocol using random angle. Comput. Eng. Appl. **52**, 1–8 (2015)
22. Liu, X., Li, J., Li, B.: Source-location privacy protocol based on the minimum cost routing. Chin. J. Sens. Actuators **27**, 394–400 (2014)
23. Wang, W., Chen, L., Wang, J.: A source-location privacy protocol in WSN based on locational angle. In: Proceedings of the IEEE International Conference Communications, pp. 1630–1634. IEEE Press, Beijing (2008)
24. Li, Y., Ren, J., Wu, J.: Quantitative measurement and design of source-location privacy schemes for wireless sensor networks. IEEE Trans. Parallel Distrib. Syst. **23**, 1302–1311 (2012)

A Robust Authentication Protocol with Privacy Protection for Wireless Sensor Networks

Xiong Li[1,2], Jianwei Niu[2(✉)], and Kim-Kwang Raymond Choo[3]

[1] School of Computer Science and Engineering,
Hunan University of Science and Technology, Xiangtan 411201, China
[2] State Key Laboratory of Virtual Reality Technology and Systems,
School of Computer Science and Engineering, Beihang University,
Beijing 100191, China
niujianwei@buaa.edu.cn
[3] Department of Information Systems and Cyber Security,
University of Texas at San Antonio, San Antonio, TX 78249-0631, USA

Abstract. As a typical application of Internet of Things (IoT), wireless sensor networks (WSNs) have been widely used in many fields, such as remote healthcare, to gather data of monitoring area. However, due to open nature of wireless channel and limited computing and storage resource of sensor node, how to guarantee the sensitive sensed data are only be accessed by valid user becomes an important issue. Many user authentication protocols for WSNs have been proposed to address this issue, however, previous work more or less have their own weaknesses. Recently, Gope and Hwang proposed a lightweight anonymity authentication for WSNs, and they claimed that their protocol is secure against most attacks. However, our analysis indicates that their protocol still has some design and security flaws. To address the security issue for WSNs, a user authentication protocol with privacy protection for WSNs has been proposed. The analysis and comparisons results show that the proposed protocol is a robust and security one for WSNs.

Keywords: Wireless sensor networks (WSNs) · Authentication · Key agreement · User anonymity

1 Introduction

Wireless sensor networks (WSNs) play an important role in Internet of Things (IoT), which have been widely used in many fields to collect data of specific monitoring area, such as in remote healthcare and environment monitoring. Typically, a wireless sensor network is formed by a gateway node and numerous sensor nodes through wireless communication, where sensor nodes are used

This work was supported by the National Natural Science Foundation of China under Grant Nos. 61300220 & 61572013 & 61572188, and the Scientific Research Fund of Hunan Provincial Education Department under Grant No. 16B089.

© Springer International Publishing AG 2017
G.P. Hancke and K. Markantonakis (Eds.): RFIDSec 2016, LNCS 10155, pp. 30–44, 2017.
DOI: 10.1007/978-3-319-62024-4_3

to collect environmental data for specific area and then these data would be forward to gateway via a wireless channel. Generally, a sensor node has limited storage, computing and power resource, while gateway usually has more powerful capability. In some applications of WSNs with high timeliness, such as remote healthcare, user needs to access the sensors' data directly by using mobile device. Therefore, how to verify the validity of the user is an important issue for security of WSNs. As a basic security mechanism for many network based applications, user authentication has also been used in verify validity of user for WSNs, and researchers have proposed many user authentication protocols for WSNs. However, the wireless sensor network is full of malicious attacks due to its open characteristic of wireless channel. Besides, the resource limitation of sensor node makes traditional public key cryptography algorithms like RSA are not suitable for WSN environments. At the same time, it is hoped that the user authentication protocol should meet more security and function features, such as mutual authentication, key agreement, user anonymity, and resist most of known attacks. Therefore, compared with traditional network environments, the design of security and efficient authentication protocol for WSNs is a big challenge.

In 2009, Das [2] first introduced a password and smart card based two-factor user authentication protocol for WSNs, which becomes foundation of the follow-up work. However, some researchers [6,7,13] pointed out that the protocol in [2] exists some function and security drawbacks, such as it cannot offer mutual authentication, user anonymity and key agreement, and it is also vulnerable to gateway bypassing, password guessing, sensor node capture and denial-of-service attacks. Later, some symmetric cryptography based user authentication protocols have been proposed to provide lightweight and efficient security protection for WSNs. However, most of these protocols are found vulnerable to potential malicious attacks. In fact, there is a contradiction between security and efficiency, i.e. traditional public cryptography based protocols can provide high level of security, however it may inefficient for WSNs, while symmetric cryptography based protocols are just the opposite. To balance this contradiction, elliptic curve cryptography (ECC) is introduced to the design of authentication for WSNs due to it is efficient than RSA and can provide the same security level as RSA with much shorter key length. In 2011, Yeh et al. [13] presented an ECC-based two-factor authentication protocol for WSNs. However, the mutual authentication cannot be achieved in their protocol. Later, Shi et al. [11] proposed an improved ECC-based authentication protocol to address the flaws of the protocol in [13]. The protocol in [11] is efficient and can provide more features than the protocol in [13]. Unfortunately, Choi et al. [1] pointed out that the protocol in [11] is suffer from unknown key share attack and stolen smart card attack, and they presented an enhanced protocol for WSNs. Recently, Gope and Hwang [4] puts forward a lightweight authentication protocol with user anonymity for WSNs, and they claimed that their protocol provides most of security and function features with high efficiency. However, we find their protocol vulnerable to some attacks and exists some design flaws. To balance the contradiction of security and efficient, we proposed an ECC based user authentication for WSNs.

The rest parts of the paper are arranged as follows: Sects. 2 and 3 give the review and cryptanalysis of the protocol in [4], respectively. The proposed protocol and the corresponding analysis are provided in Sect. 4 and 5, respectively. Finally, Sect. 6 concludes the full paper.

2 Review of Gope and Hwang's Protocol

In this section, we review Gope and Hwang's authentication protocol for wireless sensor networks [4]. Their protocol is composed of four phases, i.e. registration, authentication and key exchange, password renewal, and dynamic node addition phases. Since the last phase has no relation with our cryptanalysis, we just briefly introduce the first three phases of their protocol as follows, and the notations used in their protocol are shown in Table 1.

Table 1. The notations used in this paper

Notation	Description
U, GW, SN	User, Gateway, and Sensor node, respectively
ID_U, PW_U	Identity and password of user U
AID_U, SID	One-time alias identity and shadow identity of user U
ID_G, ω	Secret identity and secret key of gateway
SN_{id}	Identity of sensor node
N_u	Random number generated by user U
SK	Session key shared between U and S_n
K_{ug}, K_{em}	Shared key and shared emergency key between U and GW
K_{gs}	Shared secret key between GW and S_n
TS_{ug}	Transmission sequence number of U's login request message
$h(\cdot)$	One way hash function
$\oplus$	XOR operation
$\|$	Concatenation operation
$\mathcal{A}$	An attacker

2.1 Registration Phase

To access the sensor data through the wireless sensor networks, a user U needs to register at gateway GW as follows.

Step 1: User U chooses an identity ID_U, and submits it to GW via a secure channel.

Step 2: When receiving the registration request from user, GW generates a 128 bit length random number n_g, and calculates secret key $K_{ug} = h(ID_U \| n_g) \oplus$

ID_G. Besides, GW generates a 64 bit length transmission sequence number TS_{ug}, which is used to identify the login message belongs to which user, and will be increased by 1 if a session is successfully authenticated between U and GW. Furthermore, in order to handle the desynchronization problem between U and GW, GW generates a set of shadow identities $SID = \{sid_1, sid_2, \ldots\}$ for U, where $sid_j = h(ID_U \| r_j \| K_{ug})$ and r_j is a 128 bit random number. Then, GW calculates the corresponding set of emergency keys $K_{em} = \{k_{em_1}, k_{em_2}, \ldots\}$, where $k_{em_j} = h(ID_U \| sid_j \| r_j')$ and r_j' is a 128 bit random number for k_{em_j}.

Step 3: GW stores $\{K_{ug}, (SID, K_{em}), TS_{ug}, h(\cdot)\}$ into a smart card, and issues it to U securely. Besides, GW calculates $ID_U^{\#} = ID_U \oplus h(ID_G \| \omega \| TS_{ug})$, $K_{ug}^{\#} = K_{ug} \oplus h(ID_G \| ID_U \| \omega)$. For $K_{em_j} \in K_{em}$, GW produces a set $K_{em}^{\#}$ by calculating $k_{em_j}^{\#} = k_{em_j} \oplus h(ID_G \| ID_U \| \omega)$. Then, GW stores $\{ID_U^{\#}, K_{ug}^{\#}, (SID, K_{em}^{\#}), TS_{ug}\}$ in the database.

Step 4: When getting the smart card, U chooses a password PW_U, and calculates $K_{ug}^{*} = K_{ug} \oplus h(h(ID_U) \oplus h(PW_U))$ and $f_U^{*} = h(h(K_{ug}) \oplus h(PW_U) \oplus h(ID_U))$. For each $sid_j \in SID$ and $k_{em_j} \in K_{em}$, U computes $sid_j^{*} = sid_j \oplus h(h(ID_U) \oplus h(PW_U))$ and $k_{em_j}^{*} = k_{em_j} \oplus h(h(ID_U) \oplus h(PW_U))$ to form $SID^{*} = \{sid_1^{*}, sid_2^{*}, \ldots\}$ and $K_{em}^{*} = \{k_{em_1}^{*}, k_{em_2}^{*}, \ldots\}$. At last, U replaces K_{ug}, SID and K_{em} with K_{ug}^{*}, SID^{*} and K_{em}^{*}, respectively, and the parameters in the smart card are $\{K_{ug}^{*}, f_U^{*}, (SID^{*}, K_{em}^{*}), TS_{ug}, h(\cdot)\}$.

2.2 Authentication and Key Exchange Phase

When U wants to access the data of sensor node SN, the following steps are performed among U, GW and SN to achieve mutual authentication, and at last a shared session key is agreed between U and SN. Besides, in case of desynchronization between U and GW, the user is asked to use data pair of (SID, K_{em}) to perform the authentication, and we illustrate these steps as '.

Step 1: $U \rightarrow GW : M_{A_1} = \{AID_U, N_x, TS_{ug}, SN_{id}, V_1\}$.
. U inserts the smart card into a terminal, and inputs ID_U and PW_U. The smart card calculates $K_{ug} = K_{ug}^{*} \oplus h(h(ID_U) \oplus h(PW_U))$, $f_U = h(h(K_{ug}) \oplus h(PW_U) \oplus h(ID_U))$, and checks whether $f_U^{*} = f_U$. If they are not equal, the session is rejected by the smart card. Otherwise, the smart card generates a random number N_u and computes pseudonym identity $AID_U = h(ID_U \| K_{ug} \| N_u \| TS_{ug})$, $N_x = K_{ug} \oplus N_u$, and $V_1 = h(AID_U \| K_{ug} \| N_x \| SN_{id})$. At last, U submits the login request message $M_{A_1} = \{AID_U, N_x, TS_{ug}, SN_{id}, V_1\}$ to GW.

Step 1': $U \rightarrow GW : M_{A_1} = \{AID_U, N_x, SN_{id}, V_1\}$
The smart card chooses a data pair $(sid_j^{*}, k_{em_j}^{*})$, and computes $sid_j = sid_j^{*} \oplus h(h(ID_U) \oplus h(PW_U))$, $k_{em_j} = k_{em_j}^{*} \oplus h(h(ID_U) \oplus h(PW_U))$. Then, the smart card sets $AID_U = sid_j$ and $K_{ug} = k_{em_j}$. As like in step 1, the smart card submits $M_{A_1} = \{AID_U, N_x, SN_{id}, V_1\}$ to GW.

Step 2: $GW \to SN : M_{A_2} = \{AID_U, SK', T, V_2\}$.

When receiving the login request message from U, GW checks whether the transmission sequence number TS_{ug} existed in its database. If not, the session is terminated by GW, and U is asked to use shadow ID and emergency key pair to initiate the login request. Otherwise, GW decodes ID_U and K_{ug} from $ID_U^\#$ and $K_{ug}^\#$ which are corresponding to TS_{ug} by using its secret key ω. Then, GW checks whether $V_1 = h(AID_U \| K_{ug} \| N_x \| SN_{id})$. If not, the session is rejected by GW. Otherwise, GW calculates $N_u = K_{ug} \oplus N_x$ and checks $AID_U \overset{?}{=} h(ID_U \| K_{ug} \| N_u \| TS_{ug})$. If they are not equal, the session is terminated by GW. Otherwise, U is authenticated by GW, and GW generates a session key SK and a timestamp T. Then, GW computes $SK' = h(K_{gs}) \oplus SK$, $V_2 = h(AID_U \| SK' \| T \| K_{gs})$. At last, GW forwards the message $M_{A_2} = \{AID_U, SK', T, V_2\}$ to SN.

Step 2′: GW searches if $AID_U = sid_j$ is in the database, if so GW takes the multivariate data corresponding to sid_j, and perform the same process as step 2.

Step 3: $SN \to GW : M_{A_3} = \{T', SN_{id}, V_3\}$.

When receiving the message M_{A_2}, SN checks the validity of V_2 by using K_{gs} and the freshness of T. Any failure of these two verifications will deduce the termination of the session. Otherwise, SN calculates $SK = h(K_{gs}) \oplus SK'$, and generates a timestamp T' and computes $V_3 = h(SK \| K_{gs} \| SN_{id} \| T')$. Then, SN calculates $K_{gs_{new}} = h(K_{gs} \| SN_{id})$ and updates K_{gs} with $K_{gs_{new}}$. At last, SN submits the message $M_{A_3} = \{T', SN_{id}, V_3\}$ to GW.

Step 4: $GW \to U : M_{A_4} = \{SK'', V_4, T_s\}$

When receiving the message M_{A_3} from SN, GW checks the freshness of T', and checks $V_3 \overset{?}{=} h(SK \| K_{gs} \| SN_{id} \| T')$. If they are not equal, the session is terminated. Otherwise, GW sets $TS_{ug_{new}} = TS_{ug} + 1$, and computes $T_s = h(K_{ug} \| ID_U \| N_u) \oplus TS_{ug_{new}}$, $SK'' = h(K_{ug} \| ID_U \| N_u) \oplus SK$, and $V_4 = h(SK'' \| N_u \| T_s \| K_{ug})$. Then, GW calculates $K_{ug_{new}} = h(K_{ug} \| ID_U \| TS_{ug_{new}})$, $K_{gs_{new}} = h(K_{gs} \| SN_{id})$, and replaces K_{ug}, K_{gs} and TS_{ug} with $K_{ug_{new}}, K_{gs_{new}}$ and $TS_{ug_{new}}$, respectively. At last, GW forwards the message $M_{A_4} = \{SK'', V_4, T_s\}$ to U.

Step 4′: $GW \to U : M_{A_4} = \{SK'', V_4, T_s, x\}$

GW generates a new unique transmission sequence number $TS_{ug_{new}}$, and computes T_s and SK'' as step 4 by substituting k_{em_j} for K_{ug}. Then GW generates a new shared key $K_{ug_{new}}$, and computes $x = K_{ug_{new}} \oplus h(ID_U \| k_{em_j})$, $V_4 = h(SK'' \| N_u \| T_s \| x) \oplus k_{em_j}$. At last, GW submits $M_{A_4} = \{SK'', V_4, T_s, x\}$ to U.

Step 5: When receiving the message M_{A_4} from GW, the smart card checks $h(SK'' \| N_u \| T_s \| K_{ug}) \overset{?}{=} V_4$. If they are equal, the smart card derives the session key $SK = h(K_{ug} \| ID_U \| N_u) \oplus SK''$, which is used to ensuring the following secure communication between U and SN. Then, the smart card calculates $TS_{ug_{new}} = h(K_{ug} \| ID_U \| N_u) \oplus T_s$, $K_{ug_{new}} = h(K_{ug} \| ID_U \| TS_{ug_{new}})$. At last, the smart card updates TS_{ug} and K_{ug} with $TS_{ug_{new}}$ and $K_{ug_{new}}$, respectively.

Step 5': The smart card verifies V_4 and derives SK. Then, the smart card computes $TS_{ug_{new}} = h(k_{em_j} \| ID_U \| N_u) \oplus T_s$, $K_{ug_{new}} = h(ID_U \| k_{em_j}) \oplus x$. At last, the smart card updates TS_{ug} and K_{ug} with $TS_{ug_{new}}$ and $K_{ug_{new}}$, respectively.

2.3 Password Renewal Phase

By executing this phase, U can update the password without contact with GW. The user inserts the smart card into a reader, and inputs ID_U, PW_U and new password PW_U^*, and request to update the password. The smart card retrieves $K_{ug} = K_{ug}^* \oplus h(h(ID_U) \oplus h(PW_U))$, $sid_j = sid_j^* \oplus h(h(ID_U) \oplus h(PW_U))$, $k_{em_j} = k_{em_j}^* \oplus h(h(ID_U) \oplus h(PW_U))$, and calculates $K_{ug}^{**} = K_{ug} \oplus h(h(ID_U) \oplus h(PW_U^*))$, $sid_j^{**} = sid_j \oplus h(h(ID_U) \oplus h(PW_U^*))$, $k_{em_j}^{**} = k_{em_j} \oplus h(h(ID_U) \oplus h(PW_U^*))$. Finally, the smart card replaces K_{ug}^*, sid_j^* and $k_{em_j}^*$ with K_{ug}^{**}, sid_j^{**} and $k_{em_j}^{**}$, respectively.

3 Cryptanalysis of Gope and Hwang's Protocol

In this section, we analyze the weaknesses of the protocol in [4], and illustrate the design flaws of their protocol.

3.1 Stolen Smart Card Attack

Previous work [8,10] have illustrated that the information stored in smart card can be extracted by using side-channel attacks. Therefore, stolen smart card attack should be considered in the design of smart card based authentication protocol. In analysis part of Gope and Hwang's protocol [4], they said that their protocol can avoid of stolen smart card attack since an attacker cannot obtain ID_U and PW_U, but the reality is not the case. As mentioned in previous work [9,12], user usually chooses easy to remember identity and password with low entropy, so it is reasonable and realistic that an attacker can guess out user's data pair (ID, PW) within polynomial time by using the method of off-line enumeration. In Gope and Hwang's protocol, if U's smart card is stolen by an attack $\mathcal{A}$, the data $\{K_{ug}^*, f_U^*, (SID^*, K_{em}^*), TS_{ug}, h(\cdot)\}$ stored in U's smart card can be revealed by $\mathcal{A}$, where $K_{ug}^* = K_{ug} \oplus h(h(ID_U) \oplus h(PW_U))$, $f_U^* = h(h(K_{ug}) \oplus h(PW_U) \oplus h(ID_U))$, $SID^* = \{sid_1^*, sid_1^*, \ldots\}$, $K_{em}^* = \{k_{em_1}^*, k_{em_2}^*, \ldots\}$, $sid_j^* = sid_j \oplus h(h(ID_U) \oplus h(PW_U))$, $k_{em_j}^* = k_{em_j} \oplus h(h(ID_U) \oplus h(PW_U))$, and TS_{ug} is the most recent transmission sequence number. Then $\mathcal{A}$ can guess U's identity and password as follows:

Step 1: Randomly chooses a data pair (ID_U', PW_U') from $\mathcal{D}_{id} \times \mathcal{D}_{pw}$, where $\mathcal{D}_{id}$ and $\mathcal{D}_{pw}$ denote the identity dictionary and password dictionary of the system, respectively.

Step 2: Computes $K_{ug}' = K_{ug}^* \oplus h(h(ID_U') \oplus h(PW_U'))$ and $f_U' = h(h(K_{ug}') \oplus h(PW_U') \oplus h(ID_U'))$.

Step 3: Examines the validity of ID'_U and PW'_U by checking whether f'_U equals to f^*_U.

Step 4: Repeats above steps until valid data pair (ID'_U, PW'_U) is found.

When obtain U's valid (ID'_U, PW'_U), $\mathcal{A}$ can reveal $SID = \{sid_1, sid_2, \ldots\}$ and $K_{em} = \{k_{em_1}, k_{em_2}, \ldots\}$ by calculating $sid_j = sid^*_j \oplus h(h(ID'_U) \oplus h(PW'_U))$ for $sid^*_j \in SID^*$ and $k_{em_j} = k^*_{em_j} \oplus h(h(ID'_U) \oplus h(PW'_U))$ for $k^*_{em_j} \in K^*_{em}$.

From above analysis, we can see that if U's smart card is stolen by attacker $\mathcal{A}$, then not only U's identity and password can be guessed by $\mathcal{A}$, but also the shadow ID set SID and emergency key set K_{em} can be calculated by $\mathcal{A}$. Therefore the protocol in [4] is vulnerable to stolen smart card attack.

3.2 No Provision of User Anonymity

User anonymity is an important feature for authentication protocol, especially in current ubiquitous network environment. Generally, user anonymity not only protects user's real identity from being revealed, but also keeps the user from being tracked. In each login phase, U submits the login request message $M_{A_1} = \{AID_U, N_x, TS_{ug}, SN_{id}, V_1\}$ to GW. From the description of the protocol in [4], we can see that U's transmission sequence number TS_{ug} will increase 1 for each successful session, so it can be seen as a fixed indicator of U. It is true that AID_U, N_x and V_1 are all dynamically change for each session, however if he/she can continuous acquire sequence numbers set $\{TS_{ug}, TS_{ug} + 1, TS_{ug} + 2, \ldots\}$ from all eavesdropped login request messages, attacker $\mathcal{A}$ can confirm that these sessions are come from a specific user. Therefore, the protocol in [4] fails to preserve user anonymity, and an attacker can trace a specific user by checking user's transmission sequence numbers via continuous eavesdropping attack.

3.3 Unable to Provide Backward Secrecy

In the protocol in [4], the authors claimed that their scheme aimed to provide the feature of forward and backward secrecy. However, we find the protocol in [4] cannot ensure backward secrecy of session key, i.e. the compromise of GW's secret key K_{gs} in current session will result in the compromise of next session key between U and SN, and we illustrate this situation as follows:

Step 1: Assume that GW's secret key K_{gs} in current session has been compromised by an attacker $\mathcal{A}$, and the exchanged messages $\{AID_U, N_x, TS_{ug}, SN_{id}, V_1\}$, $\{AID_U, SK', T, V_2\}$, $\{T', SN_{id}, V_3\}$ and $\{SK'', V_4, T_s\}$ in current session among U, GW and SN have been eavesdropped by $\mathcal{A}$. In this session, GW and SN update the shared secret key as $K_{gs_{new}} = h(K_{gs} \| SN_{id})$.

Step 2: $\mathcal{A}$ trace next session among U, GW and SN by eavesdropping attack and checking whether $TS_{ug} + 1$ appears in the messages. If so, $\mathcal{A}$ records the messages in this session as $\{AID^*_U, N^*_x, TS_{ug} + 1, SN_{id}, V^*_1\}$, $\{AID_U, SK'^*, T^*, V^*_2\}$, $\{T'^*, SN_{id}, V^*_3\}$ and $\{SK''^*, V^*_4, T^*_s\}$, where $SK'^* = h(K_{gs_{new}}) \oplus SK^*$ and SK^* is the session key between U and SN in this session.

Step 3: Since K_{gs} is compromised by $\mathcal{A}$ and SN_{id} is known as plaintext, $\mathcal{A}$ can compute the shared secret key between U and SN as $K_{gs_{new}} = h(K_{gs} \| SN_{id})$. Therefore, $\mathcal{A}$ can extract the shared session key between U and SN of this session by computes $SK^* = h(K_{gs_{new}}) \oplus SK'^*$.

3.4   Incorrect Password Renewal Phase

From the review of the protocol in [4], we can see that U's smart card contains information $\{K_{ug}^*, f_U^*, (SID^*, K_{em}^*), TS_{ug}, h(\cdot)\}$, where $\{K_{ug}^*, f_U^*, (SID^*, K_{em}^*)$ are all related to U's identity and password, and f_U^* is used for verify the validity of U's identity and password. However, in the password renewal phase of the protocol in [4], the smart card only renewals $\{K_{ug}^*, (SID^*, K_{em}^*)\}$, and f_U^* is remain the original one. Therefore, if U updates the password according to the protocol in [4], U cannot access sensors any more since the computed f_U would not equal to the stored f_U^*. According to the review of the protocol in [4], we correct the password renewal phase of protocol in [4] as below:

U inserts the smart card into a reader, and inputs ID_U, PW_U and new password PW_U^*, and request to update the password. The smart card retrieves $K_{ug} = K_{ug}^* \oplus h(h(ID_U) \oplus h(PW_U))$, $sid_j = sid_j^* \oplus h(h(ID_U) \oplus h(PW_U))$, $k_{em_j} = k_{em_j}^* \oplus h(h(ID_U) \oplus h(PW_U))$, and calculates $K_{ug}^{**} = K_{ug} \oplus h(h(ID_U) \oplus h(PW_U^*))$, $f_U^{**} = h(h(K_{ug}) \oplus h(PW_U^*) \oplus h(ID_U))$, $sid_j^{**} = sid_j \oplus h(h(ID_U) \oplus h(PW_U^*))$, $k_{em_j}^{**} = k_{em_j} \oplus h(h(ID_U) \oplus h(PW_U^*))$. Finally, the smart card replaces K_{ug}^*, f_U^*, sid_j^* and $k_{em_j}^*$ with K_{ug}^{**}, f_U^{**}, sid_j^{**} and $k_{em_j}^{**}$, respectively.

3.5   Potential Denial-of-Service Attack

Even if the password renewal phase is corrected as in Sect. 3.4, the protocol in [4] is still vulnerable to a potential denial-of-service attack. As we know that the user may input a wrong password when we login to a system. The protocol in [4] may vulnerable to a potential denial-of-service attack if the user inputs a wrong password in password renewal phase due to the absence of wrong password change mechanism. We describe this situation as follows:

When U wants to renewal the password, he/she inserts the smart card into a reader. Suppose U inputs ID_U, a wrong password $PW_U'(\neq PW_U)$ and new password PW_U^*, and request to update the password. Then U's secret key will be updated as $K_{ug}' = K_{ug}^* \oplus h(h(ID_U) \oplus h(PW_U')) = K_{ug} \oplus h(h(ID_U) \oplus h(PW_U)) \oplus h(h(ID_U) \oplus h(PW_U'))$, which is not equal to the original K_{ug} due to $PW_U' \neq PW_U$. However, since the password renewal phase has no relation with GW, the shared secret key in GW is still K_{ug}. Therefore, the shared secret key of U is not the same with those of GW. The desynchronization of shared secret key between U and GW would cause U cannot pass the authentication of GW anymore, and the protocol in [4] may vulnerable to denial-of-services.

4   Proposed Anonymity Authentication Protocol for WSN

In this section, a strong ECC and biometric based authentication protocol with user anonymity for wireless sensor network is proposed. Due to space limitations, we don't introduce the basic knowledge about ECC and biometric, and the reader can refer [5] for ECC and [3] for fuzzy extractor. In order to initialize the system, GW chooses an elliptic curve E over prime finite field F_p, and chooses an additional subgroup G of E, which is generated by P with a large prime order n. Then, GW selects a random number $x \in Z_n^*$ as a secret key, and computes the corresponding public key $X = xP$. Besides, GW chooses a secret key ω. GW publishes $\{E, G, n, P, X\}$. Our protocol contains three phases, i.e. registration, authentication and key agreement, password change.

4.1   Registration Phase

Registration phase is divided to aspects, i.e. sensor registration and user registration, and they are both completed in a secure manner.

1. **Sensor registration:** GW selects a unique identity SN_{id} for each sensor node, and computes a secret key $K_{gs} = h(SN_{id} \| \omega)$. After that, GW stores SN_{id} in its database and (SN_{id}, K_{gs}) in SN. Then the sensor nodes can be deployed in target area to forming a network.
   Remark: To add a new sensor node into the WSN, GW just need to register the sensor node as this phase, and then it can be added into the WSN.

2. **User registration:**
   Step 1: User U chooses an identity ID_U and a password PW_U, and extracts the biometric information in the mobile device with fuzzy extractor $Gen(BIO_U) = (R_U, P_U)$. Then, U generates a random number r_U, and computes $HPW_U = h(PW_U \| r_U)$. At last, U submits the registration request (ID_U, HPW_U, R_U) to GW via a secure manner.
   Step 2: When receiving the request from U, GW first checks whether ID_U is in the database. If not, U is asked to choose a new identity. Otherwise, GW calculates $B_1 = h(ID_U \| HPW_U \| R_U)$, $B_2 = h(ID_U \| \omega)$, and $B_3 = h(HPW_U \| R_U) \oplus B_2$. At last, GW sends the data (B_1, B_3, X, ID_{GW}) to U via a secure manner.
   Step 3: Upon receiving the parameters, U stores $(P_U, r_U, B_1, B_3, X, ID_{GW}, Gen(,), Rep(,))$ into the mobile device.

4.2   Authentication and Key Agreement Phase

When U wants access the sensory data of sensor node SN with identity SN_{id}, the following authentication processes should be performed among U, GW and SN, and at last a session key will be agreed between U and SN for future communication.

Step 1: $U \rightarrow GW : M_1 = \{DID_U, ID_G, SN_{id}, D_1, D_3\}$

U inputs identity ID_U and password PW_U, and imprints the biometrics BIO'_U at the mobile device with fuzzy extractor. The mobile device calculates $R_U = Rep(BIO'_U, P_U)$, $B'_1 = h(ID_U \| h(PW_U \| r) \| R_U)$, and checks $B'_1 \overset{?}{=} B_1$. If they are not equal, at least one factor of identity, password and biometrics is not valid, and the login request is rejected by the mobile device. Otherwise, the mobile device generates a random number $a \in Z_n^*$, and computes $B_2 = B_3 \oplus h(h(PW_U \| r_U) \| R_U)$, $D_1 = aP$, $D_2 = aX$, $DID_U = ID_U \oplus D_2$, and $D_3 = h(B_2 \| ID_G \| D_2 \| SN_{id})$. At last, the mobile device submits the login request $M_1 = \{DID_U, ID_G, SN_{id}, D_1, D_3\}$ to GW.

Step 2: $GW \rightarrow SN : M_2 = \{ID_G, D_1, D_5, D_6\}$

Upon receiving the login request, GW computes $D'_2 = xD_1$, $ID'_U = DID_U \oplus D'_2$, and checks whether ID'_U is in the database. If so, GW calculates $B'_2 = h(ID'_U \| \omega)$, $D'_3 = h(B'_2 \| ID_G \| D'_2 \| SN_{id})$, and checks $D'_3 \overset{?}{=} D_3$. If they are not equal, the request is terminated by GW. Otherwise, GW generates a random number r_G, and computes $D_4 = h(SN_{id} \| \omega)$, $D_5 = D_4 \oplus r_G$, and $D_6 = h(ID_G \| D_1 \| r_G \| D_4 \| SN_{id})$. Then, GW forwards message $M_2 = \{ID_G, D_1, D_5, D_6\}$ to SN.

Step 3: $SN \rightarrow GW : M_3 = \{SN_{id}, D_7, D_8\}$

When receiving the message from GW, SN calculates $r'_G = K_{gs} \oplus D_5$, $D'_6 = h(ID_G \| D_1 \| r'_G \| K_{gs} \| SN_{id})$, and checks $D'_6 \overset{?}{=} D_6$. If they are not equal, SN terminates the session. Otherwise, SN generates a random number $b \in Z_n^*$, and computes $D_7 = bP$, $SK = h(D_1 \| D_7 \| bD_1)$, and $D_8 = h(K_{gs} \| D_7 \| r'_G \| SN_{id})$. Then, SN submits the message $M_3 = \{SN_{id}, D_7, D_8\}$ to GW.

Step 4: $GW \rightarrow U : M_4 = \{SN_{id}, D_7, D_9\}$

On receiving the message M_3, GW calculates $D'_8 = h(D_4 \| D_7 \| r_G \| SN_{id})$, and checks $D'_8 \overset{?}{=} D_8$. If they are not equal, the session is terminated. Otherwise, GW calculates $D_9 = h(ID'_U \| D_1 \| D_7 \| SN_{id})$, and then submits the message $M_4 = \{SN_{id}, D_7, D_9\}$ to U.

Step 5: When getting the message M_4, the mobile device calculates $D'_9 = h(ID_U \| D_1 \| D_7 \| SN_{id})$, and checks $D'_9 \overset{?}{=} D_9$. If they are not equal, the session is terminated. Otherwise, the mobile device computes $SK = h(D_1 \| D_7 \| aD_7)$.

4.3 Password Change Phase

This phase allows a user to update password without contact with gateway. When U wants to change the password, U inputs ID_U and PW_U, and imprints the biometrics BIO'_U at the mobile device with fuzzy extractor. The mobile device calculates $R_U = Rep(BIO'_U, P_U)$, $B'_1 = h(ID_U \| h(PW_U \| r_U) \| R_U)$, and checks $B'_1 \overset{?}{=} B_1$. If they are not equal, the request is rejected. Otherwise, U is allowed to input a new password PW_U^*. Then the mobile device calculates $B_2 = B_3 \oplus h(h(PW_U \| r_U) \| R_U)$, $B_1^* = h(ID_U \| h(PW_U^* \| r_U) \| R_U)$,

$B_3^* = h(h(PW_U^*\|r_U)\|R_U) \oplus B_2$. At last, the mobile device replaces B_1 and B_3 with B_1^* and B_3^*, respectively, which finishes the password change.

5   Analysis of the Proposed Protocol

In this section, the security and performance features of the proposed protocol are analyzed, and the comparisons with other related protocols are given.

5.1   Mutual Authentication

The proposed protocol provides mutual authentication between U and GW and between GW and SN.

In step 2 of authentication and key agreement phase, GW computes $D_2' = xD_1$, $ID_U' = DID_U \oplus D_2'$, and can check whether the identity is valid. Later, GW calculates $B_2' = h(ID_U'\|\omega)$, $D_3' = h(B_2'\|ID_G\|D_2'\|SN_{id})$, and can authenticate U by checking $D_3' \overset{?}{=} D_3$. Only U has a and can retrieve $B_2 = h(ID_U\|\omega)$ using password and biometric, then GW can ensure that U is a valid user since only U can generate valid D_3. On the contrary, in step 5, U can authenticate GW by checking whether $h(ID_U\|D_1\|D_7\|SN_{id})$ equals to D_9, this is because that only GW can reveal U's real identity ID_U with secret key x. Therefore, the mutual authentication between FW and SN is achieved in the proposed protocol.

The mutual authentication between GW and SN is relied on the shared secret key $h(SN_{id}\|\omega)$, which is stored in the memory of SN and can be calculated by GW by using SN_{id} and secret key ω. In step 3 of authentication and key agreement phase, only SN with $K_{gs} = h(SN_{id}\|\omega)$ can calculate $r_G' = K_{gs} \oplus D_5$, $D_6' = h(ID_G\|D_1\|r_G'\|K_{gs}\|SN_{id})$, and check $D_6' \overset{?}{=} D_6$ to verify the validity of GW. On the contrary, in step 4 of authentication and key agreement phase, GW can authenticate SN by checking $h(h(SN_{id}\|\omega)\|D_7\|r_G\|SN_{id}) \overset{?}{=} D_8$.

5.2   Resist Mobile Device Loss Attack

We suppose that U's mobile device is lost and obtained by an attacker $\mathcal{A}$, then $\mathcal{A}$ can retrieve the data $(P_U, r, B_1, B_3, X, ID_{GW}, Gen(,), Rep(,))$. $\mathcal{A}$ can guess a data pair $\{ID_U', PW_U'\}$, and in order to verify the validity of the guessed data pair from B_1, $\mathcal{A}$ has to know the information R_U. However, R_U is extracted from U's biometric BIO_U with the help of P_U, and it can be see as a random number with long bit length. Therefore, $\mathcal{A}$ cannot guess U's identity and password from B_1. Besides, without knowing R_U and ω, $\mathcal{A}$ has no chance to figure out U's identity and password from B_3. Therefore, the proposed protocol is free from mobile device loss attack.

5.3   User Anonymity

A login request message $M_1 = \{DID_U, ID_G, SN_{id}, D_1, D_3\}$ is submitted to GW when U wants login to SN, where $D_1 = aP$, $DID_U = ID_U \oplus D_2$, $D_2 = aX$,

$D_3 = h(B_2\|ID_G\|D_2\|SN_{id})$, and a is a random number. In order to obtain U's identity from dynamic identity DID_U, x is required information for $\mathcal{A}$ to calculate D_2. However, x is a secret key only known to GW. Therefore, U's real identity cannot be revealed by $\mathcal{A}$. Besides, in the proposed protocol, the information DID_U, D_1, and D_3 in login request are dynamically change with the random number a for each session. Therefore, $\mathcal{A}$ cannot trace a specific user by eavesdropping the login request messages. From the above analysis we can see that the proposed protocol protects user anonymity really.

5.4 Session Key Agreement and Known-Key Security

In the proposed protocol, a session key $SK = h(D_1\|D_7\|aD_7) = h(D_1\|D_7\|bD_1)$ $= h(aP\|bP\|abP)$ is shared between U and SN after the mutual authentication is achieved, which will be used to ensure subsequent secure communication between U and SN. Besides, the session key is relied on aP and bP, which are both different from each session due to the different random numbers a and b are generated by U and SN, respectively. In the proposed protocol, each session key in one session has no relation with those of other sessions. Therefore, the compromise of a session key in one session would not lead to the compromise of previous established session keys and future session keys, and the proposed protocol achieves known-key security.

5.5 Perfect Forward Secrecy and Backward Secrecy

As shown in Sect. 5.4, the session key $SK = h(aP\|bP\|abP)$ shared between U and SN is only related to the random numbers a and b, which are generated by U and SN, respectively, for each session. Even if the long term secret information of U, GW, and SN are all compromised by $\mathcal{A}$, the previous or future session key SK is still secure since $\mathcal{A}$ has to resolve intractable elliptic curve discrete logarithm problem or elliptic curve Diffie-Hellman problem to get abP from aP and bP. Therefore, the proposed protocol can achieve perfect forward secrecy and backward secrecy.

5.6 Resist Replay Attack

In the proposed protocol, the random number mechanism is used to ensure the freshness of communication messages. In each session, U, GW and SN generate random numbers a, r_G and b, respectively, which ensures that the messages exchanged among U, GW and SN are valid only for this session and different from those of other sessions. Therefore, the proposed protocol is free from replay attack without using timestamp.

5.7 Resist Impersonation Attacks

In the proposed protocol, in order to generate a valid login request message to impersonate as a user U, $\mathcal{A}$ has to know ID_U and $B_2 = h(ID_U\|\omega)$. However, as discussed in Sect. 5.2, $\mathcal{A}$ cannot reveal these information even if he/she has obtained U's mobile device. Therefore, the proposed protocol is free from user impersonation attack.

Besides, in the proposed protocol, without knowing the secret key x and ω, no one can masqueraded as the gateway. Therefore, our protocol can resist gateway impersonation attack.

5.8   Resist Sensor Node Capture Attack

Since the sensor nodes are usually deployed in the region without secure guaranteed, it can be compromised by an attacker. If the protocol can ensure that compromise of some sensor nodes has no security threat to other sensor nodes are not compromised, we say the protocol can resist sensor node capture attack. In the proposed protocol, for secure authentication, each sensor node SN stores a unique secret key $h(SN_{id}\|\omega)$, which is calculated by SN's identity and GW's secret key ω. Therefore, if $\mathcal{A}$ compromises a sensor node SN and obtains the key $h(SN_{id}\|\omega)$, he/she not only cannot reveal GW's secret key ω, but also cannot calculates other sensor nodes' secret key $h(SN_{id'}\|\omega)$. Therefore, the compromised sensor node has no security threat to other sensor nodes, and the proposed protocol can resist sensor node capture attack.

5.9   Comparisons with Other Related Protocols

In this section, we evaluate the security and performance of the proposed protocol by comparing our protocol with other related protocols. The following symbols are defined to simplify the efficiency comparison.

T_m: the time cost of one scalar multiplication;

T_h: the time cost of one hash operation;

T_s: the time cost of one symmetrical encryption/decryption operation.

The function and security features comparisons are listed in Table 2, from which we can see that the protocols in [1, 4, 11, 13] are all timestamp based protocols, and vulnerable to stolen smart card attack and cannot protect user anonymity. Besides, the protocol in [13] cannot achieve mutual authentication and lacks the function of session key agreement, and also vulnerable to sensor impersonation attack. Gope and Hwang's protocol [4] still vulnerable to denial-of-service attack and cannot achieve backward secrecy as they claimed. However, the proposed protocol can resist most of known attacks.

Table 3 shows the performance comparisons of our protocol with other related protocols, from which we can see that our protocol is efficient than the protocol in [13], and almost at the same level with the protocols in [1, 11]. In these protocols, Gope and Hwang's protocol [4] is the most efficient one. However, it can be seen in Table 2, Gope and Hwang's protocol [4] vulnerable to many attacks. Integrated both security and efficiency aspects, our protocol is most secure one with acceptable computational efficiency.

Table 2. Function and security features comparisons

	Yeh et al. [13]	Shi et al. [11]	Choi et al. [1]	Gope-Hwang [4]	Ours
Mutual authentication	No	Yes	Yes	Yes	Yes
Session key agreement	No	Yes	Yes	Yes	Yes
Perfect forward secrecy	N/A	Yes	Yes	Yes	Yes
Backward secrecy	N/A	Yes	Yes	No	Yes
Known-key security	N/A	Yes	Yes	Yes	Yes
Resist replay attack	Yes	Yes	Yes	Yes	Yes
User anonymity	No	No	No	No	Yes
Resist sensor impersonation attack	No	Yes	Yes	Yes	Yes
No timestamp	No	No	No	No	Yes
Resist DoS attack	Yes	Yes	Yes	No	Yes
Resist stolen card/device attack	No	No	No	No	Yes

Table 3. Performance comparisons

Time cost	U	GW	SN	Total
Yeh et al. [13]	$T_h + 2T_m$	$3T_h + 2T_m$	$4T_h + 4T_m$	$8T_h + 8T_m$
Shi et al. [11]	$6T_h + 3T_H$	$4T_h + 2T_m$	$4T_h + T_m$	$14T_h + 6T_m$
Choi et al. [1]	$8T_h + 3T_m$	$6T_C + 2T_m$	$45_h + 1T_m$	$19T_h + 6T_m$
Gope-Hwang [4]	$10T_h$	$11T_h$	$3T_h$	$24T_h$
Ours	$5T_h + 3T_m$	$6T_h + T_m$	$4T_h + 2T_m$	$15T_h + 6T_m$

6   Conclusions

This paper analyzed the design and security flaws of Gope and Hwang's protocol
[4], and proposed a new user authentication protocol with privacy protection for
WSNs. We analyzed the security features of the proposed protocol and compared it with some previous work in security and performance aspects, and the
comparison results show that the proposed protocol is robust and security for
WSNs with acceptable computational efficiency.

References

1. Choi, Y., Lee, D., Kim, J., Jung, J., Nam, J., Won, D.: Security enhanced user
   authentication protocol for wireless sensor networks using elliptic curves cryptography. Sensors **14**(6), 10081–10106 (2014)
2. Das, M.L.: Two-factor user authentication in wireless sensor networks. IEEE Trans.
   Wireless Commun. **8**(3), 1086–1090 (2009)
3. Dodis, Y., Reyzin, L., Smith, A.: Fuzzy extractors: how to generate strong keys
   from biometrics and other noisy data. In: Cachin, C., Camenisch, J.L. (eds.)
   EUROCRYPT 2004. LNCS, vol. 3027, pp. 523–540. Springer, Heidelberg (2004).
   doi:10.1007/978-3-540-24676-3_31
4. Gope, P., Hwang, T.: A realistic lightweight anonymous authentication protocol
   for securing real-time application data access in wireless sensor networks. IEEE
   Trans. Ind. Electron. **63**(11), 7124–7132 (2016)

5. Hankerson, D., Menezes, A.J., Vanstone, S.: Guide to Elliptic Curve Cryptography. Springer Science & Business Media, Heidelberg (2006)
6. He, D., Gao, Y., Chan, S., Chen, C., Bu, J.: An enhanced two-factor user authentication scheme in wireless sensor networks. Ad Hoc Sens. Wirel. Networks **10**(4), 361–371 (2010)
7. Khan, M.K., Alghathbar, K.: Cryptanalysis and security improvements of two-factor user authentication in wireless sensor networks. Sensors **10**(3), 2450–2459 (2010)
8. Kocher, P., Jaffe, J., Jun, B.: Differential power analysis. In: Wiener, M. (ed.) CRYPTO 1999. LNCS, vol. 1666, pp. 388–397. Springer, Heidelberg (1999). doi:10. 1007/3-540-48405-1_25
9. Ma, C.-G., Wang, D., Zhao, S.-D.: Security flaws in two improved remote user authentication schemes using smart cards. Int. J. Commun Syst **27**(10), 2215–2227 (2014)
10. Messerges, T.S., Dabbish, E.A., Sloan, R.H.: Examining smart-card security under the threat of power analysis attacks. IEEE Trans. Comput. **51**(5), 541–552 (2002)
11. Shi, W., Gong, P.: A new user authentication protocol for wireless sensor networks using elliptic curves cryptography. Int. J. Distrib. Sens. Networks (2013)
12. Wang, D., Wang, P.: Understanding security failures of two-factor authentication schemes for real-time applications in hierarchical wireless sensor networks. Ad Hoc Netw. **20**, 1–15 (2014)
13. Yeh, H.-L., Chen, T.-H., Liu, P.-C., Kim, T.-H., Wei, H.-W.: A secured authentication protocol for wireless sensor networks using elliptic curves cryptography. Sensors **11**(5), 4767–4779 (2011)

Side Channel and Hardware

Energy Optimization of Unrolled Block Ciphers Using Combinational Checkpointing

Siva Nishok Dhanuskodi$^{(\boxtimes)}$ and Daniel Holcomb

Department of Electrical and Computer Engineering,
University of Massachusetts, Amherst, USA
sdhanusk@umass.edu, holcomb@engin.umass.edu

Abstract. Energy consumption of block ciphers is critical in resource constrained devices. Unrolling has been explored in literature as a technique to increase efficiency by eliminating energy spent in loop control elements such as registers and multiplexers. However these savings are minimal and are offset by the increase in glitching power that comes with unrolling. We propose an efficient latch-based glitch filter for unrolled designs that reduces energy per encryption by an order of magnitude over a straightforward implementation, and by 28–32% over the best existing glitch filtering schemes. We explore the optimal number of glitch filters that should be used in order to minimize total energy, and provide estimates of the area cost. Partially unrolled designs also benefit from using our scheme with energies competitive to fully serialized implementations. We demonstrate our approach on the SIMON-128 and AES-256 block ciphers.

1 Introduction

Energy efficiency is one of the main concerns in low-power implementations of block ciphers, regardless of the key strength of the algorithm being implemented. Minimization of energy is important because it allows computation on scavenged energy, long-running devices on small batteries, and so forth. Aside from energy efficiency, area cost and latency are secondary concerns. In the consumer electronics market, a focus on area is justified because area cost translates directly to monetary cost of a chip. Yet, there are many interesting energy-constrained scenarios in defense and healthcare where the monetary cost of silicon area is less critical. In these scenarios, one may wish to trade area against latency by unrolling repetitive cryptographic operations to perform a larger share of the computation in each cycle in order to complete operation sooner. This is especially important for block ciphers such as SIMON that require a large number of rounds. Yet, in order to be suitable for highly-constrained devices, unrolling must be done without significantly compromising the energy efficiency of the computation.

In this work, we address the problem of efficiency in unrolled block ciphers, by presenting a new technique of combinational checkpointing to minimize their

© Springer International Publishing AG 2017
G.P. Hancke and K. Markantonakis (Eds.): RFIDSec 2016, LNCS 10155, pp. 47–61, 2017.
DOI: 10.1007/978-3-319-62024-4_4

energy. We term the approach as *checkpointing* because we are adding state-holding elements at intermediate stages of the combinational logic, and each set of these elements stores an intermediate snapshot of the entire state of the block cipher operation. The specific contributions we make are as follows:

- We present an efficient latch-based glitch filter design that reduces energy of unrolled block ciphers.
- We find the optimal spacing of glitch filters in deeply unrolled block cipher implementations.
- For the first time, we give a technique that allows partially and fully unrolled block ciphers to have an energy efficiency that is competitive with serialized implementations.

2 Background and Related Work

There are a variety of low power design techniques for integrated circuits including near-threshold and subthreshold operation [9] and adiabatic logic styles [2]. However, in this work we focus exclusively on microarchitectural techniques for reducing energy instead of exotic circuits. In the remainder of this section, we review considerations for implementing block ciphers, and existing techniques for mitigating the glitches that dominate their power consumption.

2.1 Implementing Cryptographic Block Ciphers

Block ciphers are cryptographic primitives used to encrypt and decrypt data, typically used as part of a larger encryption mode of operation. Block ciphers are almost always implemented as components of a larger overall system-on-chip design, and this prevents the block cipher from being freely optimized independently of the other SoC components. For example, the block cipher will have to use the same fabrication process and supply voltage as the other components, and typically will share a common clock frequency to avoid clock generation and clock domain crossing. Therefore, any attempt at optimizing block ciphers may be constrained by these chip-scale implementation decisions.

The block cipher algorithm iterates over a round function for a specified number of times using different subkeys. The rounds can be implemented through sequential reuse of a single combinational block for each round, or they can be unrolled. If a design is fully serialized (no unrolling), one round function is computed in each clock cycle, and the number of cycles needed to encrypt a block is the same as the number of rounds in the block cipher algorithm. Yet, small low-power SoCs will typically operate at slow clock frequencies, and therefore the clock period may far exceed the critical path delay of a block cipher round. The latency of the block-cipher is then being increased unnecessarily due to the serialization of the round function.

Unrolling a block cipher is the process of instantiating multiple rounds of the algorithm combinationally to be completed within each clock cycle. Unrolling allows the result to be computed in fewer cycles at the cost of increased area of the combinational circuit. Unrolling also saves some amount of register energy, as energy is not spent storing signals at the output of each round like the fully serialized case. The unrolling of block ciphers as an energy optimization technique has been explored in a number of recent works [5,13].

2.2 Glitches and Glitch Filtering

The limiting factor in energy minimization of block ciphers is switching energy. This is especially true in unrolled block ciphers because combinational logic glitches at the input of each round diffuse through the round to cause more glitches at the output of the round. Leakage power is negligible relative to switching power for typical clock periods and technologies used in low power designs [13]. Fundamentally, glitches occur because of mismatched arrival times of gate inputs. This causes the gate output to switch once when the first input arrives, and then switch again when the next input arrives. These two switching events then propagate to many other nodes and cause more switching events in a cascading fashion.

Several techniques to filter glitches have been proposed in literature. Pipelining [8,19] stops glitches because they cannot propagate through a register, as a register can change its output value only once per clock cycle upon arrival of the clock transition. Gate-freezing [7] stalls the computation in a gate by using an NMOS footer transistor to filter 1-to-0 transitions. The stalled gate is allowed to compute only when its inputs have reached their final state. The scheme has a limitation in that it allows 0-to-1 transitions to pass through a stalled gate. Retiming [15] by moving or adding flip-flops in the datapath to high activity nodes that have a large fanout can reduce glitches and save power. Yet another approach is delay balancing to equalize input arrival times at a gate and reduce the number of output switching events [11,12,14].

An AND gate based glitch filtering scheme (Round Gating) was proposed in [4]. The output signals of each round in this scheme are gated by AND gates that wait on an enable signal. The enable signal is derived from a delayed clock such that it goes high to propagate the round outputs through the AND gates only after they have stopped glitching and become stable. A drawback of this scheme is that the enable signals must be reset low between the end of one computation and the start of the next in order to stop propagation of the glitches in the next operation. When the enable signals go low, waves of 0 s propagate forward from the glitch filters and propagate through the circuit to charge and discharge the nodes in the round functions similar to a normal computation of the round function. Effectively, resetting the glitch filters is thus causing a second, unnecessary, power-wasting computation to occur. State-retaining barriers [16] provide a mechanism for preventing this power-wasting computation.

3   Methodology

Combinational checkpointing is a microarchitectural technique to increase energy efficiency in a combinational circuit by filtering glitches. In this section, we describe the application of latch-based checkpoints in a block cipher and the methodology used to evaluate the approach.

3.1   Proposed Use of Checkpoints for Glitch Filtering

We propose a new standard-cell compatible glitch filtering mechanism as shown in Fig. 1. The topology is similar to that of round gating using AND gates [4], except that the glitch filtering element consists of a positive latch implemented using a multiplexer (MUX) at the output of the round function. The purpose of the filter is to make sure that any glitching activity from its input is not propagated to its output.

The operation of the filter is as follows. The MUX holds on to its previous output value when the enable (select) signal is low, and becomes transparent when enable is high. This causes the latch to be transparent only during the enable pulse. The enable pulse is generated at the rising edge of the clock as the AND of the clock signal and a delayed inverted version of clock. The enable pulse is propagated to the glitch filters combinationally with timing controlled by adding a delay element per round function. If the propagation delay of the delay element (t_d) is greater than the critical delay of a round function (t_r), then round output r_i stabilizes before the rising edge of signal en_i, so the latches only become transparent after the glitching has stopped. Therefore, when this timing condition ($t_d > t_r$) is satisfied, glitches generated in round i do not propagate

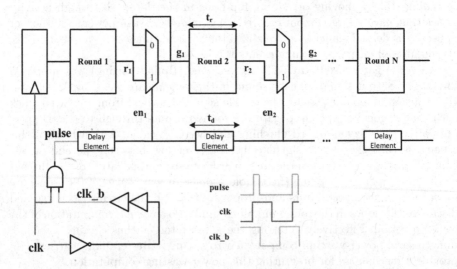

Fig. 1. Schematic of latch-based checkpoints for glitch filtering.

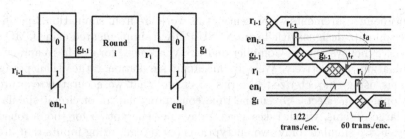

Fig. 2. Timing diagram of glitch filter operation, annotated with the number of switching events happening at each point in the circuit for SIMON-128.

through the glitch filters to round $i + 1$. Because the latch stays open for the duration of the enable pulse, the circuit will function correctly as long as the round outputs stabilize before the falling edge of en_i, but the circuit will not filter any glitches that arrive when the latch is open, and the glitch filter will not have the intended effect.

The timing waveform for a single round is shown in Fig. 2. When the enable signal pulses at the first glitch filter, the stable outputs of round $i - 1$ propagate through round i and cause a total of 122 transitions on the 128 round output signals. The round outputs wait for the enable signal to arrive at the second glitch filter, and upon its arrival, only 60 transitions occur on the inputs of round $i + 1$; these 60 transitions are single transitions on 60 of the 128 signals, which is close to the expected number of bits that would differ between two uncorrelated 128-bit signals. In this case, the filter has prevented all the spurious glitches from propagating across rounds.

3.2 Evaluation Methodology

We use the SIMON and AES block ciphers to study the effectiveness of our glitch filtering scheme. SIMON is a lightweight Feistel cipher suitable for resource constrained systems, and we use SIMON-128 [6], which has a 128-bit key, 128-bit block size, and requires 68 rounds for each encryption. Being a very simple design, the RTL for our SIMON implementation is written by us and validated for correctness against a software implementation of the same. AES refers to three standardized variants [17] of the Rijndael cipher, based on a substitution-permutation network. Relative to SIMON, AES is a more complicated design, and we specifically use the most complicated variant, AES-256; which has 128-bit block size, a 256-bit key, and requires 14 rounds per encryption. The RTL for our AES implementation is publicly available from OpenCores.org [10], and we validate its correctness against an online AES software implementation. To give an idea of the relative scales of the two ciphers, the round and key functions of fully unrolled SIMON require around 30,000 gates, whereas the round and key functions of fully unrolled AES are more than 8 times larger, requiring around 250,000 gates.

All of the measurements we present in this work are from simulation. Specifically, we simulate designs with 45 nm NCSU PDK [1] implemented using CMOS logic style. Synopsys Design Compiler and HSIM are used for synthesis and circuit simulation, respectively. We rely on circuit simulation rather than power simulations using characterized libraries to ensure that we accurately capture glitch propagation effects. Given the time consuming nature of circuit simulation on large designs, which takes several days per encryption for the unrolled AES design, we simulate only two encryptions per design, using inputs that are chosen at random. The first encryption initializes the circuit state, and the second encryption is used for measuring metrics described below. The accuracy of our results should not be compromised by the small number of encryptions simulated because a block cipher's behavior is fairly independent of the input value used. In support of this claim, the energy consumption of partially unrolled (17 rounds) SIMON for 100 random input vectors is shown in Fig. 3. The variation in energy consumption is small ($\sigma = 0.032\,\mathrm{pJ/bit}$) for the chosen input vectors.

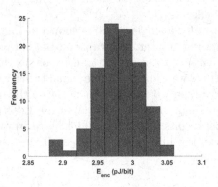

Fig. 3. SIMON-128 energy per encryption histogram for 100 random inputs.

Metrics such as toggle rate and energy consumption are measured during the circuit simulation and used to compare our scheme's performance with others. **Toggle rate** is measured as the average number of signal transitions at round outputs per encryption. For example, in SIMON-128 a round output has 128 signals. We compute the total number of signal transitions in all 128 signals that occur during an encryption operation, and divide by bit-width (128) to get the toggle rate. We present energy numbers using a metric of **energy-per-encrypted bit** denoted as E_{enc}, which is the total energy consumed to perform an encryption operation divided by the number of encrypted bits generated during the operation. When considering individual rounds of the block cipher, we use as a metric the contribution of that round to the overall E_{enc}. In our experiments, clock frequencies are chosen such that idle time is minimal, and are above 10 MHz in all cases.

4   Results

In this section we present results showing energy benefits of using checkpointing. We first demonstrate that glitch filtering using checkpointing leads to a reduction in toggle rate, which translates to energy savings. Further, we vary the number of checkpoints to explore the trade off between checkpointing overhead and glitching energy saved. Finally, we evaluate the effectiveness of checkpointing in partially unrolled designs, and also estimate area penalty incurred by checkpointing.

4.1   Comparison of Average Switching Rates

We first study the effectiveness of the proposed glitch filter by counting switching events on a fully unrolled implementation of SIMON-128. Figure 4 shows a comparison of signal toggle rates (signal transitions/encryption) for the outputs of all the 68 round and key functions. In the ideal case of no glitching activity, at the round outputs, one can expect 0.5 transitions per signal for each encryption, as round outputs are uncorrelated across encryptions.

When no glitch filtering is used (baseline design), the switching activity is observed to increase linearly with logic depth (number of rounds). This increase in switching occurs because the logic of the block cipher tends not to mask transitions as they propagate, and because the diffusion property of block ciphers tends to propagate each transition out to many nodes. Our finding of linear increase is consistent with observations made in previous works [3]. For each encryption in the baseline design, the average switching across all rounds is 14.16 transitions per signal, and in the later rounds it is $2\times$ larger than this average.

We analyze the effectiveness of checkpointing and two other techniques that mitigate switching. Compared to baseline, the Round Gating scheme [4] achieves a much lower average switching of 1.79 transitions per signal. Also, the switching activity stays fairly constant across rounds because glitches are never propagated across round boundaries. However as noted in Sect. 2, resetting the AND gates every clock cycle leads to unnecessary switching activity. Our checkpointing scheme has no such resetting and is therefore able to reduce switching to 0.95 transitions per signal, a 47% reduction relative to Round Gating. For comparison purposes, we implement SIMON-128 also using WDDL logic style [18]. WDDL is a dual-rail precharge based logic that is glitch free by design. To mitigate power side channel leakages, every signal pair in WDDL always has exactly 2 transitions per encryption; specifically, among the true and complementary representations of each signal, it is always the case that exactly one representation goes through a 1–0 transition during precharge and a subsequent 0–1 transition during evaluation.

4.2   Energy Savings from Checkpointing in Fully Unrolled Designs

The significant reduction in average switching rates implies that glitch filtering can reduce the overall energy used for encryption. In this section we study the energy savings achieved by using checkpointing to filter glitches in fully unrolled implementations of SIMON-128 and AES-256.

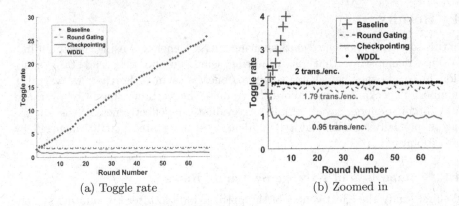

(a) Toggle rate   (b) Zoomed in

Fig. 4. Comparison of the average toggle rate of the output signals of each round of SIMON-128 for four different implementation styles.

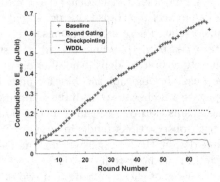

Fig. 5. Contribution of each round to the overall energy per encrypted bit in four different implementation styles of fully unrolled SIMON-128

SIMON-128. The energy use of each round in the fully unrolled SIMON-128 implementation is plotted in Fig. 5. The energy trends are similar to the toggle rate trends shown in Fig. 4. Table 1 lists the breakdown of energy per encryption (E_{enc}) for baseline (no glitch filter) designs and three glitch filtering schemes. A fully-unrolled implementation with checkpointing (4.46 pJ/bit) performs much better than fully unrolled baseline (25.91 pJ/bit) by saving glitching energy. Checkpointing is also competitive in energy with a baseline design that is not unrolled (1-unrolled, 3.78 pJ/bit) while offering single cycle latency, compared to 68 cycles in the 1-unrolled baseline. In comparison to Round Gating [4], checkpointing consumes 27.9% lower E_{enc}. The savings comes from a 47% reduction in toggle rate which leads to a 44.6% reduction in data and key computation energy specifically, while the costs of other components are similar across the two schemes. Note that WDDL and Round Gating schemes have similar toggle rates, yet WDDL consumes 2.4× more energy because it uses only positive gates, and therefore requires approximately 3× more gates to implement the same function.

Table 1. Breakdown of E_{enc} (pJ/bit) in fully unrolled SIMON-128. Glitch filters are added after every round in Round Gating and our work.

E_{enc} breakdown	Baseline		Glitch filtering scheme (68-unrolled)		
	1-unrolled	68-unrolled	Round Gating	Checkpointing	WDDL
Data	0.58	16.37	1.90	1.07	6.95
Key	0.40	9.42	1.62	0.88	7.42
Glitch Filter	–	–	2.36	2.20	–
Delay line	–	–	0.18	0.19	–
Other	2.80	0.12	0.12	0.12	0.45
Total	**3.78**	**25.91**	**6.19**	**4.46**	**14.82**

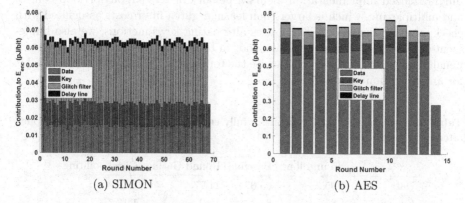

(a) SIMON   (b) AES

Fig. 6. Energy/encryption breakdown in fully unrolled implementations using checkpointing after every round.

Figure 6a shows the breakdown of energy consumption per encryption for our scheme. As can be seen in the figure, the switching energy does not increase across rounds, because each round similarly starts its computation from a single switching event. However, the glitch filters themselves consume about 50% of the total energy relative to the extremely simple combinational round function of SIMON. Hence, there is a possibility that using fewer glitch filters might reduce E_{enc} further, if the glitches do not increase significantly. We explore this in Sect. 4.3. It can also be noted that the simple delay line that propagates the enable is not costly in energy, as it is a single inverter chain relative to a 128-bit wide computation path. The delay line does not require any tuning if care is taken by adding some margin (buffers) to ensure $t_d > t_r$ even in the presence of process variation (Fig. 2).

AES-256. We also study the effectiveness of our scheme for the larger design, the fully unrolled implementation of AES-256. The energy breakdown per encryption in Fig. 6b shows that glitches are filtered effectively as there is no significant increase in switching energy with logic depth (round number). The energy cost of glitch filtering is small compared to that of actual computation. Note that the last round in AES is simpler, and therefore consumes less energy. The energy breakdown summary is tabulated in Table 2. Our scheme consumes an E_{enc} of 9.77 pJ/bit, which is 7.5x lower than fully unrolled baseline and 32.6% lower than Round Gating. These savings directly come from a lower switching activity. Unlike the extremely simple round functions of SIMON, AES round and key functions constitute about 90% of the total energy. As a result, in comparison to Round Gating our scheme saves more energy in AES-256 (32.6%) than in SIMON-128 (27.9%). It is important to note that our checkpointing scheme has similar energy efficiency as a fully serialized implementation (no unrolling, consumes 9.69 pJ/bit) while achieving single cycle latency. This is because the fully serialized implementation incurs a penalty of 2.19 pJ/bit for loop control and multiplexing, which is larger than leakage/glitch filter costs associated with checkpointing. Because AES-256 uses alternating key functions, we also implemented a 2-unrolled baseline design (not in table) that has smaller loop control penalty, but in that case glitches cause the total energy to increase to 13.7 pJ/bit for an encryption operation.

Table 2. Breakdown of E_{enc} (pJ/bit) in fully enrolled AES-256. Glitch filters applied after every round.

	No unrolling	Baseline	Round Gating	Checkpointing
Data	5.95	65.07	11.77	7.70
Key	1.55	8.64	1.82	1.13
Glitch filter	–	–	0.82	0.82
Delay line	–	–	0.03	0.07
Other	2.19	–	–	–
Total	**9.69**	**73.76**	**14.50**	**9.77**

4.3 Optimal Placement of Checkpoints for Glitch Filtering

In this section we explore the optimal number of glitch filters to use in our scheme so as to minimize the total energy consumption. Energy optimal glitch filtering requires finding the right trade-off between the cost of glitch filtering and the energy saved by filtering glitches. If too many filters are used, then the cost of the filters themselves will dominate; but if too few filters are used, then the cost of the glitches will dominate. Figure 7 shows how each round contributes to the energy per encrypted bit when different number of rounds are implemented between the checkpoints. When checkpoints are added after every round (spacing = 1) in fully unrolled SIMON-128 (Fig. 7a), more energy is spent in glitch filtering than is spent in actual computation. However, if spacing is increased to 2 where checkpointing is done every other round, the average energy per round

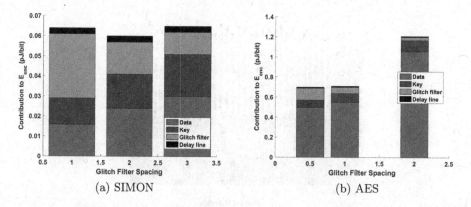

(a) SIMON   (b) AES

Fig. 7. Energy efficiency varies with the spacing between checkpoints in fully unrolled designs. Performing more computation between checkpoints reduces checkpointing energy, but allows more data switching to occur

is decreased. Increasing the spacing beyond 2 further reduces the cost of glitch filtering but the glitches increase the key and data energy by a larger amount and the total energy increases. Therefore a spacing of 2 rounds between checkpoints is optimal for SIMON-128.

The energy breakdown of E_{enc} for each round of the fully unrolled SIMON-128 with optimal glitch filter placement is shown in Fig. 8. The even rounds have more glitching, and only the even rounds spend energy on checkpointing. At the optimal spacing of 2, the design consumes 4.18 pJ/bit per encryption which is 6.3% lower than the 4.46 pJ/bit when checkpointing is applied after every round (Table 1). In addition, the area will be reduced because of the fewer checkpoints. Any block cipher implementation will have some optimal tradeoff of checkpointing energy versus glitching, but the specifics are of course design and technology dependent.

Figure 7b shows that in AES, the much larger round function justifies adding glitch filtering after every round. Given the small energy cost of the checkpoints relative to round function, one might consider adding glitch filters at half round boundaries. Doing this reduces glitches but increases the cost of glitch filter such that the total energy consumption becomes comparable to glitch filter spacing of 1. Therefore, checkpoint spacing of 1 is optimal in AES-256 as it requires fewer glitch filters for the same energy efficiency as half-round checkpointing.

4.4 Checkpointing in Partially Unrolled Designs

Partially unrolled designs, which implement some number of rounds combinationally, offer a tradeoff between area and latency of encryption. Aside from this tradeoff, partial unrolling may also be desirable due to design constraints (area, clock period) which do not allow for a fully unrolled implementation. Since the optimal spacing of checkpoints is a low number (every round for AES-256, and every second round for SIMON-128), it is beneficial to use checkpointing even

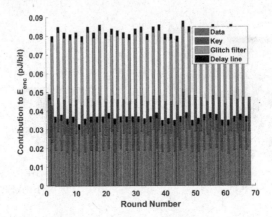

Fig. 8. Energy breakdown of E_{enc} for each round in fully unrolled SIMON-128 in the optimal configuration of checkpointing every second round.

for partially unrolled designs. Table 3 shows the energy per encryption numbers for different partially unrolled implementations of SIMON-128. Glitching in the baseline design increases with the degree of unrolling and so do the energy savings offered by checkpointing, up to 84% in the fully unrolled case. Checkpointing allows for a deeper unrolling with minimal energy penalty resulting in lower latency. In comparison to the most efficient baseline implementation (4-unrolled, 2.89 pJ/bit), checkpointing enables 34-unrolled design (3.41 pJ/bit) to be competitive in energy at a much lower latency. Fully unrolling helps save loop control energy but incurs leakage cost, leading to less efficient design (4.18 pJ/bit).

Also, 1-unrolled baseline consumes more energy than the 2-unrolled and 4-unrolled baselines because the SIMON key expansion function requires storing key_{i-2} in additional registers to compute key_i if no unrolling were done [6]. The frequencies in Table 3 are chosen conservatively to account for process variations, but the design could be optimized for performance.

Table 3. SIMON-128 E_{enc} (pJ/bit) comparison between optimal checkpointing and the baseline design for various degrees of unrolling.

	Unrollings	1	2	4	17	34	68
Baseline	E_{enc} (pJ/bit)	3.78	2.95	2.89	6.15	12.43	25.91
	$I_{leak}(\mu A)$	132.58	133.51	169.8	417.4	753.3	1419.8
	Frequency (MHz)	1667	833	417	98	49	25
Checkpointing	E_{enc} (pJ/bit)	–	–	2.92	2.99	3.41	4.18
	$I_{leak}(\mu A)$	–	–	170.4	556.6	1080.2	2016.6
	Frequency (MHz)	–	–	185	73	37	19
Either	Latency (cycles)	68	34	17	4	2	1

4.5   Area Cost of Checkpointing

Using our glitch filtering scheme does incur some area penalty as tabulated in Table 4. In terms of number of gate equivalents, we incur a small 3.7% penalty if checkpoints are added after every round in AES-256. In the case of a lightweight block cipher like SIMON-128 that has a very small round function and larger number of rounds, the penalty is more pronounced. For SIMON, we incur a 44% overhead if checkpoints are placed at the energy-optimal spacing of every second round. It is worth noting that using checkpoints after every round in SIMON-128 would incur a much higher 80% area penalty in addition to not being energy optimal.

With regard to timing, we introduce a small timing penalty because of the introduction of the glitch filters in the critical path and some timing margin to make sure the delay element is sufficiently long so that the enable pulse to a glitch filter arrives after the corresponding round output stabilizes. Though we report conservative frequency numbers in Table 3 to account for process variations, we do not have any requirements to double the clock period as in other schemes such as WDDL or Round Gating.

Table 4. Area penalty of proposed glitch filtering scheme in units of gate equivalents. Even in absolute terms, the area cost of checkpointing is significantly higher in SIMON-128 than in AES-256 because the larger number of rounds requires a larger number of checkpoints, even though the checkpoints are only applied at every second round.

	Baseline	Checkpointing	Area overhead
SIMON-128	56,488	81,321	44.0%
AES-256	342,805	355,630	3.7%

5   Conclusion

In this paper, we have presented an efficient latch-based checkpointing mechanism to reduce the energy per encryption of unrolled block cipher implementations. We demonstrated significant energy savings (28–32%) compared to the best existing scheme for glitch filtering in unrolled block ciphers. Our scheme performs well on block ciphers with simple round functions as in SIMON, and complex round functions as in AES. We also showed that optimal use of glitch filters can lead to further energy savings, resulting in energy consumption that is competitive to a fully serialized implementation while maintaining the latency advantages of an unrolled design. Further, partially unrolled implementations can also greatly benefit from our scheme in scenarios where design constraints limit the degree of unrolling. This technique has applications in improving the efficiency of different unrolled block cipher implementations.

References

1. NCSU Free PDK 45. http://www.eda.ncsu.edu/wiki/FreePDK45:Contents
2. Athas, W.C., Svensson, L.J., Koller, J.G., Tzartzanis, N., Chou, E.Y.-C.: Low-power digital systems based on adiabatic-switching principles. IEEE Trans. Very Large Scale Integr. VLSI Syst. **2**(4), 398–407 (1994)
3. Banik, S., Bogdanov, A., Regazzoni, F.: Exploring energy efficiency of lightweight block ciphers. In: Dunkelman, O., Keliher, L. (eds.) SAC 2015. LNCS, vol. 9566, pp. 178–194. Springer, Cham (2016). doi:10.1007/978-3-319-31301-6_10
4. Banik, S., Bogdanov, A., Regazzoni, F., Isobe, T., Hiwatari, H., Akishita, T.: Round gating for low energy block ciphers. In: IEEE International Symposium on Hardware Oriented Security and Trust (HOST), pp. 55–60, May 2016
5. Batina, L., Das, A., Ege, B., Kavun, E.B., Mentens, N., Paar, C., Verbauwhede, I., Yalçın, T.: Dietary recommendations for lightweight block ciphers: power, energy and area analysis of recently developed architectures. In: Hutter, M., Schmidt, J.-M. (eds.) RFIDSec 2013. LNCS, vol. 8262, pp. 103–112. Springer, Heidelberg (2013). doi:10.1007/978-3-642-41332-2_7
6. Beaulieu, R., Shors, D., Smith, J., Treatman-Clark, S., Weeks, B., Wingers, L.: The simon and speck families of lightweight block ciphers. Cryptology ePrint Archive, Report 2013/404 (2013). http://eprint.iacr.org/2013/404
7. Benini, L., Micheli, G.D., Macii, A., Macii, E., Poncino, M., Scarsi, R.: Glitch power minimization by selective gate freezing. IEEE Trans. Very Large Scale Integr. VLSI Syst. **8**(3), 287–298 (2000)
8. Boemo, E., Oliver, J.P., Caffarena, G.: Tracking the pipelining-power rule along the FPGA technical literature. In: Proceedings of the 10th FPGAworld Conference, FPGAworld 2013, New York, pp. 9:1–9:5. ACM (2013)
9. Hanson, S., Zhai, B., Bernstein, K., Blaauw, D., Bryant, A., Chang, L., Das, K.K., Haensch, W., Nowak, E.J., Sylvester, D.M.: Ultralow-voltage, minimum-energy CMOS. IBM J. Res. Dev. **50**(4.5), 469–490 (2006)
10. Hsing, H.: Tiny AES project. opencores.org/project,tiny_aes
11. Huda, S., Anderson, J.: Towards PVT-tolerant glitch-free operation in FPGAs. In: Proceedings of the 2016 ACM/SIGDA International Symposium on Field-Programmable Gate Arrays, FPGA 2016, New York, pp. 90–99. ACM (2016)
12. Karthik, H.S., Naik, B.M.K.: Glitch elimination and optimization of dynamic power dissipation in combinational circuits. In: 2014 International Conference on Advances in Electronics, Computers and Communications (ICAECC), pp. 1–6, October 2014
13. Kerckhof, S., Durvaux, F., Hocquet, C., Bol, D., Standaert, F.-X.: Towards green cryptography: a comparison of lightweight ciphers from the energy viewpoint. In: Prouff, E., Schaumont, P. (eds.) CHES 2012. LNCS, vol. 7428, pp. 390–407. Springer, Heidelberg (2012). doi:10.1007/978-3-642-33027-8_23
14. Lamoureux, J., Lemieux, G.G.F., Wilton, S.J.E.: GlitchLess: dynamic power minimization in FPGAs through edge alignment and glitch filtering. IEEE Trans. Very Large Scale Integr. VLSI Syst. **16**(11), 1521–1534 (2008)
15. Monteiro, J., Devadas, S., Ghosh, A.: Retiming sequential circuits for low power. In: IEEE/ACM International Conference on Computer-Aided Design, ICCAD 1993. Digest of Technical Papers, pp. 398–402, November 1993
16. Musoll, E., Cortadella, J.: Low-power array multipliers with transition-retaining barriers. In: Power and Timing Modeling, Optimization and Simulation (PATMOS), pp. 227–238, October 1995

17. Pub, N.F.: 197: Advanced encryption standard (AES). Federal Information Processing Standards Publication 197, 441–0311 (2001)
18. Tiri, K., Verbauwhede, I.: A digital design flow for secure integrated circuits. IEEE Trans. Comput. Aided Des. Integr. Circuits Syst. **25**(7), 1197–1208 (2006)
19. Wilton, S.J.E., Ang, S.-S., Luk, W.: The impact of pipelining on energy per operation in field-programmable gate arrays. In: Becker, J., Platzner, M., Vernalde, S. (eds.) FPL 2004. LNCS, vol. 3203, pp. 719–728. Springer, Heidelberg (2004). doi:10.1007/978-3-540-30117-2_73

LDA-Based Clustering as a Side-Channel Distinguisher

Rauf Mahmudlu[1,2(✉)], Valentina Banciu[1], Lejla Batina[2], and Ileana Buhan[1]

[1] Riscure BV, Delftechpark 49, 2628 XJ Delft, The Netherlands
{banciu,buhan}@riscure.com
[2] Digital Security Group, Radboud University, Nijmegen, The Netherlands
r.mahmudlu@student.ru.nl, lejla@cs.ru.nl

Abstract. Side-channel attacks put the security of the implementations of cryptographic algorithms under threat. Secret information can be recovered by analyzing the physical measurements acquired during the computations and using key recovery distinguishing functions to guess the best candidate. Several generic and model based distinguishers have been proposed in the literature. In this work we describe two contributions that lead to better performance of side-channel attacks in challenging scenarios. First, we describe how to transform the physical leakage traces into a new space where the noise reduction is near-optimal. Second, we propose a new generic distinguisher that is based upon minimal assumptions. It approaches a key distinguishing task as a problem of classification and ranks the key candidates according to the separation among the leakage traces. We also provide experiments and compare their results to those of the Correlation Power Analysis (CPA). Our results show that the proposed method can indeed reach better success rates even in the presence of significant amount of noise.

1 Introduction

Side-Channel Analysis (SCA) attacks have become a powerful tool for extracting secret information from cryptographic devices since the introduction of Differential Power Analysis (DPA) by Kocher et al. [18]. These attacks exploit the relationship between the side-channel measurements and the data-dependent leakage models to reveal some part of the key. The Correlation Power Analysis (CPA) method [6] is among the most efficient distinguishers when the relationship of the leakage and data can be approximated with a linear model. However, due to process variation in nano-scale devices and consequently the increase in the contribution of the leakage component of the power consumption, different leakage models become necessary. Since the performance of the CPA method strongly depends on the assumed (linear) leakage model, imprecise predictions can lead to complete failure of the method. Another major cause of the suboptimal performance of key recovery attacks is the presence of noise in leakage traces. While the performance of all SCA distinguishers are similar for a large Signal-to-Noise Ratio (SNR) [20], in real world scenarios it is common that the physical leakage

© Springer International Publishing AG 2017
G.P. Hancke and K. Markantonakis (Eds.): RFIDSec 2016, LNCS 10155, pp. 62–75, 2017.
DOI: 10.1007/978-3-319-62024-4_5

measurements contain a significant amount of noise originating from multiple sources such as the power supply, the specifics of the measurement set-up, the clock generator, parallel computations etc. As discussed by Mangard et al. [19], the success of SCA attacks is heavily dependent on the SNR, and thus multiple noise reduction methods such as filtering, Principal Component Analysis (PCA) [17], Linear Discriminant Analysis (LDA) [15], singular spectrum analysis [16] etc. have been studied in the domain of SCA attacks.

Summarizing, we note that there are two main directions for improving key recovery methods: finding optimal distinguishers, and reducing the noise level in measurements. In this work we shall address and combine both aspects.

1.1   Related Work

With respect to data (pre-)processing and transformation methods, various ideas ranging from machine learning, pattern recognition and other localization techniques have been suggested. As an example, some of the techniques have been utilized for conducting template attacks as first introduced by Chari et al. [8]. Template attacks are the strongest form of side-channel attacks from the information theoretic point of view, and can successfully extract secret information from a limited number of traces. These attacks are typically carried out in two main steps: a profiling step during which templates corresponding to each subkey candidate are derived, and a template matching step during which a new trace is matched to the templates.

LDA and PCA are among the data transformation methods that have been used [1,9,22] for feature extraction and dimensionality reduction in template attacks. While the performance of PCA-based attacks is close to that of LDA-based attacks when the measurements feature a high SNR, it deteriorates substantially when the SNR gets lower. LDA-based template attacks have been shown to lead to better templates especially in the presence of higher noise levels, because of the better separation of the classes in the transformed subspace and the near-optimal noise reduction [7]. PCA has also been studied for both data preprocessing and as a method for key recovery. Batina et al. [4] propose to utilize it as a preprocessing technique before conducting the DPA attack. The observed benefits of PCA in such scenarios are the noise reduction in the traces and the better performance of the DPA after the transformation of the traces into a lower dimension subspace spanned by eigenvectors. In contrast to this, Souissi et al. [21] have investigated the applicability of the PCA as another distinguisher by merely using the first principal component.

The Differential Cluster Analysis (DCA) technique introduced by Batina et al. [2] is also framing key recovery as a classification problem. The authors use metrics such as *sum-of-squared-error* and *sum-of-squares* to derive statistics about clusters. This method does not require an accurate leakage model, however including it would enhance the performance. The ANOVA (ANalysis Of VAriance) F-test is using a distance measure between the classes, which is similar to what we propose in this work [5]. The metric called Normalized Inter-Class Variance (NICV) is used for leakage detection in SCA. While efficient in determining the time where the sensitive information is computed, comparing different leakage models or speeding up attacks on asymmetric cryptography, this method cannot be used as a distinguisher for recovering the secret information.

1.2 Contribution

Our main contribution is a new distinguisher which exploits the near-optimal noise reduction offered by the LDA transformation. The new distinguisher is versatile and can be adapted to any leakage model. We test the performance of our distinguisher using two different low SNR trace sets and show that it has superior performance compared to CPA.

This paper is organized as follows. In Sect. 2 we discuss background information relevant to this work. In Sect. 3 we introduce our attack method. In Sect. 4 we address the caveats. In Sect. 5 we discuss the results of our experiments and compare the Global Success Rates (GSR) of our attack to that of standard CPA. We conclude in Sect. 6.

2 Background

Let X denote a random variable over a space $\mathcal{X}$ with realization x. $\mathbf{X}$ is a d-dimensional $(X_1, X_2, \ldots, X_d) \in \mathcal{X}^d$ row vector with realization $\mathbf{x}$.

2.1 Side-Channel Analysis

We adopt the terminology and notations of [3], and consider the schematic representation of a classic SCA represented in Fig. 1. In this scenario, a targeted cryptographic implementation is performing an encryption $E_k(p)$ of the plaintext p using a constant key k. During computation, the sensitive intermediate value $V_{s,p}$ that depends on a part s of the key k, and the plaintext p are handled. The physical leakage generated during the computation of $V_{s,p}$ is denoted as $Y_{k,p}$ since the leakage may potentially depend on the whole key k. The adversary acquires leakage traces by sampling or measuring the side-channel observables (power, electromagnetic emanation) at successive time instances. The value $Y_{k,p}$ can be captured in one sample or spread over multiple samples depending on the implementation details and the parameters of the acquisition. To recover the key, the adversary predicts the intermediate values handled during the computation of $E_k(p)$ and calculates the values $V_{j,p}$ for every possible subkey candidate $j \in \mathcal{S}$. The adversary maps the intermediate values $V_{j,p}$ to the hypothetical leakage value $X_{j,p}$ by applying an estimated leakage model. To recover k the same steps are repeated for all the subkeys s.

2.2 Linear Discriminant Analysis (LDA)

LDA is a dimensionality reduction technique used for classification purposes in machine learning, pattern recognition, etc. For a given data set, LDA seeks the

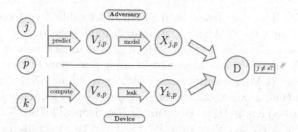

Fig. 1. Schematic illustration of a side-channel key recovery

linear combination of features which preserves the class-discriminant information. Then, the between-class (S_B) and within-class (S_W) scatter matrices are
calculated according to Eqs. (1) and (2) respectively, where μ is the mean of all
the observations.

$$S_B = \sum_{j=1}^{|\mathcal{C}|} N_j(\mu_j - \mu)(\mu_j - \mu)^T \tag{1}$$

$$S_W = \sum_{j=1}^{|\mathcal{C}|}\sum_{i=1}^{N_j}(\mathbf{x}_{i,j} - \mu_j)(\mathbf{x}_{i,j} - \mu_j)^T \tag{2}$$

The two matrix values are used to find the projection directions W which
maximize the separation between classes. The separation - J between the classes
is calculated according to Eq. (3). After determining the projection directions,
the observations are transformed to the new space as $\hat{\mathbf{x}} = \mathbf{x}W$.

$$J(W) = \frac{W^T S_B W}{W^T S_W W} \tag{3}$$

2.3   Information Theoretic Definitions

The *entropy* of a random variable X [10] represents the uncertainty or the
amount of information content and is defined as:

$$H[X] = \sum_{x \in \mathcal{X}} Pr[X = x] \cdot \log\left(\frac{1}{Pr[X = x]}\right). \tag{4}$$

The *conditional entropy*, $H[X|Y]$ of a random variable X given variable Y is the
measure of the uncertainty left about X when Y is known. Finally, *mutual information* $I(X;Y)$ is a measure of the dependence between the random variables
X and Y and the amount of information they have in common.

2.4   Experimental Setup

For this research, we consider software implementations of AES128 [14] and DES
[13] running on an ARM Cortex-M4F core based board operating at a 168 MHz

clock frequency. The board has been physically modified and programmed in order to be a target for SCA and it accurately models current 32-bit embedded devices. As discussed in Sect. 1, the SNR of side-channel traces is an indication of their quality. Since we are interested in noisy side-channel traces, we acquire electro-magnetic (EM) measurements which have lower SNR than the power measurements (i.e., a more challenging scenario). To do so, we build a standard setup (as described e.g. in [19]). We utilize a PicoScope 3207B [23] digital oscilloscope with a 500 MHz sampling rate. We carry out two measurement campaigns (one for each cryptographic algorithm implementation), as follows:

$TraceSet_1$: 50 000 traces were obtained for the implementation of the AES128 algorithm. The key was fixed and the traces were obtained for random plaintext inputs. The SNR value is 1.01 dB.

$TraceSet_2$: 50 000 traces were obtained for the implementation of the DES algorithm. The key was fixed and the traces were obtained for random plaintext inputs. The SNR value is 2.78 dB.

3   Attack Description

The key recovery attack proposed in this paper relies on the central assumption that all leakages corresponding to the processing of some fixed key dependent intermediate value are similar. In other words, when a set of physical leakages $Y_{k,p}$ is classified according to the values of $X_{s,p}$ as defined in Sect. 2.1, the between-class to within-class scatter matrices ratio is large. Note that the above requirement is indeed met in the context of side-channel attacks, as the instantaneous power consumption of a cryptographic implementation is generally expected to be data dependent. However, in practice side-channel measurements often include noise, which leads to a weaker separation amongst classes and in consequence decreases the success rate of key recovery attacks.

The approach proposed in this work targets such challenging scenarios where the SNR is low, and achieves key extraction with fewer traces. It consists of two steps: (i) the leakage transformation step; and (ii) the distinguishing step.

In the following we describe in more detail the working principles of our attack. In Sect. 3.1 we describe how parts of the plaintext can be used for classification purposes and how measured leakages can be projected into a subspace where they are maximally separated and the SNR level is higher. Then in Sect. 3.2 we propose a function that enumerates subkeys based on the separation of the model based classes.

3.1   The Leakage Transformation Step

The objective of the leakage transformation step is to identify and select time samples where the difference between mean traces corresponding to distinct classes of intermediates is maximized. In order to apply a LDA transformation in this step, information that allows for the separation of traces into classes must

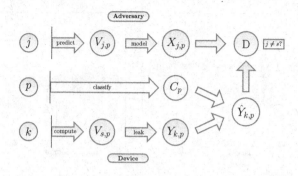

Fig. 2. Schematic illustration of the proposed attack

be available, e.g. one must know the plaintexts or ciphertexts. The sensitive key dependent intermediate variables are predicted as $V_{j,p}$, as represented in Fig. 2. Although the correct intermediate values $V_{s,p}$ depend on the unknown subkey $s \in \mathcal{S}$, they may still be classified based only on the value of the plaintext due to the fact that for any $j \in \mathcal{S}$ and $(p_1, p_2) \in \mathcal{P}$, if $p_1 = p_2$ then $V_{j,p_1} = V_{j,p_2}$. After separating the physical leakages into groups based on the plaintext or ciphertext values, the projection directions are calculated and the leakages are projected onto the new subspace. The transformed leakages are subsequently used for key recovery, as represented in Fig. 2.

3.2 The Distinguishing Step

The objective of this step is to distinguish between the key candidates. Note that because the traces have previously been linearly transformed to maximize the separation between classes, the correlation between the traces and the hypothetical power consumption may be lost. By definition, the transformation is the sum of the inner product between the leakage with the projection directions where each direction is a column of the transformation matrix $\overrightarrow{W}$. It follows that the magnitudes of the coefficients of each direction are proportional to the contribution of the corresponding samples to the transformation. Figure 3 shows the Pearson correlation coefficients and the first projection direction for $TraceSet_1$. While there are clear peaks in the $159\,\mu s$ to $164\,\mu s$ time interval, the dominating samples in the first projection direction are situated in different regions. Therefore, the need for a new distinguisher that better matches the properties of the transformed traces arises. To this end, we propose to use the ratio of the between- and the within-class scatter. The features extracted through the LDA transformation correspond to the linear combination of the leakage samples that maximally separate classes. At the same time, for a given leakage model, traces corresponding to the same values of $X_{s,p}$ are expected to have similar features. Since for each projection direction the contribution of each sample of the side-channel leakages towards this direction is the same, when the projected leakages are labelled according to the model obtained from the correct key, the separation of the clusters should be maximum. Whereas, if the model obtained from

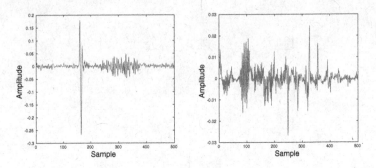

Fig. 3. Known key correlation (left) vs. the first projection eigenvector (right)

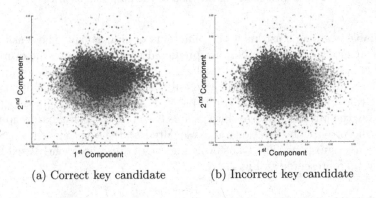

(a) Correct key candidate   (b) Incorrect key candidate

Fig. 4. Visualization of the class separation under different key candidates

the wrong key is used for labelling, the lack of similar features within classes should lead to a weaker separation as shown in Fig. 4. Since the objective of the distinguisher is to retrieve ordinal information about the variance of the ratio matrix, its largest eigenvalue can be a numerical measure for separation [24].

Summarizing, in the second stage $|\mathcal{S}|$ models (each corresponding to a different $j \in \mathcal{S}$) are computed and the transformed physical leakages are classified accordingly. After calculating between-class ($\hat{S}_B$) and within-class ($\hat{S}_W$) scatter of $\hat{Y}_{k,p}$, the diagonal matrix of eigenvalues $\hat{\Delta}$ is calculated by eigendecomposing $\hat{S}_W^{-\frac{1}{2}} \hat{S}_B \hat{S}_W^{-\frac{1}{2}} = \hat{U} \hat{\Delta} \hat{U}^T$. The eigenvalue is assigned as the candidate score. Finally, the candidate leading to the largest score is selected as the correct key.

4   Caveats

In this section we explore the two caveats of our method, which are due to intrinsic characteristics of the LDA transformation.

First, the number of side-channel traces must be larger than the number of analysed samples. To overcome the need for a very large trace set, it is possible to analyse only a selected block of samples at a time. In this case for each key candidate the number of discriminant scores will be the same as the number of blocks. If a selected block does not include samples related to the calculation of the predicted intermediate values, classification of the leakages according to possible values of the subkey candidate will not be significantly different from each other. Whereas, in the block where leakage occurs, the correct key candidate should lead to significantly better separation among the classes. In order to find the block where the leakage occurs, the scores for each block have to be normalised and the one with the highest ratio of the scores for the first and second candidates is chosen as the leaking block. The first candidate of the leaking block is subsequently chosen as the correct key.

Second, the size of the plaintext space $\mathcal{P}$ must be reasonably small. To estimate the between-class scatter, more than one trace should belong to each class. Since in the classification and transformation stage the number of classes is equal to $|\mathcal{P}|$, the number of leakage traces needed for finding the projection directions would be significantly high. This restriction can be avoided by obtaining the measurements for chosen plaintexts such that text space size is small.

5 Experimental Validation

We now validate our attack methodology using the trace sets described in Sect. 2.4 under different leakage assumptions. Section 5.1 describes the calculation of the projection directions and transformation of the traces. In Sect. 5.2 we describe the attacks where the hypothetical power consumption is linked to the Hamming weight (HW) of intermediate values, and in Sect. 5.3 we describe how the (partial) identity leakage model can be exploited. We report the performance of the attacks by looking at the GSR, i.e. the ratio of the correctly guessed subkeys to the total number of subkeys.

5.1 Leakage Transformation

As described in Sect. 2.2, the projection directions that will map the traces into a new subspace where the ratio of the between-class (S_B) and within-class(S_W) scatter matrices are maximised have to be calculated. During the calculation of these matrices the traces are classified as described in Sect. 3.1. The matrix of projection directions is built as $W = S_W^{-\frac{1}{2}}U$ [9], where U is the matrix of eigenvectors obtained by eigendecomposing $S_W^{-\frac{1}{2}}S_B S_W^{-\frac{1}{2}} = U\Delta U^T$. Δ denotes diagonal matrix of eigenvalues. The projection matrix can be truncated according to the Eckart-Young theorem [12] as $\widetilde{W} = S_W^{-\frac{1}{2}}\widetilde{U}$, where $\widetilde{U}$ is the matrix of eigenvectors corresponding to the m largest eigenvalues.

5.2 HW Leakage Model

As shown in Fig. 1, the intermediate values for both of the implementations are predicted as $V_{j,p} = \text{Sbox}(j \oplus p)$ and the leakages are modelled as the HW of the intermediate values. The subkeys of the first round key were targeted at every implementation with the goal of recovering the full round key. As studied by Doget et al. [11], when the chosen leakage model exactly corresponds to the actual leakage function of the implementation, CPA has one of the best performances for key extraction. Therefore, we have used this method as a reference for comparing the performance of the proposed attack. It should be noted that while the CPA attack is based upon an assumption of linear dependence between the HW of the intermediate values and the actual power consumption, our attack does not require such a strict relation. We only assume that the power consumption corresponding to the processing of intermediate values that have the same HW is consistent and it differs from that corresponding to other HW values.

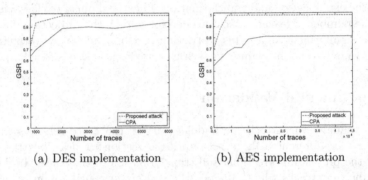

(a) DES implementation   (b) AES implementation

Fig. 5. Global Success Rate (GSR)

For CPA attacks, the hypothetical power consumption models for each possible value of the subkey were built and the Pearson correlation coefficients were calculated for each sample of the trace sets. The key candidate which maximizes the absolute value of the correlation coefficient was chosen as the correct key. Both the proposed attack and CPA were run on randomly selected subsets of the trace sets multiple times and the average results were compared. Figure 5 reports the GSR for both implementations. This figure clearly shows that the proposed attack is outperforming CPA for both implementations.

The analysis of the leakage traces after the LDA transformation shows that depending on the number of retained components, the SNR level can be significantly higher compared to the original traces. The graph in Fig. 6 shows the SNR levels as the function of the projection directions retained after the transformation. Since the increase in SNR together with the supervised classification are the reasons for the better performance of the proposed attack method, it is important to select a significantly large number of components. We have adapted the heuristics of keeping the directions corresponding to the 95th percentile of the eigenvalues after the eigendecomposition of $S_W^{-\frac{1}{2}} S_B S_W^{-\frac{1}{2}}$ [25].

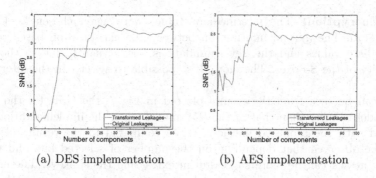

(a) DES implementation   (b) AES implementation

Fig. 6. The SNR before and after the LDA transformation

5.3   Identity Leakage Model

To further extend our experiments, we have also investigated key extraction when no assumptions about the leakage model are made. To this end, instead of classifying leakage traces according to the HW of intermediate values, we separate them according to some selected bits of the intermediate values. Due to intrinsic properties of the AES ans DES encryption algorithms (in particular: the bijectivity of the S-box), we will analyse them separately.

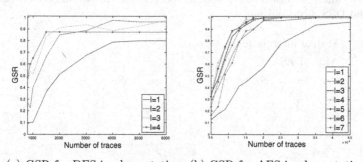

(a) GSR for DES implementation (b) GSR for AES implementation

Fig. 7. GSR for the target implementations

AES Encryption. The intermediate values in this case were also predicted as $V_{j,p} = \mathrm{Sbox}(j \oplus p)$. The classification of the leakage traces does not depend on the value of key candidate j due to the bijectivity of the S-box function. The absence of mutual information leads to the conclusion that the classification based on the hypothetical intermediate values will be the same for each key candidate. Therefore, instead of assigning identical intermediate values, we assign similar intermediate values to the same class. In this context, we define similar intermediate values as those whose preselected $l \in \{1 \dots 7\}$ bits are equal.

DES Encryption. The intermediate values were again chosen as $V_{j,p} =$ $\text{Sbox}(j \oplus p)$. The mutual information between the classification based on the intermediate values and the key candidate is larger than 0 due to the non-bijectivity of the S-boxes. Therefore, it is possible to select l in the interval of $\{1\ldots4\}$.

As can be seen from the results plotted in Fig. 7, the GSR for the Identity Model is lower than that of the HW model when the implementations are attacked with the proposed method. When compared to the results of CPA, it can be observed that depending on the number of selected bits and traces the new attack can be more successful in extracting the subkeys. The empirical study of the S-box functions of the encryption algorithms reveals that the mutual information between the key candidate and the classification increases with decreasing l (see Table 1), while the GSR does not follow the same pattern. When l gets smaller, the number of distinct intermediate values that are assigned to the same class increases, which leads to weaker separation among classes. Therefore, a compromise between getting maximum possible mutual information and keeping the classes well separable has to be made. Given that for fairly large amount of traces the performance of the attack is better than CPA even without making any assumptions about the leakage model, we can argue that the proposed attack is preferable.

Table 1. The analysis of the mutual information between the key and the classification for AES and DES S-box outputs

	Mutual information								
	AES	DES							
l	S	S_1	S_2	S_3	S_4	S_5	S_6	S_7	S_8
8	0	–	–	–	–	–	–	–	–
7	0.060	–	–	–	–	–	–	–	–
6	0.116	–	–	–	–	–	–	–	–
5	0.204	–	–	–	–	–	–	–	–
4	0.340	0.306	0.294	0.302	0.263	0.285	0.297	0.306	0.296
3	0.545	0.538	0.541	0.541	0.543	0.537	0.544	0.544	0.537
2	0.812	0.859	0.832	0.858	0.827	0.831	0.861	0.867	0.856
1	1.001	1.037	1.023	1.039	1.025	1.011	1.028	1.053	1.019

5.4 Computational Complexity

While the success rates of different key extraction attacks may be high, their adaptation in real world scenarios is also bounded by the computational complexity. Since the side-channel security evaluations of cryptographic devices can involve millions of traces, it is desirable to be able to perform the analysis within

---

Algorithm 1. Pseudo-code of the proposed attack

Input: Matrix of leakage traces: Y $(m \times d)$
Input: Vector of plaintexts: P $(m \times 1)$
Output: Vector of key candidate scores: k $(|\mathcal{S}| \times 1)$

1 $[S_W, S_B] = \text{scatter}(Y, P)$;

2 $T = S_W^{-\frac{1}{2}}$;

3 $M = TS_BT$;

4 $[U, \Delta] = \text{eig}(M)$;

5 $I = \text{sort}(\Delta)$;

6 $\widetilde{U} = U(I)$;

7 $\widetilde{W} = T\widetilde{U}$;

8 $\widehat{Y} = Y\widetilde{W}$;

9 **for** $j \in \mathcal{S}$ **do**

10     $X_P = \text{model}(P, j)$;

11     $[\widehat{S}_W, \widehat{S}_B] = \text{scatter}(\widehat{Y}, X_P)$;

12     $\widehat{T} = \widehat{S}_W^{-\frac{1}{2}}$;

13     $\widehat{M} = \widehat{T}\widehat{S}_W\widehat{T}$;

14     $[\widehat{U}, \widehat{\Delta}] = \text{eig}(\widehat{M})$;

15     $k(j) = \max(\widehat{\Delta})$;

16 **end**

---

the bounds of target time interval. We note that it is not feasible to run the analysis using the proposed method on a large number of traces.

The analysis of the attack algorithm described in Algorithm 1 shows that the costly part is the transformation of the original leakage traces to the new subspace spanned by the eigenvectors of the ratio of scatter matrices. In particular, the calculation of the between-class and within-class scatter matrices have the complexity of $\mathcal{O}(md^2)$ where m is the number of leakage traces and d is the number of samples. Similarly, the complexities of the operations in lines 2–4 are equal to $\mathcal{O}(d^3)$. Since the number of traces is larger than the number of samples as described in Sect. 4, the complexity of the attack is $\mathcal{O}(md^2)$. The linear relation between the computational complexity and the number of traces implies that the attack can indeed be carried out using large number of leakage traces if the number of samples per trace is kept small.

6   Conclusion

In this paper we have introduced a new method for conducting a key recovery side-channel attack. We have described how the matrix that transforms the side-channel leakage traces into a new subspace where the SNR is increased can be constructed. Later, a distinguisher which compares the classifications of the traces based on different values of the key candidates has been introduced.

The method has been tested against noisy trace sets with and without making assumptions about the leakage model of the implementations. We have also discussed the theoretical restrictions arising from the application of the LDA transformation and proposed a method for achieving a higher GSR with lower number of traces. The experiments conducted on the software implementations of the AES and DES encryption have confirmed the efficiency of the proposed method. We have compared the new method to the CPA and have observed that significantly less number of traces were needed to achieve the same GSR.

Acknowledgments. This work has been funded partially by Riscure BV through the Internship@Riscure program, by the Dutch government and the Netherlands Technology Foundation STW through project 13499 - TYPHOON & ASPASIA, project 12624 - SIDES, and by the Netherlands Organization for Scientific Research NWO through project 628.001.007 - ProFIL.

References

1. Archambeau, C., Peeters, E., Standaert, F.-X., Quisquater, J.-J.: Template attacks in principal subspaces. In: Goubin, L., Matsui, M. (eds.) CHES 2006. LNCS, vol. 4249, pp. 1–14. Springer, Heidelberg (2006). doi:10.1007/11894063_1
2. Batina, L., Gierlichs, B., Lemke-Rust, K.: Differential cluster analysis. In: Clavier, C., Gaj, K. (eds.) CHES 2009. LNCS, vol. 5747, pp. 112–127. Springer, Heidelberg (2009). doi:10.1007/978-3-642-04138-9_9
3. Batina, L., Gierlichs, B., Prouff, E., Rivain, M., Standaert, F.-X., Veyrat-Charvillon, N.: Mutual information analysis: a comprehensive study. J. Cryptology **24**(2), 269–291 (2011)
4. Batina, L., Hogenboom, J., Woudenberg, J.G.J.: Getting more from PCA: first results of using principal component analysis for extensive power analysis. In: Dunkelman, O. (ed.) CT-RSA 2012. LNCS, vol. 7178, pp. 383–397. Springer, Heidelberg (2012). doi:10.1007/978-3-642-27954-6_24
5. Bhasin, S., Danger, J.-L., Guilley, S., Najm, N.: Normalized inter-class variance for detection of side-channel leakage. In: International Symposium on Electromagnetic Compatibility, Tokyo-EMC 2014, pp. 310–313. IEEE (2014)
6. Brier, E., Clavier, C., Olivier, F.: Correlation power analysis with a leakage model. In: Joye, M., Quisquater, J.-J. (eds.) CHES 2004. LNCS, vol. 3156, pp. 16–29. Springer, Heidelberg (2004). doi:10.1007/978-3-540-28632-5_2
7. Bruneau, N., Guilley, S., Heuser, A., Marion, D., Rioul, O.: Less is more - dimensionality reduction from a theoretical perspective. In: Güneysu, T., Handschuh, H. (eds.) CHES 2015. LNCS, vol. 9293, pp. 22–41. Springer, Heidelberg (2015). doi:10.1007/978-3-662-48324-4_2
8. Chari, S., Rao, J.R., Rohatgi, P.: Template attacks. In: Kaliski, B.S., Koç, K., Paar, C. (eds.) CHES 2002. LNCS, vol. 2523, pp. 13–28. Springer, Heidelberg (2003). doi:10.1007/3-540-36400-5_3
9. Choudary, O., Kuhn, M.G.: Efficient template attacks. In: Francillon, A., Rohatgi, P. (eds.) CARDIS 2013. LNCS, vol. 8419, pp. 253–270. Springer, Cham (2014). doi:10.1007/978-3-319-08302-5_17
10. Cover, T.M., Thomas, J.A.: Elements of Information Theory. Wiley, Hoboken (2012)

11. Doget, J., Prouff, E., Rivain, M., Standaert, F.-X.: Univariate side channel attacks and leakage modeling. J. Cryptographic Eng. **1**(2), 123–144 (2011)
12. Eckart, C., Young, G.: The approximation of one matrix by another of lower rank. Psychometrika **1**(3), 211–218 (1936)
13. PUB FIPS. 46-3: Data Encryption Standard (DES). National Institute of Standards and Technology, **25** (1999)
14. PUB FIPS. 197: Advanced Encryption standard (AES). National Institute of Standards and Technology, **26** (2001)
15. Fisher, R.A.: The use of multiple measurements in taxonomic problems. Ann. Eugenics **7**(2), 179–188 (1936)
16. Golyandina, N., Zhigljavsky, A.: Singular Spectrum Analysis for Time Series. Springer Science & Business Media, Heidelberg (2013)
17. Jolliffe, I.: Principal Component Analysis. Wiley Online Library (2002)
18. Kocher, P., Jaffe, J., Jun, B.: Differential power analysis. In: Wiener, M. (ed.) CRYPTO 1999. LNCS, vol. 1666, pp. 388–397. Springer, Heidelberg (1999). doi:10. 1007/3-540-48405-1_25
19. Mangard, S., Oswald, E., Popp, T.: Power Analysis Attacks: Revealing the Secrets of Smart Cards, vol. 31. Springer Science & Business Media, New York (2008)
20. Mangard, S., Oswald, E., Standaert, F.-X.: One for all - all for one: unifying standard differential power analysis attacks. IET Inf. Secur. **5**(2), 100–110 (2011)
21. Souissi, Y., Nassar, M., Guilley, S., Danger, J.-L., Flament, F.: First principal components analysis: a new side channel distinguisher. In: Rhee, K.-H., Nyang, D.H. (eds.) ICISC 2010. LNCS, vol. 6829, pp. 407–419. Springer, Heidelberg (2011). doi:10.1007/978-3-642-24209-0_27
22. Standaert, F.-X., Archambeau, C.: Using subspace-based template attacks to compare and combine power and electromagnetic information leakages. In: Oswald, E., Rohatgi, P. (eds.) CHES 2008. LNCS, vol. 5154, pp. 411–425. Springer, Heidelberg (2008). doi:10.1007/978-3-540-85053-3_26
23. Pico Technology. PicoScope 3000 Series (2013). https://www.picotech.com/ download/datasheets/PicoScope3200ABSeriesDataSheet.pdf
24. Warrens, M.J.: Similarity Coefficients for Binary Data: Properties of Coefficients, Coefficient Matrices, Multi-Way Metrics and Multivariate Coefficients. Psychometrics and Research Methodology Group, Leiden University Institute for Psychological Research, Faculty of Social Sciences, Leiden University (2008)
25. Weng, L.-J., Cheng, C.-P.: Parallel analysis with unidimensional binary data. Educ. Psychol. Measur. **65**(5), 697–716 (2005)

Efficient Implementation of Ring-LWE Encryption on High-End IoT Platform

Zhe Liu[1,2], Reza Azarderakhsh[3], Howon Kim[4], and Hwajeong Seo[5(✉)]

[1] College of Computer Science and Technology,
Nanjing University of Aeronautics and Astronautics, Nanjing, China
[2] Department of Combinatorics and Optimization,
University of Waterloo, Waterloo, Canada
sduliuzhe@gmail.com
[3] Computer and Electrical Engineering and Computer Science (CEECS),
I-SENSE, Boca Raton, USA
azarderakhsh@gmail.com
[4] Pusan National University, Busan, Republic of Korea
howonkim@pusan.ac.kr
[5] Institute for Infocomm Research (I2R), Singapore, Singapore
hwajeong84@gmail.com

Abstract. ARM NEON architecture has occupied a significant share of high-end Internet of Things platforms such as mini computer, tablet and smartphone markets due to its low cost and high performance. This paper studies efficient techniques of lattice-based cryptography on ARM processor and presents the first implementation of ring-LWE encryption on ARM NEON architecture. We propose a vectorized version of Iterative Number Theoretic Transform (NTT) for high-speed computation and present a 32-bit variant of SAMS2 technique, original from Liu et al. in CHES2015, for fast reduction. Subsequently, we present a full-fledged implementation of Ring-LWE by taking advantage of proposed and previous optimization techniques. Ultimately, our ring-LWE implementation requires only 145 k clock cycles for encryption and 32.8 k cycles for decryption for $n = 256$. These results are more than 17.6 times faster than the fastest ECC implementation on ARM NEON with same security level.

Keywords: Lightweight implementation · Lattice-based cryptography · ARM NEON architecture

1 Introduction

The 32-bit ARM processor [1] is the most widely used embedded processor in almost all high-end Internet of Things (IoT) platforms, e.g., mini computer,

This work was supported by the NSERC CREATE Training Program in Building a Workforce for the Cryptographic Infrastructure of the 21st Century (CryptoWorks21), and Public Works and Government Services Canada.

G.P. Hancke and K. Markantonakis (Eds.): RFIDSec 2016, LNCS 10155, pp. 76–90, 2017.
DOI: 10.1007/978-3-319-62024-4_6

tablets and smartphones, thanks to its low cost and high performance. ARMv6 [2] architecture introduces a small set of *SIMD* instructions, operating on multiple 16-bit or 8-bit values packed into standard 32-bit general purpose registers. This nice feature permits some certain operations can be executed in at least double speed, without using any additional computation units. From ARMv7 architecture [3], ARM introduces the Advanced SIMD extension, called *"NEON"*. It extends the SIMD concept by defining groups of instructions operating on vectors stored in 64-bit D, doubleword, registers and 128-bit Q, quadword, vector registers. In the literature, many papers presented cryptography primitives on the embedded processor such as RSA [5], Elliptic Curve Cryptography (ECC) [6], pairing-based cryptography [26], AES [7] as well as lattice-based cryptography [8]. Despite recent research progress, efficient implementation of lattice based cryptographic algorithm on 32-bit ARM, in particular ARM NEON, is still an interesting and challenge topic.

1.1 Related Work

The first evaluation of cryptographic algorithm on ARM NEON architecture belonged to Bernstein and Schwabe in CHES'12 [6]. The authors showed that NEON supports high-security elliptic curve cryptography at surprised high speeds. They also summarized the useful instructions set for high-speed cryptography and presented the experimental results of NaCl library on Cortex A8 core. In 2013, Câmaraand et al. employed the VMULL.P8 instruction to describe a novel software multiplier for performing a polynomial multiplication of 64-bit binary polynomial and obtained a fast software multiplication in the binary field $\mathbb{F}_{2^m}$ [9]. Their results emphasized the advantage of NEON for high-speed binary ECC. In SAC'13, Bos et al. in [10] presented a parallel approach to compute interleaved Montgomery multiplication, which is suitable to be computed on 2-way single instruction, multiple data platforms, e.g., ARM NEON. Seo et al. revisited the work in [10], and introduced the Cascade Operand Scanning (COS) method for multi-precision multiplication with the goal of reducing Read-After-Write (RAW) dependencies in the propagation of carries and the number of pipeline stalls [11]. As a follow up work, Seo et al. proposed a novel Double Operand Scanning (DOS) method to speed-up multi-precision squaring with non-redundant representations on SIMD architecture and investigated RSA-1024 and RSA-2048 on ARM Cortex A9 and A15 cores [5]. Besides public-key algorithm, cryptographic engineers also evaluated the impact of performance for symmetric ciphers on ARM NEON architecture. In [12], Seo et al. evaluated and proposed a parallel implementation of block cipher LEA on ARM NEON and achieved a speed up of roughly 50 % compared to previous fastest implementation on ARM without NEON. In 2014, Saarinenand et al. presented the results of authenticated encryption algorithms, e.g., WHIRLBOB and STRIBOB on NEON platform [13]. In CT-RSA'15, Gouvêa and López used NEON instructions vmull to multiply two 64-bit binary polynomials and presented an optimized yet timing-resistant implementation of GCM over AES-128 on ARMv8 [14]. Similarly, Wang et al. chose the ARM NEON platform and presented a high order masked AES implementation in [7].

Another interesting research line is to evaluate lattice-based cryptography (e.g., Ring-LWE) on different platforms. The first practical evaluations of LWE and ring-LWE based encryption schemes were presented by Göttert et al. in CHES'12 [15]. The authors concluded that the ring-LWE based encryption scheme is faster by at least a factor of four and requires less memory in comparison to the encryption scheme based on the standard LWE problem. Sujoy et al. [30] proposed a complete ring-LWE based encryption processor that uses the Number Theoretic Transform (NTT) algorithm for polynomial multiplication. The architecture is designed to have small area and memory requirement, but is also optimized to keep the number of cycles small. Oder et al. in [8] presented the first efficient implementation of Bimodal Lattice Signature Schemes (BLISS) on a 32-bit ARM processor. The most optimal variant of their implementation cost 6 M cycles for signing, 1 M cycles for verification and 368 M cycles for key generation, respectively, at a medium-term security level. In DATE'15, De Clercq et al. in [18] implemented ring-LWE encryption scheme on the identical ARM processors, they investigated acceleration techniques to improve the sampler based on the architecture of the microcontroller. Namely, the platform built-in True Random Number Generator (TRNG) is used to generate random numbers. As a result, their implementation required 121 K cycles per encryption and 43.3 K cycles per decryption at medium-term security level while 261 K cycles per encryption and roughly 96.5 K cycles per decryption for long-term security level. The first time when a lattice-based cryptographic scheme was implemented on an 8-bit processor belonged to Boorghany et al. in [19,20]. The authors evaluated four lattice-based authentication protocols on both 8-bit AVR and 32-bit ARM processors. Very recently, Pöppelmann et al. [21] and Liu et al. [22] studied and compared implementations of Ring-LWE encryption and the Bimodal Lattice Signature Scheme (BLISS) on an 8-bit platform and presents efficient ring-LWE results, respectively.

1.2   Motivation

Lattice-based cryptography is often considered a premier candidate for realizing post-quantum cryptosystems [32]. Its security relies on worst-case computational assumptions in lattices that will remain hard even for quantum computers. Although some work has been done, the design and implementation of post-quantum cryptosystems and protocols is still a big challenge. For example, it has been recognized in a recent Microsoft Research project [23] and the Canada "CryptoWorks21" project [24] as well as the European project "PQCrypto" [25]. However, we were surprised to find there exists no previous work about evaluating Ring-LWE encryption or signature scheme on ARM NEON architecture, which was reported, in 2014, to be present in 95% of mini computers, tablets and smartphones [14]. This raises one interesting question that how well this "cryptosystems of the future" are suited for today's most widely used mobile devoices and one aspect of this question is the performance and memory consumption of lattice-based cryptosystems on 32-bit ARM NEON platform. In this paper, we are going to fill the implementation gap and give our answer for this open problem.

1.3 NEON PQCryto

This paper studies efficient techniques of lattice-based cryptography and presents an efficient ring-LWE implementation on ARM NEON architecture, called "NEON PQCrypto". NEON PQCrypto includes support for core ring-LWE functions necessary to implement most popular ring-LWE based schemes, i.e. encryption scheme. In particular, NEON PQCrypto supports the computation of two most important operations:

- We propose parallel Number Theoretic Transform (NTT) to reduce the execution time for coefficient multiplication. This method introduces 4-way NTT computations over SIMD architecture.
- We introduce the 32-bit wise Shifting-Addition-Multiplication-Subtraction-Subtraction (SAMS2) approach for reduction operation. The approach replaced the expensive division operation into shifting, addition and multiplication operations.
- We exploit the incomplete arithmetic for representing the coefficients and perform the reduction operation in a lazy fashion. This technique avoids one time of subtraction in each reduction stage.
- Efficient implementation of Gaussian distribution sampler. We employ Knuth-Yao sampler, LUT and byte-scanning methods. Our implementation exploits the PRNG based on block cipher, which achieved the high performance with parallel and pipelined techniques.

NEON PQCrypto achieves high performance without compromising security. By a combination of proposed and previous optimizations (e.g., Incomplete arithmetic), we present high speed implementations of ring-LWE encryption for 128-bit security level on ARM NEON. For 128-bit security level, it only requires $145,200$ and $32,800$ clock cycles for encryption and decryption. The decryption result outperforms the previous ARM implementation (without NEON) by a factor of 1.32. When compared with ECC implementation with same security level, our ring-LWE is 17.6 faster on identical platform.

The rest of this paper is organized as follows. In the next section, we review the background of Ring-LWE. In Sect. 2, we introduce the optimization techniques for Ring-LWE on ARM-NEON processors. In particular, we propose several optimization techniques to reduce the execution time in SIMD architecture. In Sect. 4, we report the implementation results and compare with the state-of-the-art implementations.

2   Implementation of NTT

In this section, we describe several optimization techniques to reduce the execution time of Ring-LWE on ARM NEON architectures. We choose the parameter sets (n, q, σ) with $(256, 7681, 11.31/\sqrt{2\pi})$ for security level of 128-bit. These parameter sets were also used in most of the previous hardware implementations, e.g., [15,30] and software implementations, e.g., [18–22]. This also helps us to compare our work with previous works.

2.1   Vectorized Iterative Algorithm

Previous implementations on RISC processors, e.g., [18,21,22], executed the NTT computation in a sequential fashion. Namely, the coefficient multiplication is performed in sequence in each iteration. In the following, we propose a vectorized variant of iterative NTT algorithm, which significantly speeds up the execution time of NTT operations on ARM NEON. The core idea is to take the advantages of SIMD instruction set and implement NTT computation in a hybrid fashion. In particular, when the number of consecutive coefficient multiplication satisfies the minimum width of SIMD, we compute the SIMD based vectored computations. Otherwise, when the number of consecutive coefficient multiplication is smaller than width of SIMD, we simply adopt the sequential fashion in ARM instruction.

The vectorized variant of NTT computation is given in Algorithm 1. As shown in steps 3 to 12, in the innermost k loop, the index value of consecutive coefficient multiplication between two coefficients $(a[k+j], a[k+j+i/2])$ are only 1 and 2 for $i = 2$ and $i = 4$ cases, respectively. Thus, we conduct these coefficient multiplication in a sequential way. On the other hand, the cases $i > 4$ have at least four consecutive coefficient multiplication operations, we perform these coefficient multiplications in a parallel fashion. Specifically, we first conduct the whole twiddle factors (ω) in consecutive array form (steps 15–18). Observing that the twiddle factors are fixed variables, we simply compute these values off-line and store them into a look-up table. Thereafter, in steps 19–28, the coefficient variables are loaded into registers in consecutive array form such as U_{array}, V_{array} and ω_{array}. We conduct the four different modular multiplications with $\omega_{array}[p : p+3] \cdot a[k+j+i/2 : k+j+3+i/2]$. After then, the pointer address of p increases by 4 (i.e. the SIMD width)[1]. Finally, the multiple number of coefficient variables are added and subtracted each other, simultaneously.

2.2   Parallel Coefficient Multiplication

The coefficient multiplication is one of the most expensive operations of NTT computation, since each NTT computation requires $\frac{n}{2} log_2 n$ coefficient multiplications. In our implementation, the coefficient is at most 13-bit long, which can be kept in one 32-bit ARM register. As mentioned before, it is possible to store two coefficients into one register as De Clercq did in [18]. However, we decide to store only one coefficient in a register since the product of a coefficient multiplication can be (at most) 26-bit long. In this case, storing 26-bit in a register will result in some extra cost to extract the 13-bit operand out of 26-bit before performing the next step. For ARM NEON, the 128-bit Q register is able to store

---

[1] For AVX256 and AVX512, we can extend to 8 and 16 respectively.

Algorithm 1. Vectorized iterative number theoretic transform

Require: A polynomial $a(x) \in \mathbb{Z}_q[x]$ of degree $n-1$ and n-th primitive $\omega \in \mathbb{Z}_q$ of unity

Ensure: Polynomial $a(x) = NTT(a) \in \mathbb{Z}_q[x]$

1: $a = BitReverse(a)$ {BitReverse computation}

2: **for** i from 2 by $i = 2i$ to n **do**

3:     $\omega_i = \omega_n^{n/i}$, $\omega = 1$ {Setting twiddle factors}

4:     **if** $i = 2$ or $i = 4$ **then**

5:        **for** j from 0 by 1 to $i/2 - 1$ **do**

6:           **for** k from 0 by i to $n - 1$ **do**

7:             $U = a[k+j]$ {sequential computations}

8:             $V = \omega \cdot a[k+j+i/2]$ {single multiplication}

9:             $a[k+j] = U + V$ {single addition}

10:             $a[k+j+i/2] = U - V$ {single subtraction}

11:           **end for**

12:           $\omega = \omega \cdot \omega_i$ {computation of single twiddle factors}

13:        **end for**

14:     **else**

15:        $\omega_{array}[0] = \omega$

16:        **for** p from 1 by 1 to $i/2 - 1$ **do**

17:           $\omega = \omega \cdot \omega_i$, $\omega_{array}[p] = \omega$ {computations of multiple twiddle factors}

18:        **end for**

19:        **for** j from 0 by i to $n - 1$ **do**

20:           $p = 0$

21:           **for** k from 0 by 4 to $i/2 - 1$ **do**

22:             $U_{array} = a[k+j : k+j+3]$ {parallel computations}

23:             $V_{array} = \omega_{array}[p : p+3] \cdot a[k+j+i/2 : k+j+3+i/2]$ {multiple multiplications}

24:             $p = p + 4$ {index increment}

25:             $a[k+j : k+j+3] = U_{array} + V_{array}$ {multiple additions}

26:             $a[k+j+i/2 : k+j+3+i/2] = U_{array} - V_{array}$ {multiple subtractions}

27:           **end for**

28:        **end for**

29:     **end if**

30: **end for**

31: **return** a

---

four 32-bit wise variables. We load four different aligned consecutive variables and then conduct the four different multiplications with one single vectorized vmull instruction.

2.3 Fast Reduction

In NTT computation, the majority of the execution time is spent on computing reduction operation since it is performed in the innermost k-loop (three times nested). Thus, fast reduction operation is an essential for high-speed implementation of NTT algorithm. Our implementation chooses the prime modulus $q = 7681$ (i.e. 0x1e01 in hexadecimal representation).

One of the efficient method for reduction belongs to SAMS2 method, which was originally proposed in an 8-bit AVR implementation [22]. This method has optimized the register usages and computation complexity. Since it replaces expensive operation (e.g., division) with relatively cheaper instructions (e.g., addition, shifting, multiplication), the execution time is significantly improved. However, compared to RISC architecture, ARM NEON has more distinguished features. First, the length of a word is bigger, i.e. 32-bit per word. This feature allows us to readily compute the 13-bit wise multiplication in single instruction and up-to 31-bit shifting can be performed in single cycle. Second, ARM NEON supplies SIMD instructions, which perform multiple operations (up-to four 32-bit multiplications) in parallel using single instruction. Therefore, we have craftily design an enhanced variant of SAMS2 method on ARM NEON architecture.

We propose an optimized 32-bit wise SAMS2 reduction technique for performing the mod 7681 operation. The SAMS2 method is introduced in [22] and the method is highly optimized in 8-bit AVR processors in terms of register utilization and the number of operations. However, ARM NEON processor has two distinguished features over 8-bit AVR. First the processor provide 32-bit word size. We can readily compute the 13-bit wise multiplication in single instruction and up-to 31-bit shift is available within single cycle. Second multiple number of operations are conducted at once by exploiting SIMD instructions. With these features in mind, we redesign the original SAMS2 for ARM NEON architecture.

This main idea of SAMS2 is to first estimate the quotient of $t = \frac{a}{q}$, and then perform the subtraction $a - t \cdot q$ where the value of t is $(a \gg 13) + (a \gg 17) + (a \gg 21)$. The reduction process consists of four different basic operations, namely, 32-bit wise Shifting $\rightarrow$ Addition $\rightarrow$ Multiplication $\rightarrow$ Subtraction $\rightarrow$ Subtraction (SAMS2). As shown in Fig. 1, one Q register consists of four 32-bit registers. Among them, multiplication over one 32-bit long register ($r0$, a quarter of NEON register) is described in detail. Since remaining three 32-bit registers and $r0$ register is packed in the Q register, four identical SAMS2 method is conducted simultaneously. The colorful parts mean that the storage has been occupied while the white part is not. The reduction with 7681 using SAMS2 approach can be performed as follows:

1. Shifting. We right shift $r0$ by 13-bit, 17-bit and 21-bit. This outputs results $t0$, $t1$ and $t2$.
2. Addition. We then perform the addition of $t0 + t1 + t2$.
3. Multiplication and Subtraction. The third step is to multiply the constant 0x1e01 by $(t0 + t1 + t2)$, which is a 16×13-bit multiplication and then subtract the product from $r0$.
4. Multiplication and Subtraction. However, the result we get in step 3 may still be larger than $p = 7681$, thus, we do the correction by subtracting the modulus p multiplied by intermediate result larger than 13-bit.

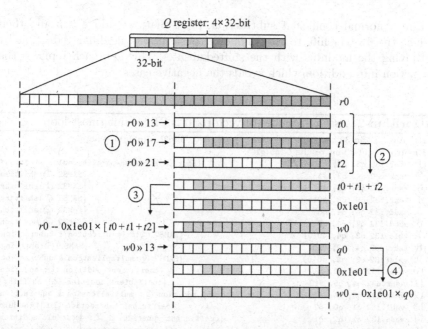

Fig. 1. Fast reduction operation with 32-bit wise SAMS2 method for $q = 7681$. ①: shifting; ②: addition; ③: multiplication & subtraction; ④: multiplication and subtraction.

In Algorithm 2, pseudo codes for vectorized NTT computation with constant time reduction is described. Firstly four coefficients (q3) and four twiddle factors (q1) are multiplied in Step 1. From Steps 2–6, the intermediate results are shifted to right by 13, 17 and 21-bit and accumulated. In Step 7, we conduct multiplication with modulo (d0[0]) and intermediate result (q4). This process is readily available by using vmls instruction, which conducts four different multiplication and then subtract operations from the destination (q3). From Steps 8–9, results over 13-bit are shifted and then reduced once again. In case of coefficient addition, two operands (q2 and q3) are added and then one time of reduction is follows in Steps 10–12. For subtraction, we firstly calculate the value (4 × modulus) in Step 13. After then the value is added to operand (q2). Since the operand (q3) is placed within $[0, 2^{\lceil log_2 p \rceil}]$, the subtraction in Step 15 does not introduce negative values. Conveniently we can conduct one time of reduction that is same with addition case.

2.4 Coefficient Addition and Subtraction

We employ the incomplete arithmetic to represent the intermediate result of coefficient. Our implementation of coefficient addition works as follows. We first perform a normal coefficient addition, after that, we conduct the 13-bit shift to the right and perform the modular reduction by multiplying the modulus with the shifted results. Similarly, for incomplete coefficient subtraction, we first perform a normal coefficient subtraction, after that, we add $4 \times p$ and then conduct the 13-bit shift to the right and perform the modular reduction by multiplying the modulus with the shifted results. This approach replaces the subtraction into addition which avoids the negative cases.

Algorithm 2. Assembly codes of vectorized NTT for innermost loop

Require: Eight 32-bit coefficients $A[0:3]$(q2), $B[0:3]$(q3), ω(q1), modulo(q0).
Ensure: Eight 32-bit results C(q5,q10).

```
 1: vmul.i32 q3, q3, q1          {Four 32-bit wise parallel multiplications}
 2: vshr.u32 q4, q3, #13                              {SAMS2 ①:shifting}
 3: vshr.u32 q5, q3, #17                              {SAMS2 ①:shifting}
 4: vshr.u32 q6, q3, #21                              {SAMS2 ①:shifting}
 5: vadd.i32 q4, q4, q5                               {SAMS2 ②:addition}
 6: vadd.i32 q4, q4, q6                               {SAMS2 ②:addition}
 7: vmls.i32 q3, q4, d0[0]           {SAMS2 ③:multiplication & subtraction}
 8: vshr.u32 q4, q3, #13                              {SAMS2 ④:shifting}
 9: vmls.i32 q3, q4, d0[0]           {SAMS2 ④:multiplication & subtraction}
10: vadd.i32 q5, q2, q3                   {coefficient addition ①: addition}
11: vshr.u32 q4, q5, #13                  {coefficient addition ②: shifting}
12: vmls.i32 q5, q4, d0[0]     {coefficient addition ③: multiplication & subtraction}
13: vshl.i32 q1, q0, #2                {coefficient subtraction ①: 4×modulo}
14: vadd.i32 q2, q2, q1           {coefficient subtraction ②: 4×modulo addition}
15: vsub.i32 q10, q2, q3              {coefficient subtraction ③: subtraction}
16: vshr.u32 q14, q10, #13              {coefficient subtraction ④: shifting}
17: vmls.i32 q10, q14, d0[0]  {coefficient subtraction ⑤: multiplication & subtraction}
```

2.5 Look-Up Table for the Twiddle Factors

A straightforward computation of $\omega = \omega \cdot \omega_i$ on-the-fly needs to perform $n - 1$ times of coefficient modular multiplications. Both of the computations of the power of ω_n in i-loop and twiddle factor $\omega = \omega \cdot \omega_i$ in j-loop can be considered as fixed costs. We can pre-compute the all twiddle factors ω into RAM which is similar to the technique used in [22]. Fortunately, ARM-NEON process provides huge RAM size (1–4 GB) and the storing all the intermediate twiddle factors ω into RAM is very cheap approach. We only need to transfer the twiddle factor that is required for the current iteration. For vectorized operation, whole twiddle factors are stored in aligned vector form which ensures efficient memory access pattern and vector operations as well.

3   Implementation of Gaussian Sampler

Both key-generation and encryption require the operation of Gaussian samplers, thus efficient implementation of the Knuth-Yao sampler is another important factor for a high-speed ring-LWE encryption scheme. In this section, we describe optimization techniques that can be used to reduce the execution time of the Knuth-Yao sampler on ARM NEON processors.

3.1 Pseudo-Random Number Generation

Gaussian sampler needs random sequences. As ARM NEON does not support the build-in TRNG, our implementation adopts the PRNG algorithm, which runs the block cipher in counter mode, i.e. it encrypts successive values of an incrementing counter. There are a number of lightweight block ciphers that can be used for generating random numbers. Recently, ATmel company introduced AES peripheral based PRNG [34]. This module is available in modern XMega products which can be used for high performance of PRNG and Seo et al. in WF-IoT'14 implemented the AES accelerator based PRNG implementation on XMega processor [35].

Our implementation exploits the LEA block cipher [33] for random generations. LEA is a new lightweight and low-power encryption algorithm. This algorithm has a certain useful features which are especially suitable for parallel hardware and software implementations, i.e., simple ARX operations, non-S-BOX architecture, and 32-bit word size. We follow the parallel implementation of LEA introduced by [12]. ARM NEON processor supports 128-bit register which consists of four different 32-bit registers. By assigning four different 128-bit wise data into four 128-bit registers, we can conduct four different encryption computations in parallel fashion. Finally, the implementation results achieved 10.06 cycle/byte for encryption by computing four different encryptions at once.

3.2 Look-Up Table for Probability Matrix

In order to ensure a precision of 2^{-90} for dimension $n = 256$, the Knuth-Yao algorithm is suggested to have a probability matrix P_{mat} of 55 rows and 109 columns [18]. On 32-bit ARM processor, we stored each 55-bit column in two words, where each word size is 32-bit long. In this case, 9-bit is wasted per each column and the probability matrix only occupies 872 bytes in total.

3.3 Byte-Wise Scanning

The bit-scanning operation requires to check each bit and decreases the distance (d) whenever the bit is set. Instead of executing the scanning operation in a bit-level, we perform the scanning operation in a byte-wise fashion [22]. The byte-wise scanning method counts the number of bits in the byte and decreases the distance by the number of bits. Since the byte-wise method does not conduct the subtraction by each bit, it only requires eight additions, one subtraction and one conditional branch statements, saving seven conditional branch statements at the cost of one subtraction rather than bit-wise scanning.

3.4 Efficiently Skip the Consecutive Leading Zeros

The probability matrix includes an occurrence of consecutive leading zeros. In order to skip the consecutive leading zeros, we conduct the simple comparison between zero and bit counter. One time of byte comparison can decide that the probability matrix has leading zeros or not by byte wise. This approach can skip one byte-scanning at the cost of one conditional branch statement, if the counter is zero.

3.5 Look-Up Table in DDG Tree

We exploit the Look-Up Table (LUT) approaches proposed in [18] into byte-wise scanning implementations. First, we perform sampling with an 8-bit random number as an index to the LUT in the first 8 levels for a Gaussian distribution with $\sigma = 11.31/\sqrt{2\pi}$. If the most significant bit of the lookup result is reset, then the algorithm returns the LUT result successfully. Otherwise, the most significant bit of the LUT result is one, then a LUT failure occurs, and the next level of sampling will execute. Similarly, a second LUT will be used for level 9–13 in the same Gaussian distribution. Since two levels of LUT method shows about 99% hit ratio, this is the computation efficient approach.

4 Performance Evaluation and Comparison

4.1 Experimental Platform

The ARM Cortex A9 is full implementations of the ARMv7 architecture including NEON engine. Register sizes are 64-bit and 128-bit for double(D) and quadruple(Q) word registers, respectively. Each register provides short bit size computations such as 8-bit, 16-bit, 32-bit and 64-bit. This feature provides more precise operation and benefits to various word size computations. We complied our implementation with speed optimization option -O3. In order to obtain accurate timings, we ran each operation at least 1000 times and calculated the average cycle count for one operation (Table 1).

4.2 Experimental Results

Table 2 summarizes the execution times of Number Theoretic Transform, Gaussian sampling, key generation, encryption and decryption of the proposed implementation for medium-term security level. Our parallel NTT operations only require 25,574 clock cycles for 128-bit security level. We also compare software implementations of Number Theoretic Transform on different processors. For the 8-bit AVR and 32-bit platforms, the previous works [8, 18–21] and our implementations adopt the same parameter sets. The most suitable comparison is 32-bit ARM implementations, since the target processor shares similar ARM instructions of ARMv7. A comparison of our implementation (parallel) with De Clercq's implementation (sequential) clearly show the advantage of NEON engine, roughly 19% enhancements can be achieved for NTT computation. For Gaussian sampling, our current implementation is slower than the work in [18]. This can be explained that the authors in [18] adopted build-in true random number generator (in hardware) and our implementation simply adopts the

Table 1. Performance comparison of software implementation of Number Theoretic Transform on different processors.

Implementations	NTT/FFT
8-bit AVR processors, e.g., ATxmega64, ATxmega128	
Boorghany et al. [20]	1,216,000
Boorghany et al. [19]	754,668
Pöppelmann et al. [21]	334,646
Liu et al. [22]	193,731
32-bit ARM processors, e.g., Cortex-M4F, ARM7TDMI	
Boorghany et al. [19]	109,306
DeClercq et al. [18]	31,583
32-bit ARM-NEON processors, e.g., Cortex-A9	
This work	**25,574**

Table 2. Performance comparison of software implementation of lattice-based cryptosystems on different processors (clock cycle 10^3).

Implementations	NTT/FFT	Sampling	Gen	Enc	Dec
Implementations on 8-bit AVR processors, e.g., ATxmega64, ATxmega128					
Boorghany et al. [20]	1,216.0	N/A	N/A	5,024.0	2,464.0
Boorghany et al. [19]	754.7	N/A	2,770.6	3,042.7	1,369.0
Pöppelmann et al. [21]	334.6	N/A	N/A	1,315.0	381.3
Liu et al. [22]	193.7	26.8	589.9	671.6	275.6
Implementations on 32-bit ARM processors					
DeClercq et al. [18]	31.6	7.3	117.0	121.2	43.3
Implementations on 32-bit ARM-NEON processors, e.g., Cortex-A9					
This work	**25.5**	**18.8**	**123.2**	**145.2**	**32.8**

pseudo random number generator using software implementation. For 128-bit security level, our ring-LWE implementation requires only $145, 200$ clock cycles for encryption and $32, 800$ cycles for decryption. Comparing with the implementation on ARM Cortex M4 in [18], the key generation and encryption are slightly slower while the decryption is faster.

Table 3 compares the results of our ring-LWE encryption scheme with some classical public-key encryption algorithms, in particular recent RSA and ECC implementations for ARM NEON platform. The to-date fastest RSA software for an ARM NEON processor was reported in [5]; it achieves an execution time of approximately 20.9 M clock cycles for RSA-2048 decryption at the 96-bit security level. For comparison, our LWE-256 implementation requires only 32.8 k cycles for decryption, which is more than 639 times faster despite a much higher (i.e. 128-bit) security level. The fastest implementation ECC software implementations on

Table 3. Comparison of Ring-LWE encryption schemes with RSA and ECC on ARM NEON processors (Enc and Dec in clock cycles)

Implementation	Scheme	Enc	Dec
Seo et al. [5]	RSA-2048	535,020	20,977,660
Bernstein et al. [6]	ECC-255	1,157,952	578,976
This work	LWE-256	**145,200**	**32,800**

NEON belongs to Bernstein et al. [6]. For comparison, our implementation of ring-LWE is roughly 8 times faster for encryption and 17.6 for decryption.

5 Conclusion

This paper presented several optimizations for efficiently implementing ring-LWE encryption scheme on high-end IoT platform, 32-bit ARM NEON architecture. In particular, we proposed three optimizations to accelerate the execution time of the NTT-based polynomial multiplication. A combination of these optimizations results in a very efficient NTT computation, which is 19% faster than the previous best implementation. All of these achieved results set new speed records for ring-LWE encryption implementation on 32-bit ARM NEON platforms. Finally, a comparison of our implementation with traditional public-key cryptography (i.e. RSA, ECC) also sheds some new light on practical application of ring-LWE on 32-bit ARM NEON processors.

References

1. ARM Architectures. http://www.arm.com/products/processors/index.php
2. ARM Limited: Cortex-V6 technical reference manual. http://ecee.colorado.edu/ecen3000/labs/lab3/files/DDI0419C_arm_architecture_v6m_reference_manual.pdf
3. ARM Limited: Cortex-V7 technical reference manual. https://web.eecs.umich.edu/prabal/teaching/eecs373-f10/readings/ARMv7-M_ARM.pdf
4. Introducing NEON Development Article. https://software.intel.com/sites/default/files/m/b/4/c/DHT0002A_introducing_neon.pdf
5. Seo, H., Liu, Z., Großschädl, J., Kim, H.: Efficient arithmetic on ARM-NEON and its application for high-speed RSA implementation (2015). IACR ePrint http://eprint.iacr.org/2015/465.pdf
6. Bernstein, D.J., Schwabe, P.: NEON crypto. In: Prouff, E., Schaumont, P. (eds.) CHES 2012. LNCS, vol. 7428, pp. 320–339. Springer, Heidelberg (2012). doi:10.1007/978-3-642-33027-8_19
7. Wang, J., Vadnala, P.K., Großschädl, J., Xu, Q.: Higher-order masking in practice: a vector implementation of masked AES for ARM NEON. In: Nyberg, K. (ed.) CT-RSA 2015. LNCS, vol. 9048, pp. 181–198. Springer, Cham (2015). doi:10.1007/978-3-319-16715-2_10
8. Oder, T., Pöppelmann, T., Güneysu, T.: Beyond ECDSA and RSA: lattice-based digital signatures on constrained devices. In: 51st Annual Design Automation Conference - DAC 2014 (2014)

9. Câmara, D., Gouvêa, C.P.L., López, J., Dahab, R.: Fast software polynomial multiplication on ARM processors using the NEON engine. In: Cuzzocrea, A., Kittl, C., Simos, D.E., Weippl, E., Xu, L. (eds.) CD-ARES 2013. LNCS, vol. 8128, pp. 137–154. Springer, Heidelberg (2013). doi:10.1007/978-3-642-40588-4_10

10. Bos, J.W., Montgomery, P.L., Shumow, D., Zaverucha, G.M.: Montgomery multiplication using vector instructions. In: Lange, T., Lauter, K., Lisoněk, P. (eds.) SAC 2013. LNCS, vol. 8282, pp. 471–489. Springer, Heidelberg (2014). doi:10.1007/978-3-662-43414-7_24

11. Seo, H., Liu, Z., Großschädl, J., Choi, J., Kim, H.: Montgomery modular multiplication on ARM-NEON revisited. In: Lee, J., Kim, J. (eds.) ICISC 2014. LNCS, vol. 8949, pp. 328–342. Springer, Cham (2015). doi:10.1007/978-3-319-15943-0_20

12. Seo, H., Liu, Z., Park, T., Kim, H., Lee, Y., Choi, J., Kim, H.: Parallel implementations of LEA. In: Lee, H.-S., Han, D.-G. (eds.) ICISC 2013. LNCS, vol. 8565, pp. 256–274. Springer, Cham (2014). doi:10.1007/978-3-319-12160-4_16

13. Saarinenand, M.J.O., Brumley, B.B.: Lighter, Faster, and Constant-Time: WhirlBob, the Whirlpool variant of StriBob (2014). IACR ePrint https://eprint.iacr.org/2014/501.pdf

14. Gouvêa, C.P.L., López, J.: Implementing GCM on ARMv8. In: Nyberg, K. (ed.) CT-RSA 2015. LNCS, vol. 9048, pp. 167–180. Springer, Cham (2015). doi:10.1007/978-3-319-16715-2_9

15. Göttert, N., Feller, T., Schneider, M., Buchmann, J., Huss, S.: On the design of hardware building blocks for modern lattice-based encryption schemes. In: Prouff, E., Schaumont, P. (eds.) CHES 2012. LNCS, vol. 7428, pp. 512–529. Springer, Heidelberg (2012). doi:10.1007/978-3-642-33027-8_30

16. Güneysu, T., Lyubashevsky, V., Pöppelmann, T.: Practical lattice-based cryptography: a signature scheme for embedded systems. In: Prouff, E., Schaumont, P. (eds.) CHES 2012. LNCS, vol. 7428, pp. 530–547. Springer, Heidelberg (2012). doi:10.1007/978-3-642-33027-8_31

17. Pöppelmann, T., Ducas, L., Güneysu, T.: Enhanced lattice-based signatures on reconfigurable hardware. In: Batina, L., Robshaw, M. (eds.) CHES 2014. LNCS, vol. 8731, pp. 353–370. Springer, Heidelberg (2014). doi:10.1007/978-3-662-44709-3_20

18. De Clercq, R., Roy, S.S., Vercauteren, F., Verbauwhede, I.: Efficient software implementation of ring-LWE encryption. In: 18th Design, Automation & Test in Europe Conference & Exhibition - DATE 2015 (2015)

19. Boorghany, A., Sarmadi, S.B., Jalili, R.: On constrained implementation of lattice-based cryptographic primitives and schemes on smart cards. Cryptology ePrint Archive, Report 2014/514 (2014). https://eprint.iacr.org/2014/514.pdf

20. Boorghany, A., Jalili, R.: Implementation and comparison of lattice-based identification protocols on smart cards and microcontrollers. Cryptology ePrint Archive, Report 2014/078 (2014). https://eprint.iacr.org/2014/078.pdf

21. Pöppelmann, T., Oder, T., Güneysu, T.: Speed records for ideal lattice-based cryptography on AVR. http://eprint.iacr.org/2015/382.pdf

22. Liu, Z., Seo, H., Sinha Roy, S., Großschädl, J., Kim, H., Verbauwhede, I.: Efficient ring-LWE encryption on 8-Bit AVR processors. In: Güneysu, T., Handschuh, H. (eds.) CHES 2015. LNCS, vol. 9293, pp. 663–682. Springer, Heidelberg (2015). doi:10.1007/978-3-662-48324-4_33

23. Microsoft Research: Latticed-based cryptography. http://research.microsoft.com/en-us/projects/lattice/

24. University of Waterloo, Canada: CryptoWork21. http://cryptoworks21.albertoconnor.ca/about/

25. Post-quantum cryptography for long-term security PQCRYPTO ICT-645622. http://pqcrypto.eu.org/index.html

26. Grewal, G., Azarderakhsh, R., Longa, P., Hu, S., Jao, D.: Efficient implementation of bilinear pairings on ARM processors. In: Knudsen, L.R., Wu, H. (eds.) SAC 2012. LNCS, vol. 7707, pp. 149–165. Springer, Heidelberg (2013). doi:10.1007/978-3-642-35999-6_11

27. Bos, J.W., Lauter, K., Loftus, J., Naehrig, M.: Improved security for a ring-based fully homomorphic encryption scheme. In: Stam, M. (ed.) IMACC 2013. LNCS, vol. 8308, pp. 45–64. Springer, Heidelberg (2013). doi:10.1007/978-3-642-45239-0_4

28. Cormen, T., Leiserson, C., Rivest, R.: Introduction to Algorithms. http://staff.ustc.edu.cn/~csli/graduate/algorithms/book6/toc.htm

29. Yanık, T., Savaş, E., Koç, Ç.K.: Incomplete reduction in modular arithmetic. IEE Proc. Comput. Digit. Techn. **149**(2), 46–52 (2002)

30. Roy, S.S., Vercauteren, F., Mentens, N., Chen, D.D., Verbauwhede, I.: Compact ring-LWE cryptoprocessor. In: Batina, L., Robshaw, M. (eds.) CHES 2014. LNCS, vol. 8731, pp. 371–391. Springer, Heidelberg (2014). doi:10.1007/978-3-662-44709-3_21

31. Ducas, L.: Lattice based signatures: attacks, analysis and optimization. Ph.D. Thesis (2013). http://cseweb.ucsd.edulducas/Thesis/index.html

32. Regev, O.: On lattices, learning with errors, random linear codes, and cryptography. In: Proceedings of the Thirty-Seventh Annual ACM Symposium on Theory of Computing, STOC 2005, pp. 84–93. ACM, New York (2005)

33. Hong, D., Lee, J.-K., Kim, D.-C., Kwon, D., Ryu, K.H., Lee, D.-G.: LEA: a 128-bit block cipher for fast encryption on common processors. In: Kim, Y., Lee, H., Perrig, A. (eds.) WISA 2013. LNCS, vol. 8267, pp. 3–27. Springer, Cham (2014). doi:10.1007/978-3-319-05149-9_1

34. Prescott, T.: Random number generation using AES. http://www.atmel.com/zh/cn/Images/article_random_number.pdf

35. Seo, H., Choi, J., Kim, H., Park, T., Kim, H.: Pseudo random number generator and hash function for embedded microprocessors. In: IEEE World Forum on Internet of Things, WF-IoT 2014, Seoul, pp. 37–40. IEEE (2014)

Side-Channel Analysis of Lightweight Ciphers: Does Lightweight Equal Easy?

Annelie Heuser[1]([✉]), Stjepan Picek[2], Sylvain Guilley[3,4], and Nele Mentens[2]

[1] IRISA/CNRS, Rennes, France
annelie.heuser@irisa.fr
[2] ESAT/COSIC and IMinds, KU Leuven, Leuven-Heverlee, Belgium
[3] TELECOM-ParisTech, Paris, France
[4] Secure-IC S.A.S., Rennes, France

Abstract. Side-channel attacks represent a powerful category of attacks against cryptographic devices. Still, side-channel analysis for lightweight ciphers is much less investigated than for instance for AES. Although intuition may lead to the conclusion that lightweight ciphers are weaker in terms of side-channel resistance, that remains to be confirmed and quantified. In this paper, we consider various side-channel analysis metrics which should provide an insight on the resistance of lightweight ciphers against side-channel attacks. In particular, for the non-profiled scenario we use the theoretical confusion coefficient and empirical correlation power analysis. Furthermore, we conduct a profiled side-channel analysis using various machine learning attacks on PRESENT and AES. Our results show that the difference between AES and lightweight ciphers is smaller than one would expect. Interestingly, we observe that the studied 4-bit S-boxes have a different side-channel resilience, while the difference in the 8-bit ones is only theoretically present.

Keywords: Lightweight cryptography · Machine learning · Comparison · Confusion coefficient · CPA

1   Introduction

With the advent of the Internet of Things, we are surrounded with smart objects (aka things) that have the ability to communicate with each other and with centralized resources. The two most common and widely noticed artifacts are RFID and Wireless Sensor Networks which are used in supply-chain management, logistics, home automation, surveillance, traffic control, medical monitoring, and many more. Most of these applications have the need for cryptographic secure components which inspired research on cryptographic algorithms for constrained devices. Accordingly, lightweight cryptography has been an active research area

This work has been supported in part by Croatian Science Foundation under the project IP-2014-09-4882. In addition, this work was supported in part by the Research Council KU Leuven (C16/15/058) and IOF project EDA-DSE (HB/13/020).

G.P. Hancke and K. Markantonakis (Eds.): RFIDSec 2016, LNCS 10155, pp. 91–104, 2017.
DOI: 10.1007/978-3-319-62024-4_7

over the last 10 years. A number of innovative ciphers have been proposed in order to optimize various performance criteria and have been subject to many comparisons. Lately, the resistance against side-channel attacks has been considered as an additional decision factor.

Side-channel attacks analyze physical leakage that is unintentionally emitted during cryptographic operations in a device (e.g., power consumption [1], electromagnetic emanation [2]). This side-channel leakage is statistically dependent on intermediate processed values involving the secret key, which makes it possible to retrieve the secret from the measured data. So-called profiled side-channel distinguishers assume that the attacker is able to possess an additional device to the one he wants to attack, and on which he has the freedom of nearly full control. In this advanced setting, Machine learning (ML) techniques have shown to be effective in various scenarios (e.g., [3,4]).

Side-channel analysis for lightweight ciphers is of particular interest not only because of the apparent lack of research so far, but also because of the interesting properties of S-boxes. Since the nonlinearity property for S-boxes usually used in lightweight ciphers (i.e., 4×4) can be maximally equal to 4, the difference between the input and the output of an S-box is much smaller than for instance for AES [5]. Therefore, one could conclude that from that aspect, SCA for lightweight ciphers must be more difficult. However, the number of possible classes (e.g., Hamming weight (HW) or key classes) is significantly lower, which may indicate that (profiled) SCA must be easier than for standard ciphers. Besides the difference in the number of classes and consequently probabilities of correct classification, there is also a huge time and space complexity advantage (for the attacker) when dealing with lightweight ciphers.

Our Contributions. In this paper we give a detailed study of lightweight ciphers in terms of side-channel resistance, in particular for software implementations. As a point of exploitation we concentrate on the non-linear operation (S-box) during the first round. Our comparison includes SPN ciphers with 4-bit S-boxes such as KLEIN [6], PRESENT [7], PRIDE [8], RECTANGLE [9], Mysterion [10] as well as ciphers with 8-bit S-boxes: AES, Zorro [11], Robin [12].

In the non-profiled scenario we investigate first the relationship between different key hypotheses with the confusion coefficient [13,14]. Using specific properties of the confusion coefficient (like the minimum value and the variance) we give a preliminary classification regarding the side-channel resistance. Furthermore, using simulated data for various signal-to-noise ratios (SNR) we present empirical results for Correlation Power Analysis (CPA) [15] and discuss the difference between attacking 4-bit and 8-bit S-boxes. Finally, we compare several supervised (i.e., profiled) machine learning techniques for PRESENT and AES.

Road Map. This paper is organized as follows. Section 2 gives basic information on the ciphers and exploitations we investigate. Next, in Sect. 3 we discuss Correlation Power Analysis (CPA), confusion coefficient, and profiled side-channel analysis. Section 4 concludes and offers directions for future work.

2   Ciphers and Exploitations

2.1   Investigated Ciphers

AES [5]. The Advanced Encryption Standard (AES) has been standardized by NIST in 2001 [16]. It has an SPN structure with an internal fixed block size of 128-bits represented as a 4×4 byte matrix. At the beginning, the plaintext state is xor-ed with the secret key. Subsequently, each encryption round consists of the application of SubBytes, ShiftRows, MixColumns, and AddRoundKey; in the last round, MixColumns is omitted.

KLEIN [6]. KLEIN is an AES-like lightweight block cipher. The substitution stage uses 16 similar involutive 4-bit S-boxes. Similar to AES, each encryption round consists of AddRoundKey, SubNibbles, RotNibbles, and MixNibbles, followed by a final key addition.

PRESENT [7]. PRESENT has a 64-bit block size with a bit oriented permutation layer. The non-linear layer is based on a single 4-bit S-box which was designed to be optimal in hardware. An encryption round consists of AddRoundKey, a substitution (sBoxLayer), and a permutation layer (pLayer). A final key addition is performed after the encryption rounds.

PRIDE [8]. PRIDE has been optimized for 8-bit microcontrollers with a special focus on the linear layer of the cipher. It is designed in a bit-sliced fashion to minimize the number of instructions necessary to evaluate it. The 4-bit S-box is an involution.

RECTANGLE [9]. The state of RECTANGLE is represented as a 4×16 matrix. The non-linear layer consists of the parallel application of a 4-bit S-box on the columns of the state and the linear layer is a fixed rotation over a different amount of steps in each row.

Robin [12]. Robin is one instance of the so-called LS-design, in which the internal state of the cipher is a matrix of $s \times L$ bits. The non-linear layer consists of the parallel applications of a $s \times s$ bits ($s = 8$) permutation on each column, which is chosen to be efficiently implemented in a bit-sliced fashion. The linear layer consists of the application of a linear $L \times L$ bit ($L = 16$) permutation on each row of the matrix.

Mysterion [10]. The Mysterion cipher is also based on the LS-design principles. The internal state of the block cipher is organized into a 4×32 bit matrix for Mysterion-128, which is further subdivided into 4 4×8 blocks. A round contains the following operations: S-box layer, L-Box layer and ShiftColumns. The S-box layer is a 4-bit S-box called "Class 13", as introduced in [17], that is applied in parallel to each column of the internal state.

Zorro [11]. Zorro is a modified version of AES with a variant of the S-box that is easier to mask. Fewer S-box calls are performed and the number of multiplications has been minimized. Besides, the execution is split into "steps" of 4 rounds and the key (simply the master key) is added only at the end of each step.

2.2 Exploitations

In this paper, our main targets are the weaknesses arising in software implementations on serial microprocessors. In these applications, the Hamming weight (HW) and the Hamming distance (HD) leakage model are most commonly found in practice. More precisely, the loading and storing of data in memory (e.g., S-box calls) is usually causing HW leakage, whereas the register updating (e.g., writing of intermediate round states) is causing HD leakage. Typically the latter is less significant than the former, which is why we concentrate on a specific memory operation.

We focus on side-channel attacks targeting the key processed within the first round using a divide and conquer strategy. The main common operation all previous described ciphers share, is first the addition (xor) of the roundkey/masterkey followed by (at least one) S-box call. Our study therefore concentrates on leakage measurements X arising from an S-box lookup operation within the first round, i.e.,

$$X = \text{HW}(\text{Sbox}[T \oplus k^*]) + N, \tag{1}$$

where N is independent additive noise, k^* one chunk of the secret key (round key or master key), and T a plaintext chunk (byte or nibble).

Note that our study does not include leakages from all operations in the specific ciphers, nor (in case the cipher uses a key scheduling algorithm) the complexity to go from a round key to the master key, which may be an interesting next step for future work.

3 (Empirical) Side-Channel Evaluation

3.1 CPA and Confusion Coefficient

Correlation Power Analysis (CPA) [15] is one of the most common non-profiled side-channel distinguishers that is also integrated in common criteria evaluations. For CPA in order to reveal the secret key k^*, the attacker makes hypothetical predictions depending on a key guess k on the deterministic part of the leakage. More precisely, let n denote the number of bits of one key chunk (n bits), for each key hypothesis $k \in \mathbb{F}_2^n$ one has:

$$Y(k) = \text{HW}(\text{Sbox}[T \oplus k]). \tag{2}$$

Given a set of Q leakage measurements $X_1, \ldots, X_Q$ corresponding to $T_1, \ldots, T_Q$ plaintexts, the attacker computes the correlation between the measurements and the hypothetical model $Y(k)$ for all key hypotheses. Finally, the key $\hat{k}$ that maximizes the correlation is selected, i.e.:

$$\hat{k} = \arg\max_{k} \rho(X, Y(k)) \tag{3}$$

with ρ being the Pearson correlation coefficient [18].

Before presenting the results from the empirical evaluation of CPA, we first want to further analyze the predictions in Eq. (2) for different ciphers. Interestingly, the predictions for different keys, $Y(0), \ldots, Y(2^n-1)$, are not independent. Considering the model in Eq. (2), the relationships depend on the choice of the S-box and can be described by the so-called confusion coefficient [13,14]

$$\kappa(k^*, k) = \mathbb{E}\left\{\left(\frac{Y(k^*) - Y(k)}{2}\right)^2\right\}, \tag{4}$$

where the expectation is taken over T.

Figures 1a to e show the confusion coefficient for 4-bit S-boxes and Figs. 1f to h for 8-bit S-boxes. Note that, the distribution of $\kappa(k^*, k)$ is independent on the particular choice of k^* (in the case there are no weak keys) and the values are only permuted. For our experiments we choose $k^* = 0$ and furthermore order $\kappa(k^*, k)$ in an increasing order of magnitude. One can observe that the distribution is indeed different for the investigated ciphers. But how to judge what is easier and harder to attack from a side-channel point of view?

Recent works [13,14] showed that the theoretical success rate of CPA can be divided into three factors: confusion coefficient, signal to noise ratio (SNR), and the number of measurements, but without further investigating the confusion coefficient in particular. The authors in [19] give a first-order approximation of the success rate of CPA (for a low SNR) which only depends on the minimum value of $\kappa(k^*, k)$, where the higher the minimum, the lower the side-channel security. Another approach has been taken in [20] using $var(\kappa(k^*, k))$ as a criterion, where smaller values indicate lower side-channel security. All values for 4-bit S-boxes are given in Table 1 on the left, where both criteria show the same trend, in particular, Mysterion should be the easiest to attack and KLEIN the most difficult. Note that PRESENT, PRIDE, and RECTANGLE have the same minimum value but different variances. Interestingly, the values given for 8-bit S-boxes in Table 1 on the right indicate that the side-channel resistance of the investigated 8-bit S-boxes is lower than for the ones with 4-bit S-boxes. Recall that the confusion coefficient measures the relationship between different key hypotheses. Now, as for 8-bits we have 256 possible values for $T \in \mathbb{F}_2^8$ and $Y(k) \in [0, 1, \ldots, 8]$ it is easier to distinguish than for 4-bit S-boxes with $T \in \mathbb{F}_2^4$ and $Y(k) \in [0, 1, \ldots, 4]$.

However, in practice we cannot straightforwardly conclude that due to the properties of the confusion coefficient, 4-bit S-boxes are harder to attack than 8-bit S-boxes. One reason is that the confusion coefficient is theoretical (i.e., holding for $Q \to \infty$). But, especially for low noise scenarios Q might be small (below 100). So, naturally the 4-bit variant with only 16 inputs should converge faster than with 256 inputs. Or in other words, considering $Q = 100$, one can

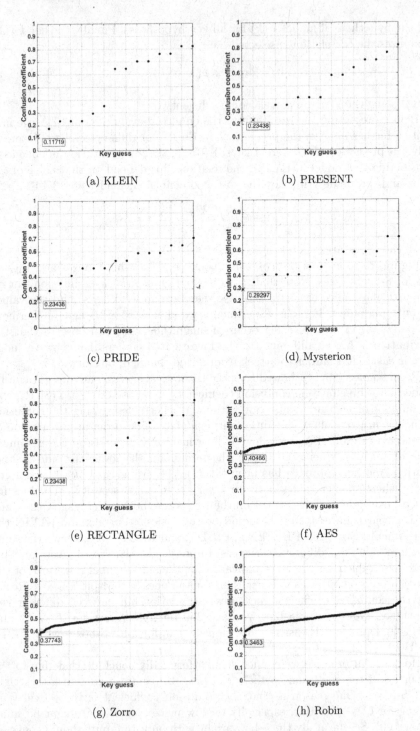

Fig. 1. Confusion coefficients

Table 1. Properties of $\kappa(k^*, k)$

	4-bit					8-bit		
	KLEIN	PRESENT	PRIDE	Mysterion	RECT.	AES	Zorro	Robin
$\mathrm{var}(\kappa(k^*, k))$	0.071	0.038	0.018	0.015	0.035	0.0017	0.0019	0.0023
$\min_k \kappa(k^*, k)$	0.117	0.234	0.234	0.292	0.234	0.4046	0.3774	0.3462

observe each plaintext for 4-bit S-boxes approximately 6.25 times, whereas for the 8-bit case more than the half has not been observed yet. Another reason is that the variance of the signal is not equivalent. In particular, as the HW follows a binomial distribution, we have $Var(\mathrm{HW}(\mathrm{Sbox}[T \oplus k]))$ with $T, k \in \mathbb{F}_2^4$ equal to 1 for 4-bit S-boxes and equal to 2 for 8-bit S-boxes. Accordingly, given the same amount of independent additional noise, the SNR using 8-bit S-boxes is twice as high as for 4-bit S-boxes.

Figures 2 and 3 give the success rate for CPA for various levels of noise, where we simulated the traces as in Eq. (1) with $N \sim \mathcal{N}(0, \sigma^2)$. To be reliable, we use 5 000 independent experiments with randomly chosen T. For 4-bit S-boxes, Fig. 2 confirms the ranking given by the confusion coefficient: Mysterion is the easiest to attack and KLEIN the hardest, which is independent of the noise level. Figure 3 shows that all three ciphers behave similarly even for different levels of noise. Accordingly, the (small) differences in the confusion coefficients in Table 1 do not influence the side-channel resistance in practice.

There are two ways to compare the success rates for 4-bit and 8-bit S-boxes in Figs. 2 and 3, either having the same additional independent noise (environmental noise) σ or the same SNR. Using the same amount of σ (Figs. 2b vs. 3a and 2d vs. 3c), we can observe that AES, Zorro, and Robin perform better than KLEIN and similar to or slightly worse than the others. On the other hand, when comparing the SNR, we observe that AES, Zorro, and Robin behave in a similar way as KLEIN.

3.2 Profiled Side-Channel Analysis

Machine learning (ML) is a term encompassing a number of methods that can be used for clustering, classification, regression, feature selection, and other knowledge discovering methods [21]. In supervised machine learning, the algorithm is provided with a set of data instances (i.e., measurements) and data classes (i.e., values of $Y(k^*)$) in a training phase. The goal of this phase is to "learn" the relationship between the instances and the classes in order to be able to reliably map new instances to the classes in the testing phase.

For our study, we use one algorithm per ML family based on the form in which the output function is represented. In particular, we use Naive Bayes as the simplest algorithm that does not have any parameters to tune. Next, from the decision tree family we use the C4.5 algorithm, which is an algorithm considered to be robust to noise. From the perceptron family, we use the Multi

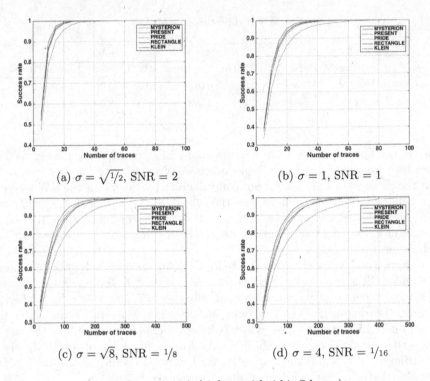

(a) $\sigma = \sqrt{1/2}$, SNR = 2   (b) $\sigma = 1$, SNR = 1

(c) $\sigma = \sqrt{8}$, SNR = $1/8$ (d) $\sigma = 4$, SNR = $1/16$

Fig. 2. Success rates (ciphers with 4-bit S-boxes)

Layer Perceptron (MLP) algorithm, which represents an advance over the simple perceptron algorithm.

Our experiments are divided in two phases: training and testing (i.e., attacking) with datasets containing 10 000, 30 000, and 50 000 instances. As common for ML techniques we use $2/3$ of the instances for training and $1/3$ for testing (e.g., results for 10 000 instances are obtained with 6 650 training instances and 3 350 instances in the testing phase). On the training set we conduct a 10-fold cross-validation with all the considered parameters. Note that the training phase contains a tuning phase in which we select the best parameters for each algorithm. Due to the lack of space, we do not present results from the training phase but we mention the best obtained parameters that are then used in the testing phase. We also conducted the same set of experiments with more advanced ML techniques – Rotation Forest and Support Vector Machines, but the results did not differ significantly from those presented here.

Note that our simulated measurements only contain one feature (time instance), which is commonly accepted for simulated data, but not usual when using ML techniques or profiled SCA (at least before dimension reduction). If one has at his disposal a sufficient number of measurements with many features and the level of noise is low, previous results confirm that such a scenario is easy for profiled attack. However, if the level of noise is high or the number of

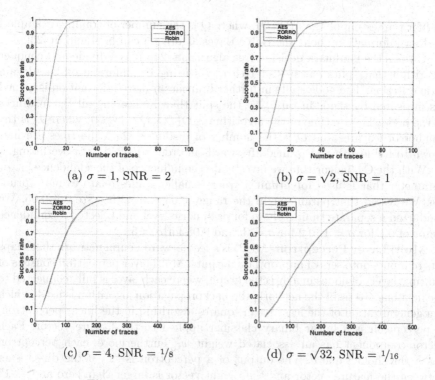

(a) $\sigma = 1$, SNR $= 2$

(b) $\sigma = \sqrt{2}$, SNR $= 1$

(c) $\sigma = 4$, SNR $= 1/8$

(d) $\sigma = \sqrt{32}$, SNR $= 1/16$

Fig. 3. Success rates (ciphers with 8-bit S-boxes)

measurements is too low, then the process becomes more cumbersome. Our study shows that even if only a single feature is available (with sufficient information), the attack can be very powerful. Moreover, with the increase in the number of features, the "curse of dimensionality" can appear: as the number of features grow, the classification effort grows exponentially. Common ways to overcome this problem in SCA are dimension reduction techniques like PCA and LDA. Finally, we note that working with only a single feature also makes theoretical analysis, such as probably approximately correct (PAC) learning, easier; we leave this for future work.

Naive Bayes (NB) classifier is a method based on the Bayesian rule (similar to template attacks [22]). Naive Bayes works under the simplifying assumption that the predictor attributes (measurements) are mutually independent among the features given the target class. The existence of highly correlated attributes in a dataset can thus influence the learning process and reduce the number of successful predictions. Additionally, Naive Bayes assumes a normal distribution for predictor attributes and outputs posterior probabilities.

The space complexity for the Naive Bayes algorithm for both the training and the testing phase equals $O(|\mathcal{Y}|Dv)$, where $|\mathcal{Y}|$ is the number of classes, D is the number of features, and v is the average number of values for a feature. On the other hand, for the training phase, the time complexity equals $O(QD)$

and for the testing phase $O(|\mathcal{Y}|D)$, where Q is the number of training examples. Further information about the Naive Bayes algorithm can be found in [23].

C4.5 is the landmark decision tree algorithm [24]. It is a divide-and-conquer algorithm that splits features at tree nodes using the information-based gain ratio criterion. The node splits in further branches if more information is gained (as measured by the gain ratio) by the split than by keeping all the instances at the node. The runtime of the algorithm is $O(D \times Q \times \log Q)$, where D is the number of features and Q is the number of instances [25]. The trees are first grown to full length and pruned afterwards in order to avoid data overfitting.

With the C4.5 algorithm we investigate the influence of the confidence factor parameter that is used for pruning, where smaller values relate to more pruning. We tested that parameter in the range $[0.05, 0.4]$ with a step of 0.05. We conducted a separate tuning phase for each noise level and selected a confidence factor of 0.1 for $\sigma = 1$, 0.2 for $\sigma = 3$, and 0.05 for $\sigma = 5$.

Multi Layer Perceptron (MLP) is a feedforward neural network that maps sets of inputs onto sets of appropriate outputs. Multi layer perceptron consists of multiple layers of nodes in a directed graph, where each layer is fully connected to the next one. To train the network, the backpropagation algorithm is used, which is a generalization of the least mean squares algorithm in the linear perceptron. A perceptron is a linear binary classifier applied to the feature vector. Each vector component has an associated weight w_i. Furthermore, each perceptron has a threshold value θ. The output of a perceptron is "1" if the direct sum between the feature vector and the weight vector is larger than zero and "−1" otherwise. A perceptron classifier works only for data that are linearly separable, i.e., if there is some hyperplane that separates all the positive points from all the negative points [21].

MLP must consist of 3 or more layers (since input and output represent two layers) of nonlinearly-activating nodes [26]. We investigate a learning rate parameter in range $[0.05, 0.4]$ with a step of 0.05, a momentum with values $[0.1, 0.2, 0.3, 0.4]$, a training time with values $[400, 500, 600]$, and a validation threshold with values $[10, 20, 30]$. In our experiments we set the number of hidden layers to be equal to $(number\_of\_classes + number\_of\_attributes)/2$, the learning rate is set to 0.1, the momentum applied to the weights during the update is set to 0.2, the training time is set to 500, and the validation threshold to 20.

4-Bit vs. 8-Bit. We highlight with a gray cell if the Area Under Curve (AUC) [18] is close to 0.5 which means that the algorithm is closer to random guessing. Note that in our study we use PRESENT and AES. However, the results (in particular the accuracy) are not specific to these ciphers but rather to the fact of using 4-bit/8-bit S-boxes, the intermediate states and the binomial distribution of the HW.

In addition to the previous scenario of attacking the HW of the output of the S-box, we first perform classifications on key chunks, directly resulting in 16 and 256 classes. The results are presented in Table 2, showing that the accuracy (given in percentages) for PRESENT is higher than for AES for all levels of noise, which seems natural since PRESENT has a significantly smaller number of classes than AES. However, when comparing the best values directly, one can observe that the difference is rather small (e.g., for $\sigma = 1$: 41.55 vs. 38.33). What is interesting to observe, is that the level of noise has much less impact when comparing $\sigma = 3$ and $\sigma = 5$ than when comparing $\sigma = 1$ and $\sigma = 3$. Finally, we observe that the number of measurements does not play a significant role in this case.

Table 2. Testing results for classifying a key chunk (nibble or byte)

PRESENT: 16 classes

Algorithm	10,000			30,000			50,000		
	$\sigma = 1$	$\sigma = 3$	$\sigma = 5$	$\sigma = 1$	$\sigma = 3$	$\sigma = 5$	$\sigma = 1$	$\sigma = 3$	$\sigma = 5$
NB	41.55	19.94	12.06	42.62	18.68	13.86	41.72	18.53	14.04
C4.5	40.73	14.85	11.79	41.88	15.79	12.05	41.9	16.08	12.76
MLP	40.67	19.3	11.15	41.4	18.3	14.15	40.82	18.24	13.85

AES: 256 classes

Algorithm	10,000			30,000			50,000		
	$\sigma = 1$	$\sigma = 3$	$\sigma = 5$	$\sigma = 1$	$\sigma = 3$	$\sigma = 5$	$\sigma = 1$	$\sigma = 3$	$\sigma = 5$
NB	38.33	12.67	7.42	37.43	13.04	8.23	38.84	13.29	8.47
C4.5	34.88	9.67	7.69	35.71	10.94	7.18	36.25	10.98	7.04
MLP	35.21	10.94	7.11	37.27	13	7.85	38.67	13.2	8.05

Table 4 gives the results for attacking the HW output of the S-box. Again, we observe that the accuracy is higher for PRESENT than for AES, but we notice that for AES the algorithm is rather "randomly" guessing than predicting meaningful classes. This is mainly due to the imbalance of the HWs since they follow a binomial distribution (see Table 3). In particular, for AES with randomly distributed inputs, the HW value 4 is occurring in 27.34% of all events, which is rather high. Therefore, the classifier mainly outputs class 4, giving an accuracy between 27% and 28%. For PRESENT we can see that HW class 2 is occurring in 37.5% of all cases. However, as there are fewer classes in total, the algorithm seems to try to find a reasonable classification.

Table 3. Occurrences of Hamming weights in %

HW	0	1	2	3	4	5	6	7	8
4-bit	6.25	25	37.5	25	6.25	–	–	–	–
8-bit	0.39	3.12	10.93	21.87	27.34	21.87	10.93	3.12	0.39

Table 4. Testing results for classifying the HW of the S-box output

Algorithm	10,000			30,000			50,000		
	$\sigma = 1$	$\sigma = 3$	$\sigma = 5$	$\sigma = 1$	$\sigma = 3$	$\sigma = 5$	$\sigma = 1$	$\sigma = 3$	$\sigma = 5$
NB	51.27	38.55	37.12	51.17	38.57	37.1	51.04	38.92	37.81
C4.5	50.06	38.82	37.03	51.05	38.16	37.19	50.72	38.73	37.59
MLP	51.27	39.12	37.03	51.07	38.47	37.31	50.57	39	38
AES: 9 classes									
Algorithm	10,000			30,000			50,000		
	$\sigma = 1$	$\sigma = 3$	$\sigma = 5$	$\sigma = 1$	$\sigma = 3$	$\sigma = 5$	$\sigma = 1$	$\sigma = 3$	$\sigma = 5$
NB	27.67	27.63	28.18	27.07	27.04	27.52	27.94	27.93	28.04
C4.5	27.76	26.91	27.64	27.07	26.77	27.26	27.94	27.94	28.15
MLP	27.64	27.64	27.21	27.03	27.03	27.47	27.93	27.93	28.33

We additionally investigate the scenario of chosen plaintexts during the profiling phase. Table 5 presents the results for both PRESENT and AES with exactly 1 000 measurements for each class, i.e., the total number of measurements equals 5 000 for PRESENT and 9 000 for AES. We can see that the problem of predicting only a subset of classes is not present and again we observe that classifying PRESENT is more accurate than AES.

Table 5. Results with 1 000 measurements per class, HW model

Algorithm	PRESENT (5 classes)			AES (9 classes)		
	$\sigma = 1$	$\sigma = 3$	$\sigma = 5$	$\sigma = 1$	$\sigma = 3$	$\sigma = 5$
NB	49.7	30.55	24.97	45.32	21.85	19.19
C4.5	50.73	30.79	24.06	43.67	21.26	19.36
MLP	50.12	29.7	24.18	44.14	21.82	19.02

4   Conclusions

In this paper, we investigate whether side-channel analysis is easier for lightweight ciphers than e.g. for AES. We cover both profiled and non-profiled techniques. In the case of non-profiled attacks, we evaluate a number of S-boxes appearing in lightweight ciphers using the confusion coefficient and empirical simulations. Interestingly, we see that the 8-bit S-boxes from AES, Zorro, and Robin perform similarly, whereas for 4-bit S-boxes we have a clear ranking, with the S-box of Mysterion being the weakest to attack and the S-box of KLEIN the hardest. Further, we cannot conclude that the 4-bit S-boxes are generally significantly less resistant than the investigated 8-bit S-boxes. For profiled attacks, we analyze several machine learning techniques for PRESENT and AES. Note that in this scenario our results are applicable to all 4-bit and 8-bit S-boxes. Our results show that attacking PRESENT is somewhat easier than attacking AES, with the difference mainly stemming from the varying number of classes in one or the other scenario. Still, that difference is not so apparent as one could imagine. Since we work with only a single feature and yet obtain a good accuracy in a number of test scenarios, we are confident (as our experiments also confirm) that adding more features will render classification algorithms even more powerful, which will result in an even higher accuracy.

Finally, we did not consider any countermeasures for the considered lightweight algorithms, since the capacity for adding countermeasures is highly dependent on the environment (which we assume to be much more constrained than in the case of AES). However, our results show that a smart selection of S-boxes results in an inherent resilience (especially for 4-bit S-boxes).

References

1. Kocher, P., Jaffe, J., Jun, B.: Differential power analysis. In: Wiener, M. (ed.) CRYPTO 1999. LNCS, vol. 1666, pp. 388–397. Springer, Heidelberg (1999). doi:10. 1007/3-540-48405-1_25
2. Gandolfi, K., Mourtel, C., Olivier, F.: Electromagnetic analysis: concrete results. In: Koç, Ç.K., Naccache, D., Paar, C. (eds.) CHES 2001. LNCS, vol. 2162, pp. 251–261. Springer, Heidelberg (2001). doi:10.1007/3-540-44709-1_21
3. Hospodar, G., Gierlichs, B., De Mulder, E., Verbauwhede, I., Vandewalle, J.: Machine learning in side-channel analysis: a first study. J. Cryptogr. Eng. 1, 293–302 (2011). doi:10.1007/s13389-011-0023-x
4. Lerman, L., Bontempi, G., Markowitch, O.: A machine learning approach against a masked AES - reaching the limit of side-channel attacks with a learning model. J. Cryptogr. Eng. 5(2), 123–139 (2015)
5. Daemen, J., Rijmen, V.: The Design of Rijndael: AES - The Advanced Encryption Standard. Springer, Heidelberg (2002)
6. Gong, Z., Nikova, S., Law, Y.W.: KLEIN: a new family of lightweight block ciphers. In: Juels, A., Paar, C. (eds.) RFIDSec 2011. LNCS, vol. 7055, pp. 1–18. Springer, Heidelberg (2012). doi:10.1007/978-3-642-25286-0_1
7. Bogdanov, A., et al.: PRESENT: an ultra-lightweight block cipher. In: Paillier, P., Verbauwhede, I. (eds.) CHES 2007. LNCS, vol. 4727, pp. 450–466. Springer, Heidelberg (2007). doi:10.1007/978-3-540-74735-2_31
8. Albrecht, M.R., Driessen, B., Kavun, E.B., Leander, G., Paar, C., Yalçın, T.: Block ciphers – focus on the linear layer (feat. PRIDE). In: Garay, J.A., Gennaro, R. (eds.) CRYPTO 2014. LNCS, vol. 8616, pp. 57–76. Springer, Heidelberg (2014). doi:10.1007/978-3-662-44371-2_4
9. Zhang, W., Bao, Z., Lin, D., Rijmen, V., Yang, B., Verbauwhede, I.: Rectangle: a bit-slice lightweight block cipher suitable for multiple platforms. Sci. China Inf. Sci. 58(12), 1–15 (2015)
10. Journault, A., Standaert, F.X., Varici, K.: Improving the security and efficiency of block ciphers based on LS-designs. Codes Cryptogr. Des. 1–15 (2016)
11. Gérard, B., Grosso, V., Naya-Plasencia, M., Standaert, F.: Block ciphers that are easier to mask: how far can we go? [27] 383–399

12. Grosso, V., Leurent, G., Standaert, F.-X., Varıcı, K.: LS-designs: bitslice encryption for efficient masked software implementations. In: Cid, C., Rechberger, C. (eds.) FSE 2014. LNCS, vol. 8540, pp. 18–37. Springer, Heidelberg (2015). doi:10.1007/978-3-662-46706-0_2

13. Fei, Y., Luo, Q., Ding, A.A.: A statistical model for DPA with novel algorithmic confusion analysis. In: Prouff, E., Schaumont, P. (eds.) CHES 2012. LNCS, vol. 7428, pp. 233–250. Springer, Heidelberg (2012). doi:10.1007/978-3-642-33027-8_14

14. Thillard, A., Prouff, E., Roche, T.: Success through confidence: evaluating the effectiveness of a side-channel attack. [27] 21–36

15. Brier, E., Clavier, C., Olivier, F.: Correlation power analysis with a leakage model. In: Joye, M., Quisquater, J.-J. (eds.) CHES 2004. LNCS, vol. 3156, pp. 16–29. Springer, Heidelberg (2004). doi:10.1007/978-3-540-28632-5_2

16. NIST/ITL/CSD: Advanced Encryption Standard (AES). FIPS PUB 197, November 2001. http://csrc.nist.gov/publications/fips/fips197/fips-197.pdf

17. Ullrich, M., De Cannière, C., Indesteege, S., Mouha, N., Preneel, B.: Finding Optimal Bitsliced Implementations of 4 × 4-bit S-Boxes. In: SKEW 2011 Symmetric Key Encryption Workshop, February 2011

18. Hastie, T., Tibshirani, R., Friedman, J.: The Elements of Statistical Learning. Springer Series in Statistics. Springer, New York (2001)

19. Guilley, S., Heuser, A., Rioul, O.: A key to success. In: Biryukov, A., Goyal, V. (eds.) INDOCRYPT 2015. LNCS, vol. 9462, pp. 270–290. Springer, Cham (2015). doi:10.1007/978-3-319-26617-6_15

20. Picek, S., Papagiannopoulos, K., Ege, B., Batina, L., Jakobovic, D.: Confused by confusion: systematic evaluation of DPA resistance of various S-boxes. In: Meier, W., Mukhopadhyay, D. (eds.) INDOCRYPT 2014. LNCS, vol. 8885, pp. 374–390. Springer, Cham (2014). doi:10.1007/978-3-319-13039-2_22

21. Mitchell, T.M.: Machine Learning, 1st edn. McGraw-Hill Inc., New York (1997)

22. Chari, S., Rao, J.R., Rohatgi, P.: Template attacks. In: Kaliski, B.S., Koç, K., Paar, C. (eds.) CHES 2002. LNCS, vol. 2523, pp. 13–28. Springer, Heidelberg (2003). doi:10.1007/3-540-36400-5_3

23. Friedman, N., Geiger, D., Goldszmidt, M.: Bayesian network classifiers. Mach. Learn. 29(2), 131–163 (1997)

24. Quinlan, J.R.: C4.5: Programs for Machine Learning. Morgan Kaufmann Publishers Inc., San Francisco (1993)

25. Frank, E., Witten, I.H.: Generating accurate rule sets without global optimization. In: Shavlik, J. (ed.) Fifteenth International Conference on Machine Learning, pp. 144–151. Morgan Kaufmann (1998)

26. Collobert, R., Bengio, S.: Links between perceptrons, MLPs and SVMs. In: Proceedings of the Twenty-First International Conference on Machine Learning (ICML 2004), p. 23. ACM, New York (2004)

27. Bertoni, G., Coron, J.-S. (eds.): CHES 2013. LNCS, vol. 8086. Springer, Heidelberg (2013)

Cards and Tokens

Enhancing EMV Tokenisation with Dynamic Transaction Tokens

Danushka Jayasinghe[✉], Konstantinos Markantonakis,
Raja Naeem Akram, and Keith Mayes

Smart Card Centre, Information Security Group, Royal Holloway,
University of London, Egham, Surrey TW20 0EX, UK
Danushka.Jayasinghe.2012@live.rhul.ac.uk,
{K.Markantonakis,R.N.Akram,Keith.Mayes}@rhul.ac.uk

Abstract. Europay MasterCard Visa (EMV) Tokenisation specification details how the risk involved in Personal Account Number (PAN) compromise can be prevented by using tokenisation. In this paper, we identify two main potential problem areas that raise concerns about the security of tokenised EMV contactless mobile payments, especially when the same token also called a static token is used to pay for all transactions. We then discuss five associated attack scenarios that would let an adversary compromise payment transactions. It is paramount to address these security concerns to secure tokenised payments, which is the main focus of the paper. We propose a solution that would enhance the security of this process when a smart phone is used to make a tokenised contactless payment. In our design, instead of using a static token in every transaction, a new dynamic token and a token cryptogram is used. The solution is then analysed against security and protocol objectives. Finally the proposed protocol was subjected to mechanical formal analysis using Scyther which did not find any feasible attacks within the bounded state space.

Keywords: Tokenisation · Security · Dynamic transaction token · EMV contactless mobile payments · Cryptography · Scyther · Formal analysis

1 Introduction

EMV is a globally accepted standard, initially introduced for "Chip & PIN" payment transactions [2,3] and contactless transactions [6]. However, compromising the Personal Account Number (PAN) sent during EMV transactions to be used in card-holder not present or magnetic-stripe transactions was a problem. EMV Tokenisation was adopted as a countermeasure to PAN compromise [4]. Tokenisation replaces the PAN by a substitutive value called the Token which is a 13–19 digit numeric value that does not reveal the PAN and passes validation checks set by the payment scheme [4]. Since its introduction, EMV tokenisation has seen early adoption in contactless mobile payment applications [5,7,16].

© Springer International Publishing AG 2017
G.P. Hancke and K. Markantonakis (Eds.): RFIDSec 2016, LNCS 10155, pp. 107–122, 2017.
DOI: 10.1007/978-3-319-62024-4_8

Near Field Communication (NFC) modules in smart phones and portable devices enable users to carry out close proximity communication which also include contactless payments. Here the mobile emulates a contactless smart card. In this paper, the payment device that emulates a contactless smart card is referred to as a mobile. Mobiles let users store a number of payment applications in one place and have hardware or software secure element technologies. Secure elements provide a secure execution environment to carry out sensitive executions. Compared to a contactless smart card, one of the additional capabilities of a mobile is the readily available communication channels via the network operator or Wi-Fi.

In this study, we identify two problem areas that raise concerns about the security of tokenised contactless mobile payments. The first problem area is that the payment terminal is assumed to be a trusted device and during a transaction, the terminal authenticates the card/mobile but the card/mobile does not authenticate the terminal. Because of this lack of mutual authentication, an adversary at a rogue terminal, can carry out a number of attacks during a tokenised payment transaction. The second problem area is that similar indelible trust assumptions are placed on the intermediary entities between the terminal and the Scheme Operator (SO)/Card Issuing Bank (CIB). When this trust assumption is disregarded, an adversary compromising one of the intermediaries is able to compromise payment transaction details. The acronyms used in this paper are listed in Table 1.

Table 1. Acronyms used in the paper

ARC: Authorisation Response Code	PAN: Primary Account Number
CDA: Combined Data Authentication	SDA: Static Data Authentication
CIB: Card Issuing Bank	SO: Scheme Operator
DDA: Dynamic Data Authentication	SPDL: Security Protocol Description
DTD: Dynamic Token Data	Language
DTT: Dynamic Transaction Token	TAR: Token Authorisation Request
EMV: Europay MasterCard Visa	TSP: Token Service Provider
NFC: Near Field Communication	TVR: Terminal Verification Result

The main contributions of this paper are threefold. They are: (1) The proposed solution provides mutual-authentication, so that both the mobile and the terminal is able to authenticate each other. (2) The protocol uses a new Dynamic Transaction Token (DTT) that is unique to a particular transaction instead of using a static token for improved security. (3) The protocol also provides end-to-end encryption between the terminal and the Token Service Provider (TSP) as well as the terminal and the mobile, eliminating the need of placing indelible trust assumptions on intermediary nodes between the terminal and the TSP.

The paper is structured as follows. In Sect. 2, the use of tokenisation in the current contactless mobile payment architecture is introduced. In Sect. 3 the two potential problem areas and the corresponding attack scenarios are discussed. The proposed protocol is introduced in Sect. 4 and evaluated in Sect. 5 against protocol objectives. Finally the protocol is subject to mechanical formal analysis in Sect. 6.

2   EMV Tokenisation

In this section, we expand our discussion to tokenisation on contactless mobile payments. One potential security issue in contactless payments is PAN compromise, where PAN related data is compromised by adversaries during EMV point-of-sale transactions or from merchants' databases. The compromised payment card details are then used to carry out cross channel fraud[1]. PAN compromise can be prevented by mapping the PAN with a substitute value. The process that manages the conversion from a PAN to a token and vice-versa is called tokenisation and the substitute value is called a token. The EMV Tokenisation Specification details requirements to support payment tokenisation in EMV transactions [4]. From the merchants' perspective, storing and managing tokens as opposed to PANs in databases, simplifies compliance audits such as the Payment Card Industry-Data Security Standard (PCI-DSS) [8,23]. The tokenisation discussed in this study refers to the EMV Tokenisation Specification [4]. The payment architecture and the transaction message flow of a generic EMV contactless mobile transaction based on tokenisation is illustrated in Fig. 1.

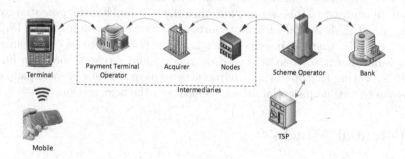

Fig. 1. Generic EMV tokenised payment architecture

At the start of the transaction, the mobile passes the token and token related data to the terminal. The terminal then sends the additional token related data in the transaction authorisation message to the SO/CIB via a number of intermediaries that engage in key-translation for approval. This means that two entities

---

[1] Cross-Channel Fraud: capturing card details in a point-of-sale transaction and using the details fraudulently in other payment channels such as e-commerce payments.

connected with arrows on both ends in Fig. 1 share a symmetric key to communicate with each other. When the message is forwarded to the next entity, it is deciphered and enciphered using the shared symmetric key with the next entity. Once the authorisation request is received at the SO, the TSP is contacted to de-tokenise the token in order to retrieve the corresponding PAN of the token and to validate the token cryptogram [4,16]. The retrieved PAN and validation results are forwarded to the SO. The SO then forwards the authorisation request with the mapped PAN to the bank. Following this, the bank generates an Authorisation Response Code (ARC) and sends it in an authorisation response message to the SO [4,19]. The SO now forwards the authorisation response to the terminal. The terminal then approves or declines the transaction.

2.1   Operating Environment

In this section, we discuss the operating environment of tokenised EMV contactless mobile payments in its current architecture as illustrated in Fig. 1. The SO has a direct communication channel to the TSP and the bank. The payment terminal operator supplies terminals to a number of merchants. It also engages in collecting transactions originating from the merchant's terminals and forwards them towards the SO/CIB. A payment terminal operator can either be a third party, or an acquirer's subcontractor. However, this does not change our attack scenarios discussed later. The same communication path between the terminal and the SO that was taken to send the transaction authorisation request is also taken in reverse to send the transaction authorisation response back to the terminal.

In this study, we consider the bank, SO, mobile and TSP as secure and trusted. In contrast to this, we consider that the terminal has the potential to be compromised. This is evident from reports and research shown in [11,13,18,24]. We also consider that the intermediaries have the potential to be compromised. This assumption is reasonable, based on reports and research shown in [9,19, 21,22,25]. Taking this operating environment into consideration, we expand the discussion to outline potential attack scenarios in the next section.

3   Potential Attacks

In this section, we outline potential attack scenarios associated with two main problem areas in tokenised contactless mobile payments.

3.1   Adversary Compromises a Terminal

In this problem area, there are three different potential attacks. The attack scenarios are outlined and discussed in Attacks 1, 2 & 3 given below. The terminal is considered to be a trusted device but, there is no mutual-authentication between the terminal and the card/mobile. When the trust assumption is taken out, a rogue terminal controlled by an adversary could be in EMV contactless payment process. For these attacks, we assume an adversary with the following capabilities. An adversary:

- can gain full control of the terminal including what is displayed on screen for the payer.
- can change transaction related details such as the amount.
- cannot break standardised encryption algorithms.
- might collude with another adversary that compromises and controls an intermediary between the terminal and the SO/CIB.

Attack 1: *Over Charging*
In this attack scenario, the adversary fraudulently enters a large payment amount (within the contactless limit) for a transaction but displays the correct purchasing product price on the terminal screen for the consumer. It is not possible for the mobile to detect whether the terminal is genuine or rogue as the transaction amount is not displayed on the mobile at the time of payment. Therefore the user does not have any alternative option other than to believe the amount displayed on the merchants terminal is true. So the user continues the payment unaware of the fraudulently over charged amount.

Attack 2: *Capturing Static Token & Related Data*
In this attack scenario, an accomplice controlling the rogue terminal transacts with a genuine mobile making a tokenised contactless mobile payment. The genuine mobile sends the static token and token cryptogram to the rogue terminal. The accomplice captures the static token, its associated cryptogram and other transaction related data. The rogue terminal may display an authentication failed message on the terminal and refuse purchase for the consumer. The captured details are used by the adversary in Attack 4.

Attack 3: *Capturing The Unpredictable Number*[2]
The EMV tokenisation specification does not specify whether offline data authentication needs to be carried out by the terminal [4]. Because tokenised payments operate in an online setting, at first, it is not apparent as to why offline data authentication is actually needed. However, we highlight why failing to carrying out offline data authentication aggregates the identified security concern. In this attack scenario, an adversary attempts a payment at a genuine terminal to obtain the unpredictable number generated by the genuine terminal. At the absence of offline data authentication, the terminal is unable to verify whether the payment application related data presented by the mobile is genuine. Therefore, the terminal nonce is sent to the mobile as a challenge to be signed by the mobile in order to carry out dynamic data authentication. The nonce forms part of the dynamic application data which is later signed by the mobile to generate the digital signature expected by the terminal. Soon as the nonce is received, the adversary captures the nonce and halts any further communication with the terminal.

---

[2] The EMV Specification defines the Unpredictable Number as a "Value to provide variability and uniqueness to the generation of a cryptogram [3]". In this paper we refer to this as the terminal nonce.

In some instances, even if Static Data Authentication (SDA) is carried out by the terminal, it may still be possible to compromise the terminal nonce if SDA is not carried out before the nonce is sent. For example, as explained in [12], Visa's payWave qVSDC protocol sends the terminal generated nonce before SDA. This would enable an adversary to obtain the terminal unpredictable number. Potential attacks and other security concerns related to compromising terminal unpredictable numbers are shown in [10,11].

3.2   Adversary Compromises an Intermediary

In the current EMV architecture, indelible trust assumptions are placed on the intermediaries between the terminal and the SO/CIB. When this trust assumption is disregarded, an adversary compromising one of the intermediaries has a potential attack scenario to infiltrate transaction details and make fraudulent transactions. The adversary at the compromised intermediary observes all transaction data passing through it, which also include transaction authorisation requests, tokens and token related data. For these attacks, we assume the following adversary's capabilities. An adversary:

- can compromise any of the intermediaries.
- can gain access to transaction data at the compromised intermediary.
- can break standardised and strong encryption algorithms.
- cannot compromise smart cards, the SO or the CIB.
- might collude with the adversary that compromises a terminal.

Attack 4: *Adversary Replays An Authorisation Response For Cloned Token Data*

The attack scenario is realised when the transacting terminal fails to carry out adequate offline data authentication method such as Dynamic Data Authentication (DDA) or Combined Data Authentication (CDA) [2], but sends the transaction data for online transaction authorisation. The adversary at the compromised intermediary gets to observe all transaction data passing through it and these include transaction authorisation requests intended for the SO/CIB. The attack steps are described below.

1. The adversary works together with the accomplice, who captured the static token and the corresponding token data in the precursor Attack 2.
2. The accomplice chooses a terminal that has an established communication path to the SO/CIB via the compromised intermediary and makes a contactless payment with the captured static token data.
3. The terminal carries out SDA on the presented static token data. As the data were captured from a genuine mobile, the SDA verification at the terminal completes successfully. However, without DDA or CDA where a dynamic signature is generated by the mobile and verified by the terminal, the terminal is not able to detect the cloned data.
4. The terminal sends the transaction data online for transaction authorisation.

5. The adversary, instead of passing the transaction authorisation request to the authorising entity, stops the request from reaching the authorising entity by identifying static token included in the message.
6. Instead, the adversary replays an ARC pretending to have come from the authorising entity. Once the authorisation response is received, the terminal approves the transaction.
7. Unlike in a contact-based EMV transaction, the transaction authorisation response cryptogram is not sent to the contactless card/mobile [2]. One of the reasons for this is that in contactless EMV, there is no assurance that the card is kept in the reader's field by a cardholder, so the transaction authorisation response is not enciphered by the bank with a key shared between the card/mobile and the bank.

Attack 5: *Replaying An Authorisation Response For DDA/CDA*
In Attack 4, the attack was realised when the terminal did not carry out DDA/CDA as offline data authentication. However, in this attack scenario, we assume that the terminal is carrying out DDA/CDA and identify a similar compromise. The attack steps are described below.

1. The adversary works together with an accomplice, who is in possession of a number of lost & stolen contactless mobiles. The attack is carried out during the time-slot between the cards/mobiles are lost/stolen and the relevant issuing banks are notified by the owners.
2. The accomplice chooses a terminal that has an established communication path to the SO/CIB via the compromised intermediary and makes a contactless payment.
3. The terminal carries out the dynamic offline data verification. As the dynamic signature is generated by a genuine mobile, the terminal verification finishes successfully. The terminal then sends the transaction data online for authorisation.
4. The adversary, instead of passing the transaction authorisation request to the authorising entity, captures it.
5. The adversary replays a previously communicated ARC generated by the authorising entity. Once the authorisation response is received, the terminal approves the transaction.

4 Proposed Solution

In this section, a solution that addresses the security concerns discussed in Sect. 3 is proposed. The main objectives of the protocol are listed below.

1. Should prevent Attacks 1, 2, 3, 4 & 5.
2. Mutual authentication should be carried out between the terminal and the mobile.
3. End-to-end encryption should be provided between the secure element and the terminal, as well as between the terminal and the TSP.

4.1   Protocol Assumptions

The following have been assumed in our proposed solution:

- The communication between the mobile and the TSP is carried out using a secure channel.
- The TSP is a trusted entity that provides transaction token issuing, detokenisation, token updates and management on behalf of the CIB.
- The SO acts as the TSP in the payment architecture.

   The notation used in the proposed solution is given in Table 2. The tokenised contactless mobile payment architecture of the proposed protocol is illustrated in Fig. 2. The protocol proposed in this study has a setup stage and a payment stage. In the *Setup Stage*, the payment app and related data are securely provisioned to the mobile. The *Payment Stage* is used when making a contactless mobile payment. The transaction scenario focused in this paper is when both the terminal and the mobile are online capable to reach the TSP. Providing offline tokenised payments is not the focus of this paper and related work can be found in [20].

Table 2. Notation used in the proposed protocols

T/SE/x: Terminal/Secure Element/Identity of X
TATC: Token Application Transaction Counter, count of token transactions since personalisation. It is shared between $mobile, bank$ & TSP and used during key derivations
K: SE generated Symmetric Session Key
K_{s1}: Symmetric Encryption Session Key shared between TSP and SE
K_{s2}: TSP generated Symmetric Encryption Session Key used by the terminal to communicate with the TSP
$K_{T_{o'}}$: Token Cryptogram Generation Symmetric Session Key derived by a key derivation function used by TSP
$E_K\{Z\}$: Symmetric Encryption of data string Z using key K
S_X: Private Signature Key of entity X
$sS_X[Z]$: Digital signature outcome (without message recovery) from applying the private signature transformation on data string Z using S_X of X
P_X, P_X^{-1}: Public Encryption/Decryption Key Pair of entity X
$eP_X\{Z\}$: Encryption of data string Z using a public algorithm with P_X
$Cert_Y(X)$: Public Key Certificate of X issued and certified by Y
$h(Z)$: Hash of data string Z
n_X/n_{2X}: First/second nonce issued by entity X
$A\|\|B$: Concatenation of A and B in that order

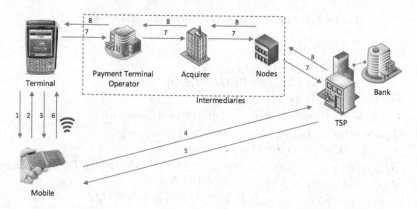

Fig. 2. Tokenised contactless mobile payment architecture of the proposed protocol

4.2 Setup Stage

During the setup phase of the protocol, the personalisation of the payment application and provisioning of security sensitive data elements of the payment application and credentials are carried out using a secure channel. Following the application personalisation, the security sensitive data elements of the payment application reside in the SE and the user interface part of the payment application reside in the mobile platform. The data elements in the SE consist of all cryptographic keys needed by the mobile e.g.: K_{SE}, K_{s1}, S_{SE} & P_{SE}/P_{SE}^{-1}. The SE also stores: $Cert_{bank}(TSP)$, $Cert_{bank}(SE)$, Token Application Transaction Counter ($TATC$). Following personalisation of the payment app, the user is required to enter a strong pass-code on first access which is used for future authentication of the user to the payment app. The subsequent transaction protocols are constructed based upon the above mentioned data elements.

Terminals and secure elements participating in the payment scheme can verify certificates issued by the SO or entities that have been certified to be trusted in the certificate hierarchy. The TSP also takes part in the payment scheme.

4.3 Payment Phase

The protocol messages of the proposed solution are illustrated in Table 3 and explained as follows. To make a payment, the user opens the payment application by entering the pass-code and taps the device on the terminal.

Message 1: The T provides its identity, n_t and $Cert_{SO}(T)$ to the SE.

Message 2: The SE obtains P_T after verifying $Cert_{SO}(T)$. A message is constructed that includes: both identities, n_{se}, n_t, the Processing Options Data Object List (PDOL) that instructs the T what information to send back to the T [6], a session key generated by the SE to be used in further communication between the T and the identity of the TSP. The SE enciphers the message using P_T. A digital signature of the message is generated by the SE and both the

Table 3. Dynamic transaction token protocol messages.

1	$T \rightarrow SE$: $t\|n_t\|Cert_{SO}(T)$
2	$SE \rightarrow T$: $V\|sS_{SE}[h(V)]\|Cert_{Bank}(SE)$ $\quad V = eP_T\{se\|t\|n_{se}\|n_t\|PDOL\|K\|tsp\}$
3	$T \rightarrow SE$: $W\|sS_T[h(W)]$ $\quad W = E_K\{t\|se\|n_{se}\|n_{2t}\|amount\|\ eP_{TSP}\{t\|amount\|n_{3t}\}\}$
4	$SE \rightarrow TSP$: $E_{K_{s1}}\{se\|tsp\|n_{2se}\|TokenR\text{-}ID\|amount\|$ $\quad TATC\|Cert_{SO}(T)\|eP_{TSP}\{t\|amount\|n_{3t}\}\}$
5	$TSP \rightarrow SE$: $E_{K_{s1}}\{tsp\|se\|n_{2se}\|n_{tsp}\|eP_T\{DTD\}\|sS_{TSP}[h(DTD)]\}$ $\quad DTD = tsp\|se\|t\|n_{2tsp}\|n_{3t}\|DTT\|K_{s2}$
6	$SE \rightarrow T$: $E_K\{se\|t\|n_{3se}\|n_{2t}\|eP_T\{DTD\}\|sS_{TSP}[h(DTD)]\}$
7	$T \rightarrow TSP$: $Token\|E_{K_{s2}}\{t\|tsp\|Token\|n_{2tsp}\|n_{4t}\|DTT\|POSem\|TVR\}$
8	$TSP \rightarrow T$: $Token\|E_{K_{s2}}\{tsp\|t\|n_{3tsp}\|n_{4t}\|Token\|TokenAssuranceLevel\|$ $\quad PANlast4digits\|ARC\}$

enciphered part and the digital signature is sent to the T. The SE's public key
certificate is also sent in the same message.

Message 3: The T authenticates the device by verifying the signature using
the certificate hierarchy, then deciphers message 2. The T encrypts and signs a
message which includes: the identities, n_{se}, n_{2t}, the amount of the transaction
and an encipherment carried out using P_{TSP} on the T's identity, amount and
n_{3t}. The full message and the signature is then sent to the SE.

Message 4: Using the certificate hierarchy, the SE verifies the signature, authenticates the T and deciphers message 3. To request a token from the TSP, a
message is constructed which includes: the identities, n_{2se}, Token Requester ID,
amount, the Token Application Transaction Counter (TATC), $Cert_{SO}(T)$ and
$eP_{TSP}\{t\|amount\|n_{3t}\}$. The message is then encrypted using the symmetric key
K_{s1} shared between the TSP and the SE before sending.

Message 5: The TSP, first verifies the $Cert_{SO}(T)$ and obtains the T's pub-
lic key. The TSP deciphers $eP_{TSP}\{t\|amount\|n_{3t}\}$ and checks whether the
amount recovered from this matches the amount requested by the SE. If satisfied, the TSP queries the CIB and verifies the user credibility for a new token.
Then the TSP generates a DTT and a session key K_{s2}. The TSP then creates Dynamic Token Data (DTD) which includes: the identities, n_{2tsp}, DTT
and K_{s2}. The TSP signs the hash of DTD. The DTD is then enciphered
using P_T. The TSP then creates a message that includes: the identities, n_{2se},
n_{tsp}, $eP_T\{DTD\}$ and $sS_{TSP}[h(DTD)]$. The message is then enciphered using
K_{s1} before sending. DTT is constructed as follows;

$$DTT = TokenData\|TokenCryptogram$$
$$TokenData = TokenID\|TokenExpiry\|TokenR-ID$$
$$TokenCryptogram = E_{K_{To'}}\{TokenData\|amount\|n_{3t}\}$$

Message 6: The SE, prepares a message to send the $eP_T\{DTD\}$ and $sS_{TSP}[h(DTD)]$ to the T. The message includes: the identities, n_{3se}, n_{2t}, $eP_T\{DTD\}$ and $sS_{TSP}[h(DTD)]$. The message is then enciphered using K before sending. If the SE is not in the NFC field, the user taps the SE on the T again to transmit the message. The SE may leave the NFC field once the message is successfully sent to the T.

Message 7: After deciphering the message received from the SE, the T first examines the nonces to detect any replay attempts. Then deciphers the $eP_T\{DTD\}$ to obtain DTD and verifies $sS_{TSP}[h(DTD)]$ to have been generated by the TSP. Once satisfied the T carries out *dynamic token data authentication* to verify the authenticity of the presented data. For this the T generates the hash of the DTD received in the previous message and compares this with the hash recovered in the $sS_{TSP}[h(DTD)]$. If the two hashes match, *dynamic token data authentication* is verified successfully, otherwise the transaction is declined due to the potential of a replay attack.

Depending on the outcome of the *dynamic token data authentication*, the T constructs a Token Authorisation Request (TAR) and forwards it to the TSP for payment authorisation. To construct the payment authorisation message, the T first constructs a message which includes: identities, Token, n_{2tsp}, n_{4t}, DTT, Point-Of-Sale Entry Mode (POSem)[3] and the Terminal Verification Result (TVR) indicating the outcome of the offline dynamic token data verification. This message is then enciphered using K_{s2}. The T before forwarding the message to the TSP also appends the $Token$ to the encipherment. The T uses the key translation mechanism to forward the TAR to the TSP via the Intermediaries, for financial transaction authorisation.

The only data sent in the clear is the $Token$, which on its own cannot be used by the *Intermediary* to obtain any useful information corresponding to the PAN. In the operating environment of the proposed solution, the SO acts as the TSP, therefore the message is received at the TSP.

Message 8: After receiving the TAR, the TSP carries out the following checks to validate the token:

- queries its database records in-relation to the issued tokens and checks details such as: expiry, requester ID, amount and the token cryptogram.
- if the token related data is validated properly, the TSP conducts payment token de-tokenisation to map the token details into PAN details.

Following these verifications the TSP retrieves the PAN details and contacts the CIB to obtain an ARC. The TSP provides information such as: the PAN, PAN expiry date, amount, POSem, token, token expiry, token requester ID and the Token Authorisation Request Result (TAR_{result}) in order to obtain the ARC. The TAR_{result} contains three main components. They are: the outcome

---

[3] The POSem acts as a Token Domain Restriction Control [4] to prevent other cross channel fraud by restricting the tokens to a specific payment channel (contactless mobile payments in this scenario).

of TSP's token verification has passed or failed, *TokenAssuranceLevel* which indicates the level of assurance that the TSP has assigned to the token depending on the confidence of the TSP and *TokenAssuranceData* which indicates the data used by the TSP to assign a token assurance level. The CIB before issuing the *ARC* carries out the following account level validations:

– retrieve account details corresponding to the PAN.
– check whether there are sufficient funds available and no account restrictions.
– verify POSem and the token has not been presented for authorisation before.
– check the outcome of the TAR_{result} validation carried out by the TSP.

Following all the validation steps, the *ARC* is issued and the TSP constructs a message that includes: the identities, n_{3tsp}, n_{4t} the Token, Token Assurance Level, the last 4 digits of the PAN and the ARC generated by the CIB. The message is then enciphered using K_{s2}. The TSP also appends the *Token* to the encipherment before the message is sent to the T via the Intermediaries. The Intermediary cannot deduce any information corresponding to the PAN or the authorisation response other then the *Token*.

Once the message is received, the T deciphers the message using the session key and examines the results in order to approve/decline the transaction. The outcome is displayed on the T. The merchant may produce a receipt that includes transaction details such as the amount, last 4 digits of the PAN, date, time and ARC to be given to the user upon request.

5   Analysis

In this section, the proposed protocol is analysed for its security and protocol objectives. The operating environments outlined in Sect. 2.1, adversary capabilities outlined in Sects. 3.1 and 3.2 and protocol assumptions outlined in Sect. 4.1 have been taken into consideration in this analysis.

At the beginning of the protocol, both the secure element and the terminal are authenticated to each other. This establishes a mutual-authentication before security sensitive transaction data are communicated. Due to the unforgeability of the digital signature algorithm used, only a genuine secure element and the terminal is able to generate their own signatures. The signatures can be verified using the certificate hierarchy.

The proposed protocol provides end-to-end encryption between the terminal and the secure element. This eliminates the need for placing indelible trust assumptions on the intermediaries. The protocol also provides end-to-end encryption for the communication between the terminal and the TSP which provides confidentiality to token transaction related data by preventing adversaries from eavesdropping. Below we describe how the identified attacks that compromise token transaction data in Sect. 3 are prevented in the proposed protocol. Table 4 categorises different countermeasures used for each attack.

Attack 1 *(Over Charging)*: In the proposed protocol, message 3 sent by the terminal to the secure element has transaction related data including the amount which is displayed on the users mobile. The mobile contacts the TSP to request the dynamic token, only after the user authorises the amount displayed on the user's mobile screen. If the merchant is trying to overcharge the user, this will be detected and the transaction can be cancelled. Furthermore, the corresponding token is requested by the mobile using the data received in message 3, hence a rogue merchant is not in a position to change the amount to a different value. The DTD also includes the amount and any changes to the transaction amount can be detected TSP.

Attack 2 *(Capturing Static Token & Related Data)*: In the proposed protocol, before the token and token related data is given to the terminal, a mutual authentication process is carried out. The mobile sends n_{se} as a challenge in message 2 for the terminal to sign with other related data. The signature is verified by the mobile after receiving message 3 where the terminal is authenticated. If the terminal is not authenticated at this stage the mobile aborts the protocol. Furthermore, the token used in the proposed protocol is a dynamic transaction token, meaning the token issued by the TSP is unique and can only be used in the particular transaction. A replay of DTT can be detected by a genuine terminal due to a replayed message 6 not having the terminal-generated n_{3t} in the $sS_{TSP}[h(DTD)]$. These countermeasures prevent rogue terminals from carrying out Attack 2. In case the token was compromised and attempted on another fraudulent transaction, the TSP would not authorise the transaction for the second time. As the mobile requests a DTT for every transaction, the TSP is aware of a transaction even before a payment authorisation request is made by a terminal, this introduces an additional layer of security to prevent unauthorised transactions, as well as facilitating accurate approvals & risk assurance levels for the tokenised payment transaction.

Attack 3 *(Capturing The Unpredictable Number)*: Due to the unforgeability of the digital signature scheme used, the terminal can verify the signature to have been generated by a genuine secure element. Furthermore, n_t included in the signature prevents a signature from being replayed and indicates to the terminal that the transaction is fresh. If the verification fails, then the terminal declines the overall transaction which prevents the terminal from generating the third nonce n_{3t} which is used in the DTT. Furthermore, the protocol provides end-to-end encryption between the terminal and the SO which also prevents any malicious entity from compromising n_{3t}.

Attack 4 *(Adversary Replays An Authorisation Response For Cloned Token Data)*: The proposed protocol uses the following countermeasures. Firstly, mutual authentication is established at the beginning of the protocol. This way the terminal only proceeds to the transaction by sending transaction related details in message 3, only if the secure element is authenticated in message 2. Secondly, the solution uses a DTT rather than a static token. This means that the token is specific for a transaction and it includes nonces from both the transacting terminal and the TSP. A replay of DTT can be detected by the terminal due to a replayed message 6 not having the terminal-generated n_{3t} in the

$sS_{TSP}[h(DTD)]$. Furthermore, the protocol provides end-to-end encryption for the communication between the terminal and the TSP. This prevents the adversary at the compromised intermediary from replaying an authorisation response back to the terminal and any such attempts are detected by the terminal.

Attack 5 (Replaying An Authorisation Response For DDA/CDA): Unlike Attack 4 where only SDA is carried out, this attack scenario is even possible with DDA/CDA. To prevent this attack, the solution provides end-to-end encryption which prevents the adversary at the compromised intermediary from learning the data communicated between the terminal and the TSP. Also, nonces generated from both the terminal and the TSP are included in messages communicated between each other as well as in the DTT. This prevents any replay attempts detectable for the terminal in the event of any authorisation response replay attempts. Furthermore, the payment application needs the user to enter a passcode before use. It must be also noted that as the mobile requests a DTT online before each transaction, in the event of the mobile being lost or stolen, the user can inform the CIB in order to deny access to token requests.

Table 4. Attacks and countermeasures used in the proposed protocol

Attack	Mutual authentication	End-To-End encryption	DTT	Other
1: Over charging	✓		✓	Amount displayed on mobile
2: Capturing static token & related data	✓		✓	
3: Capturing the unpredictable number	✓	✓	✓	
4: Adversary replays an authorisation response for cloned token data	✓	✓	✓	
5: Replaying an authorisation response For DDA/CDA	✓	✓	✓	Passcode for payment app

6   Mechanical Formal Analysis

In this section, the proposed protocol is subject to mechanical formal analysis using Scyther [15]. The proposed protocol was modelled and provided as input to Scyther using the Security Protocol Description Language (spdl) defined in [14]. The spdl provides three main protocol modelling features: *roles, events and claims*. The roles define the entities in a protocol, which characterise events. The send and receive operations are classed as `send` and `recv` events respectively; each corresponding `send` and `recv` event has the same sequence number. The security goals and objectives of a protocol that require verification are specified using `claim` events. We used the Dolev-Yao model as the adversarial model used in this analysis [17]. The following security claims are verified in the analysis: *Aliveness (`Alive`), Weak agreement (`Weakagree`), Non-injective agreement (`Niagree`) Non-injective synchronisation (`Nisynch`) and Secrecy of data (`Secret`) for: DTT, ARC, K, K_{s2}* [14,15].

The script was run on an Intel CORE-i7 2 GHz machine with 8 GB of RAM. When the security claim events were run together during protocol analysis, Scyther tool was crashing. We identified that the reason for this was the RAM getting full after a few hours of protocol analysis. To overcome this issue, the security claims were analysed one by one. Following successful execution of the script, the security of data in the claim events were verified and Scyther did not find any feasible attacks within the bounded state space. The Scyther script can be downloaded from [1].

7   Conclusion and Future Work

The work carried out in this paper first looked into the current architecture of EMV contactless mobile payments based on tokenisation. Then five potential attack scenarios in two problem areas that would compromise tokenised contactless mobile payments were discussed. To meet the objectives of the paper and to address the raised security concerns a protocol was proposed in the paper. The proposed protocol was analysed for its security and objectives. Finally the protocol was subjected to mechanical formal analysis which did not find any feasible attacks within bounds. In our further research directions, we are in the process of implementing the protocol in order to carry out measurements. We also aim to extend to include additional transaction modes and expand our threat model to include the mobile being compromised by an adversary.

References

1. Scyther script for the protocol. https://www.dropbox.com/s/euqnwf0ds17zd6v/DTT%20Protocol%20Scyther%20Script.spdl?dl=0
2. EMV integrated circuit card specifications for payment systems, Book 2: security and key management, Version 4.3, EMVCo, LLC, November 2011
3. EMV integrated circuit card specifications for payment systems, Book 3: application specification, Version 4.3, EMVCo, LLC, November 2011
4. EMV payment tokenisation specification: technical framework, Version 1.0, EMVCo, LLC, March 2014
5. Apple pay, July 2015. http://www.apple.com/uk/apple-pay/
6. EMV contactless specifications for payment systems, EMVCo, LLC, March 2015
7. Android pay, June 2016. https://developers.google.com/android-pay/
8. Askoxylakis, I., Pramateftakis, M., Kastanis, D., Traganitis, A.: Integration of a secure mobile payment system in a GSM/UMTS SIM smart card. System 12, 13 (2007)
9. BBC News: US and UK accused of hacking SIM card firm to steal codes (2015). http://www.bbc.co.uk/news/technology-31545050
10. Bond, M., Choudary, O., Murdoch, S.J., Skorobogatov, S., Anderson, R.: Chip and Skim: cloning EMV cards with the pre-play attack. In: 2014 IEEE Symposium on Security and Privacy, pp. 49–64. IEEE (2014)
11. Bond, M., Choudary, O., Murdoch, S.J., Skorobogatov, S., Anderson, R.: Be prepared: the EMV pre-play attack. IEEE Secur. Priv. 13, 56–64 (2015)

12. Chothia, T., Garcia, F.D., Ruiter, J., Breekel, J., Thompson, M.: Relay cost bounding for contactless EMV payments. In: Böhme, R., Okamoto, T. (eds.) FC 2015. LNCS, vol. 8975, pp. 189–206. Springer, Heidelberg (2015). doi:10.1007/978-3-662-47854-7_11

13. Computerworld.com: Vulnerabilities found in three popular payment terminal models can result in credit card data theft (2012). http://www.computerworld.com/article/2504956/security0/payment-terminal-flaws-shown-at-black-hat.html

14. Cremers, C., Mauw, S.: Operational semantics of security protocols. In: Leue, S., Systä, T.J. (eds.) Scenarios: Models, Transformations and Tools. LNCS, vol. 3466, pp. 66–89. Springer, Heidelberg (2005). doi:10.1007/11495628_4

15. Cremers, C.J.F.: The scyther tool: verification, falsification, and analysis of security protocols. In: Gupta, A., Malik, S. (eds.) CAV 2008. LNCS, vol. 5123, pp. 414–418. Springer, Heidelberg (2008). doi:10.1007/978-3-540-70545-1_38

16. Crowe, M., Pandy, S., Lott, D., Mott, S.: Is payment tokenization ready for prime-time? Perspectives from industry stakeholders on the tokenization landscape. Technical report, Federal Reserve Bank of Boston & Federal Reserve Bank of Atlanta (2015)

17. Dolev, D., Yao, A.C.: On the security of public key protocols. IEEE Trans. Inf. Theory 29(2), 198–208 (1983)

18. Drimer, S., Murdoch, S.J., et al.: Keep your enemies close: distance bounding against smartcard relay attacks. In: USENIX Security, vol. 2007 (2007)

19. Jayasinghe, D., Akram, R.N., Markantonakis, K., Rantos, K., Mayes, K.: Enhancing EMV online PIN verification. In: 2015 IEEE Trustcom/BigDataSE/ISPA, vol. 1, pp. 808–817, August 2015

20. Jayasinghe, D., Markantonakis, K., Gurulian, I., Akram, R., Mayes, K.: Extending emv tokenised payments to offline-environments. The 15th IEEE International Conference on Trust, Security and Privacy in Computing and Communications (IEEE TrustCom 2016). IEEE Computer Society (2016)

21. Kaspersky Lab: Equation group: the crown creator of cyber-espionage (2015). http://www.kaspersky.com/about/news/virus/2015/equation-group-the-crown-creator-of-cyber-espionage

22. Kaspersky Lab: The great bank robbery (2015). http://www.kaspersky.com/about/news/virus/2015/Carbanak-cybergang-steals-1-bn-USD-from-100-financial-institutions-worldwide

23. PCI Security Standards Council: Information Supplement: PCI DSS Tokenization Guidelines, Version 2.0, PCI Data Security Standard (PCI DSS), August 2011

24. Symantec: a special report on: attacks on point-of-sales systems, November 2014

25. TheHackerNews: 324,000 financial records with CVV numbers stolen from a payment gateway (2016). http://thehackernews.com/2016/09/bluesnap-payment-gateway-hack.html?m=1

Bias in the Mifare DESFire EV1 TRNG

Darren Hurley-Smith[(✉)] and Julio Hernandez-Castro

School of Computing, University of Kent,
Canterbury, Kent CT2 7NF, UK
{dh433,jch27}@kent.ac.uk

Abstract. The limited computational capabilities of low-cost RFID cards may induce security weaknesses stemming from concessions made in hardware. In particular, RFID cards with weak pseudo-random number generators (PRNGs) can leak secret information. Current generation RFID cards, such as the Mifare DESFire EV1, improve on the cryptographic and random number generation capabilities of previous cards such as the Mifare Classic. However, there is not yet a published analysis on the quality of the true random number generator (TRNG) used in Mifare DESFire EV1 cards. This paper represents the first study of the randomness of the DESFire EV1, and shows preliminary results that highlight a distinct pattern of biases in its TRNG.

Keywords: RFID · Security · Randomness · Cryptography · Authentication

1 Introduction

Radio Frequency IDentification (RFID) has become ubiquitous in many areas. Many transport, fare collection and locking systems have come to rely on RFID systems [1]. Contactless payments using RFID-enabled phones and cards have become common, requiring strong cryptographic protocols to ensure the privacy and confidentiality of communication between the card and reader. Mifare Classic, one of the first generation of widespread RFID cards, has proven vulnerable to attacks against its NXP proprietary cipher, CRYPTO-1 [2]. A flawed pseudo-random number generator (PRNG) further contributed in these attacks [3,4]. A later product, the Mifare DESFire EV1, has improved some security features, including the use of a true random number generator (TRNG) and AES-128 encryption capabilities. To the authors' knowledge, there has not yet been a publicly available evaluation of the EV1 TRNG's quality. The aim of this paper is to report on our study and the preliminary findings obtained.

The rest of the paper is organised as follows: Sect. 2 will discuss the background, literature and key issues in RFID security and the role that random number generation plays. Section 3 outlines the experimental set-up and tests chosen to analyse the DESFire EV1 TRNG. Section 4 reports and examines our preliminary results. The paper concludes in Sect. 5, closing on with a discussion of ongoing and related future work.

© Springer International Publishing AG 2017
G.P. Hancke and K. Markantonakis (Eds.): RFIDSec 2016, LNCS 10155, pp. 123–133, 2017.
DOI: 10.1007/978-3-319-62024-4_9

2 Background

RFID cards can be vulnerable to attacks that exploit their use of radio communication. Though short-ranged, the 13.56 MHz frequency used by RFID devices that comply with NFC standards allows remote attacks to be launched. Portable readers can allow an attacker to eavesdrop communications between a card and a legitimate reader, or be used more actively to usurp a communication session or clone a previously observed card [5].

2.1 Mifare RFID Cards

Mifare is the brand name of a family of chips developed by NXP Semiconductors Ltd. They are used in transport, access control and closed-loop payment systems. Mifare products include the Classic, Ultralight, Plus and DESFire (EV1 and EV2). Each type of Mifare chip implements security features for its target use cases.

Mifare Classic has been shown to rely on a weak cipher (CRYPTO-1) and flawed PRNG. The CRYPTO-1 cipher has been comprehensively broken due to a manipulable PRNG [6] and vulnerabilities in the algorithm itself [3]. The DESFire family aims to be one of the most secure of all the Mifare product line, targeting use cases where security is a critical requirement.

Attacks against RFID cards, such as the Mifare Classic, are widely published. Typical practical attacks on RFID systems combine multiple security vulnerabilities. These can be found, for example, in the authentication protocol, cryptographic primitives or the generation of nonces [7]. Even patched Mifare Classic and Plus cards have been shown to be vulnerable to practical attacks [8]. For example, the PRNG used in the authentication protocol of the Mifare Classic has been shown to be predictable [4]. The weak PRNG implementation made the authentication process highly vulnerable, by exposing trivially deduced random values that could be determined even after encryption, weakening multiple security services [6].

2.2 Mifare DESFire EV1

The Mifare DESFire EV1 is a closed-loop payment and access control card. The intended use cases include multi-use travel cards and access key cards. Transport for London issued approximately 8 million Oyster cards just in the 2015/16 financial year, all using DESFire EV1 chips. Security is improved, relative to its predecessors, with an AES-128 enabled crypto co-processor and a TRNG.

Authentication Protocol. The same challenge-response authentication protocol is used in all Mifare DESFire Cards, including the EV1. It consists of a mutual three-pass challenge-response protocol which is shown in Fig. 1. In this example, the encryption used is AES-128. This authentication scheme is one of the means by which random values can be collected from Mifare cards [9].

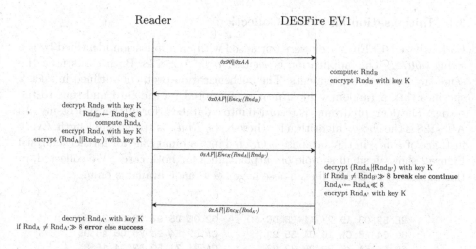

Fig. 1. Mifare DESFire EV1 authentication protocol.

TRNGs are also known as hardware random number generators. They rely on underlying physical processes to generate random data, that is used in several key security services [10]. Publications dealing with the hardware profiling of the DESFire EV1 have not yet focused on the TRNG. Oswald and Paar analyse the 3DES authentication process in terms of power and signal output to a high degree of precision, but do not study the nonces used during authentication [11]. Randomly generated values are vital for cryptography, random ID (RID) generation and the three-pass mutual authentication protocol described in Fig. 1 [12]. It is of the utmost importance that the TRNG be sufficiently random to avoid prediction, and resistant to manipulation.

3   Experimental Setting

The experimental set-up includes a Toshiba Laptop (i7 processor, 8 GB RAM), an ACR122U RFID reader and two Mifare DESFire RFID cards. The unique identifiers (UID) for the RFID cards used are 04742c32973580 and 04743732973580. To preserve readability throughout this paper, only the first 4 bytes of the UIDs will be used from this point to label the two cards. Both were randomly selected from the same pack of 100 cards. We collect the output of the TRNG during the authentication phase. To obtain it, a python script[1] was used to select an application and perform authentication, logging all exchanged values in a database. A bash script was used to repeatedly perform this procedure.

---

[1] https://www.cs.kent.ac.uk/people/staff/dh433/RFIDsec2016/sourcecode.zip.

3.1 Initialisation and Data Collection

Both Mifare DESFire cards were initialised with an application identified by the string *0007c1*. This application is secured with AES-128. Both cards used the same key for these experiments. The authentication protocol outlined in Sect. 2 specifies that a random value Rnd_B is encrypted by the card and sent to the reader. The decrypted value is recorded into a database for further processing. As AES-128 is the chosen algorithm for these tests, Rnd_B is 16 bytes in length. Every instance of Rnd_B in the database is entered into a binary file for further analysis. Figure 2 shows a small sample of output values for both cards. We collected, in this manner, two 64 MB files. These have been made available online[2].

```
2E E3 03 AB 27 41 EB DC        62 0E D5 97 53 02 24 B0
80 04 A8 C1 10 CA 35 99        CA 62 F4 98 76 06 A5 95
6C F4 6A 37 B9 2B 32 C3        CA 91 71 50 D2 2A 15 84
32 E3 EC 5E 03 3B 2F 34        E2 75 39 F7 9D 49 54 DE
95 25 0B 33 C4 9A 21 5D        12 20 FD F5 C7 4C 6E 7F
   (a) UID 04742c32               (b) UID 04743732
```

Fig. 2. Mifare DESFire EV1 TRNG sample output in hexadecimal format.

This data collection procedure is very time-consuming. To collect 4,000,000 instances of the TRNG output (64 MB of data), 9 days were needed per card. The bottleneck is the speed with which the reader and card communicate and the number of instructions required to repeatedly retrieve these values. Full authentication must be completed for every Rnd_B, collected, to prevent errors that interfere with automated data collection.

3.2 Randomness Tests

The collected data was subjected to a battery of randomness tests. For this experiment, the National Institute of Statistical Tests (NIST) Statistical Testing Suite (STS) version 2.1.2 was used alongside selected tests from Diehard, and ENT. All tests that returned a borderline (weak) or failed result were re-tried to double-check those outputs.

Terminology. In the interests of clarity, some technical terms must be further explained. P-values represent the probability of subsequent test results equal to or greater than the observed output, when the null hypothesis is true. T-samples is a shortening of *test samples* as defined in the Dieharder test description [13].

---

[2] https://www.cs.kent.ac.uk/people/staff/dh433/RFIDsec2016/datafiles.zip.

NIST STS 2.1.2. The National Institute of Standards and Technology (NIST) offers the Statistical Testing Suite (STS) for the analysis of randomness [14]. This software subjects ASCII or binary files of random values to a variety of tests. The purpose of these tests is to determine the independence and unpredictability of the data [15]. The version used in this experiment is 2.1.2.

Diehard Tests. The Diehard test battery is a collection of widely used tests of randomness. Diehard tests require more data (using default settings) than ENT and NIST STS 2.1.2, requiring up to 1.92 GB for the Squeeze test if rewinds are to be avoided. To accommodate the sample size of 64 MB, the t-sample values for tests relying on sequence comparisons had to be reduced. This prevents file rewinds from creating artificial patterns in the sampled data. Where possible tests use their default t-sample values. The Sums, OPSO, OQSO and DNA tests have been omitted from this experiment, due to their suspect reliability [13]. The selected tests and t-samples used are outlined in the results section.

ENT. ENT is a utility for evaluating pseudo-random number generators [16]. The entropy, compression, chi-square test, arithmetic mean, Monte Carlo value for π and serial correlation coefficient are tested. The most stringent of these tests is the chi-square test, which is used to determine if a data source is uniform [13].

4 Analysis

Decrypted random numbers were saved into a binary file for each card. These files were then subject the NIST STS 2.1.2, Diehard and ENT test batteries.

4.1 NIST STS Results

Table 1 shows the pass rates for both RFID cards. The NIST tests, with the exception of the random excursion (variant), have a minimum pass rate of 0.96 for a sample size of 100 binary sequences. Random excursion requires 50 out of 53 binary sequences to pass. UID 04742c32 marginally fails one of the non-overlapping template tests in each run. This indicates a small probability of a recurring pattern in the data, but with only one failed test, it is not a strong indication of non-randomness. UID 04743732 passes all tests within acceptable bounds and all p-values remain within the 1% to 99% range. Due to the length of NIST STS 2.1.2 reports, the full results have not been reproduced here. Due to the length of the NIST STS reports, results for both cards are available online[3].

---

[3] https://www.cs.kent.ac.uk/people/staff/dh433/RFIDsec2016/NISTresults.zip.

Table 1. NIST STS 2.1.2 results for 64 MB of TRNG output from two DESFire EV1 RFID cards.

NIST	UID 04742c32	UID 04743732
Pass	187/188	188/188

4.2 Diehard Results

Table 2 shows the results of the Diehard tests over the two 64 MB TRNG output files. Almost all listed tests are passed by both cards, with p-values between 0.01 and 0.99. The 32×32 Binary Rank test reported weak results, likely due to the low t-sample size. These results are a good indication of the randomness of the TRNG output. It should be noted that the relatively small sample size of 64 MB, makes it inappropriate for some tests to be applied without modification of the t-sample value to prevent rewinds. Rewound files may create artificial patterns not present in the stored data, failing tests due to perceived repetition instead of genuine weaknesses in the RNG.

Table 2. Diehard results for 64 MB of TRNG output.

Diehard test	t-samples	UID 04742c32 p-values	UID 04743732 p-values
Birthday Spacings	Default	0.18194520	0.61105583
Overlapping permutations	125,000	0.38044164	0.58693289
32×32 Binary rank	4,750	*0.9979203	*0.234095
6×8 Binary rank	25,000	0.31311490	0.32387215
Bitstream	Default	0.97724174	0.18743536
Count the 1's (stream)	Default	0.17108396	0.74984724
Count the 1's (byte)	Default	0.86481241	0.92578024
Parking Lot	Default	0.18078043	0.24200626
Minimum distance (2d sphere)	Default	0.76328000	0.95091635
3d sphere (minimum distance)	Default	0.23871272	0.20826216
Squeeze	Default	0.62598919	0.08843989
Runs	Default	0.63756836	0.80941394
Craps	20,000	0.54077256	0.92769962

4.3 ENT Results

Table 3 displays the output of ENT for both DESFire EV1 cards. The results show that the source files display good entropy (greater than 7.9999 bits per byte), and hence sufficient complexity to be incompressible. Arithmetic mean,

Table 3. Mifare DESFire EV1 ENT results for 64 MB of TRNG output.

ENT	UID 04742c32	UID 04743732	Optimal/expected
Entropy	7.999969	7.999989	8
Optimal compress	0	0	0
Chi-square	2709.10	973.07	255
Arith. Mean	127.492921	127.500582	127.5
Monte Carlo π est	3.14167	3.142019	3.14159
S. Correlation	0.000008	0.000045	0.0

Monte Carlo π estimation and Serial Correlation similarly show acceptable results, with some minor (but expected) variability between the two data sources.

However, both cards show consistent and significantly high values for the chi-square test. A figure of 2709.10 (returned by UID 04742c32) is far beyond the expected value of 255. This is an indicator of a strong bias in the distribution of byte values throughout the sample. UID 04743732 has a lower chi-square result of 973.07, which is still far in excess of the expected value. Both sets of results show that these files are significantly non-uniform.

Analysis of Bias. The occurrence of values within both files was used to compute the bias, as the difference between the observed and the expected number of occurrences. This can be seen in Fig. 3(a) and (b). Both of these graphs show a clear pattern. A sinusoid, clearest in (a) but also evident in (b), is revealed. Sixteen distinct peaks and troughs are apparent, forming a recurring pattern of eight oscillations.

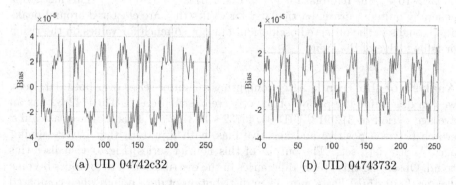

(a) UID 04742c32   (b) UID 04743732

Fig. 3. Observed bias (two 64 MB sets of TRNG data).

Figure 4(a) compares the two cards. The shared trend is clearly visible. UID 04742c32 has a maximum positive bias of 4.1754×10^{-5} and a maximum negative bias of -3.9246×10^{-5}. UID 04743732 has a maximum positive bias of 3.9785×10^{-5} and a maximum negative bias of -3.1242×10^{-5}.

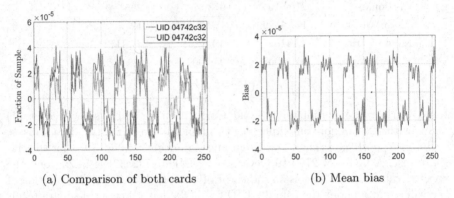

(a) Comparison of both cards   (b) Mean bias

Fig. 4. Comparison and mean of bias in two 64 MB sample files.

The mean bias, shown in Fig. 4(b), better highlights the underlying trend. A Fourier series for the mean bias can be used to estimate the expected bias, as shown in Eq. 1:

$$P(x) \approx a0 + (a1 \cdot cos(x \cdot w) + b1 \cdot sin(x \cdot w + (...) + a8 \cdot cos(8 \cdot x \cdot w) + b8 \cdot sin(8 \cdot x \cdot w) \quad (1)$$

An example approximation, for $x \doteq 177$ yields an estimated bias of $-3.342 \cdot 10^{-5}$. The real bias for 177 in Fig. 4(b) is $-3.3287 \cdot 10^{-5}$. This method is generally quite accurate, particularly for values that are clustered around peaks and troughs in the observed oscillation, but not so much for values on the rising or falling edge of the trend.

Analysis of the Trend. After computing a Fourier series over both data sets, we can determine the period of the observed oscillations. UID 04742c32 has an average period of 31.9918, UID 04743732's is 31.8782. This indicates a regular switch between positive and negative bias, with a pattern that is very similar across both data sets. The output of this Fourier series (Fig. 5) visualises this trend. Observing this graph, differences in the distribution of byte values become clearer. Figure 5(b) has a more even distribution of data points when compared with (a). The bias away from the expected occurrence of values is present, but not as pronounced. No byte values occur at exactly the expected rate, but the range between the lowest positive and highest negative bias is far smaller: 7.5781×10^{-7} to -2.4219×10^{-7}. The switching between high and low values, however, remains consistent across the same groups of byte values. Interestingly, the distribution of

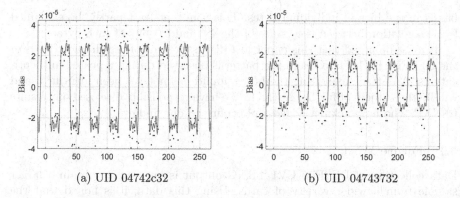

(a) UID 04742c32   (b) UID 04743732

Fig. 5. Two fourier series of the bias from the 2 cards.

byte values between positive and negative bias values is remarkably uniform for UID 04742c32. 128 values are positively biased, 128 are negative. UID 04743732 is marginally different, with 125 positive and 131 negatively biased. In both cases, approximately 16 values appear in each peak and trough. The positive and negative biases appear to correspond with the setting of bits 4 and 5 in a proportion of bytes. When both bit share the same value, the bias is positive. A difference between the two bits indicates a negative bias. Though the trend in Fig. 5(b) is less pronounced, both sets of results demonstrate this behaviour. The results presented in this paper show that the bias is not restricted to one of the two cards, but shared by both. This implies a weak TRNG, an issue to be shared by their batch. With further analysis of DESFire EV1 cards from different batches, it may be possible to determine whether this issue holds across the whole family. This could have serious security repercussions and may affect the robustness of authentication protocols and the anonymisation Random ID (RID) scheme implemented in DESFire EV1 cards.

5   Conclusion

This paper reports a preliminary analysis of the DESFire EV1 TRNG, specifically a study of its randomness. Data (64 MB) was collected from two different cards, and subject to the NIST STS 2.1.2, Diehard and ENT randomness tests. NIST and Diehard tests seem to confirm good randomness from both cards in most tests. Both cards performed poorly on the Diehard 32 × 32 binary rank test (weak but not fail results), which in light of the ENT results and subsequent analysis is unsurprising, but not strongly indicative of non-random output. The TRNG output of the EV1 exhibited good entropy under ENT and passed all but one of the other tests within acceptable bounds. The chi-square test, however, reported anomalously high values with corresponding p-values below 10^{-4}. This indicates a distinctly non-uniform distribution. Pattern-seeking tests have, however, not failed or even reported weak results, so further analysis was performed to find an explanation for this. Detailed analysis found 32 value wide bands in the bias of individual bytes. This could, at least partly, be explained by a correlation between the values of the 4th and 5th bits of each byte.

It must be noted that this paper just discusses some of the characteristics of the DESFire EV1 TRNG, and the patterns observed during repeated authentications. An attack exploiting the biases found has not yet been identified, and will be the subject of further research. We have responsibly disclosed our results to NXP, who have acknowledged and confirmed our findings.

5.1 Future Work

Data collection of DESFire EV1 TRNG output is ongoing, to obtain a larger sample from a wider variety of cards. Using this data, it is hoped that the shared trend identified in the two cards can be further analysed. Modelling of the observed bias to determine a potential root-cause is an important aspect of our ongoing work. Further investigation of the biases in the EV1 TRNG will be undertaken to understand why they have thus far eluded detection. In addition, data will be collected from DESFire EV2 cards to determine whether these biases carry over to newer products. We will also study attack scenarios in the intended EV1 use cases that could exploit these biases.

Acknowledgements. This work was funded by InnovateUK as part of the authenticatedSelf project, under reference number 102050. This work was partly sponsored by the ICT COST Action IC1403 Cryptacus in the EU Framework Horizon 2020. We would also like to thank NXP Semiconductors Ltd. for their timely and professional communication following the responsible disclosure of our findings.

References

1. Lee, S.M., Hwang, Y.J., Lee, D.H., Lim, J.I.: Efficient authentication for low-cost RFID systems. In: Gervasi, O., Gavrilova, M.L., Kumar, V., Laganà, A., Lee, H.P., Mun, Y., Taniar, D., Tan, C.J.K. (eds.) ICCSA 2005. LNCS, vol. 3480, pp. 619–627. Springer, Heidelberg (2005). doi:10.1007/11424758_65
2. Kasper, T., Oswald, D., Paar, C.: New methods for cost-effective side-channel attacks on cryptographic RFIDs. In: The 5th Workshop on RFID Security (RFID-Sec). Citeseer (2009)
3. Garcia, F.D., Koning Gans, G., Muijrers, R., Rossum, P., Verdult, R., Schreur, R.W., Jacobs, B.: Dismantling MIFARE classic. In: Jajodia, S., Lopez, J. (eds.) ESORICS 2008. LNCS, vol. 5283, pp. 97–114. Springer, Heidelberg (2008). doi:10.1007/978-3-540-88313-5_7
4. Merhi, M., Hernandez-Castro, J., Peris-Lopez, P.: Studying the PRNG of a low-cost RFID tag. In: 2011 IEEE International Conference on RFID-Technologies and Applications (RFID-TA), pp. 381–385. IEEE (2011)
5. Garcia, F.D., Van Rossum, P., Verdult, R., Schreur, R.W.: Wirelessly pick pocketing a mifare classic card. In: 2009 30th IEEE Symposium on Security and Privacy, pp. 3–15. IEEE (2009)
6. Koning Gans, G., Hoepman, J.-H., Garcia, F.D.: A practical attack on the MIFARE classic. In: Grimaud, G., Standaert, F.-X. (eds.) CARDIS 2008. LNCS, vol. 5189, pp. 267–282. Springer, Heidelberg (2008). doi:10.1007/978-3-540-85893-5_20

7. Kasper, T., Silbermann, M., Paar, C.: All you can eat or breaking a real-world contactless payment system. In: Sion, R. (ed.) FC 2010. LNCS, vol. 6052, pp. 343–350. Springer, Heidelberg (2010). doi:10.1007/978-3-642-14577-3_28

8. Chiu, Y.-H., Hong, W.-C., Chou, L.-P., Ding, J., Yang, B.-Y., Cheng, C.-M.: A practical attack on *Patched* MIFARE classic. In: Lin, D., Xu, S., Yung, M. (eds.) Inscrypt 2013. LNCS, vol. 8567, pp. 150–164. Springer, Cham (2014). doi:10.1007/978-3-319-12087-4_10

9. Verdult, R., de Koning Gans, G., Garcia, F.D.: A toolbox for RFID protocol analysis. In: 2012 Fourth International EURASIP Workshop on RFID Technology (EURASIP RFID), pp. 27–34. IEEE (2012)

10. Liu, Z., Peng, D.: True random number generator in RFID systems against traceability. In: 2006 3rd IEEE Consumer Communications and Networking Conference (CCNC 2006), vol. 1, pp. 620–624. IEEE (2006)

11. Oswald, D., Paar, C.: Breaking mifare DESFire MF3ICD40: power analysis and templates in the real world. In: Preneel, B., Takagi, T. (eds.) CHES 2011. LNCS, vol. 6917, pp. 207–222. Springer, Heidelberg (2011). doi:10.1007/978-3-642-23951-9_14

12. NXP Semiconductors. Mifare DESFire EV1 4K: Mifare DESFire EV1 contactless multi-application IC. NXP Semiconductors. http://www.nxp.com/products/identification-and-security/mifare-ics/mifare-desfire/. Accessed 5 Sep 2016

13. Anderson, W.: A study of entropy. https://sites.google.com/site/astudyofentropy/background-information/the-tests. Accessed 7 Sep 2016

14. National Institute of Standards and Technology. NIST computer security resource center (CSRC). http://csrc.nist.gov/groups/ST/toolkit/rng/index.html. Accessed 7 Sep 2016

15. Rukhin, A., Soto, J., Nechvatal, J., Smid, M., Barker, E.: A statistical test suite for random and pseudorandom number generators for cryptographic applications. Technical report, DTIC Document (2001)

16. Walker, J.: Ent. A pseudo-random number sequence testing program. https://www.fourmilab.ch/random/. Accessed 07 Sep 2016

Proximity

Optimality Results on the Security of Lookup-Based Protocols

Sjouke Mauw[1,2], Jorge Toro-Pozo[1(✉)], and Rolando Trujillo-Rasua[2]

[1] CSC, University of Luxembourg, 6, Rue Richard Coudenhove-Kalergi,
1359 Luxembourg, Luxembourg
{sjouke.mauw,jorge.toro}@uni.lu
[2] SnT, University of Luxembourg, 6, Rue Richard Coudenhove-Kalergi,
1359 Luxembourg, Luxembourg
rolando.trujillo@uni.lu

Abstract. Distance-bounding protocols use the round-trip time of a challenge-response cycle to provide an upper-bound on the distance between prover and verifier. In order to obtain an accurate upper-bound, the computation time at the prover's side should be as short as possible, which can be achieved by precomputing the responses and storing them in a lookup table. However, such lookup-based distance bounding protocols suffer from a trade-off between the achieved security level and the size of the lookup table. In this paper, we study this security-memory trade-off problem for a large class of lookup-based distance bounding protocols; called *layered protocols*. Relying on an automata-based security model, we provide mathematical definitions for different design decisions used in previous lookup-based protocols, and perform general security analyses for each of them. We also formalize an interpretation of *optimal trade-off* and find a non-trivial protocol transformation approach towards optimality. That is to say, our transformation applied to any layered protocol results in either an improved or an equal protocol with respect to the optimality criterion. This transformation allows us to provide a subclass of lookup-based protocol that cannot be improved further, which means that it contains an optimal layered protocol.

Keywords: Distance bounding · RFID · Security · Mafia-fraud · Relay attack

1 Introduction

Secure physical proximity checking in wireless technologies is a well-established field within computer security. As the speed of light represents a hard limit on the speed of radio waves, it has been used to accurately compute an upper bound on the distance between a transmitter (e.g., a satellite or an RFID reader) and a receiver (e.g., a GPS receiver or an RFID tag). The equation is simple: the distance to the receiver is half the round-trip time (RTT) multiplied by the speed of light. Nonetheless, this computation ought to be embedded into a

© Springer International Publishing AG 2017
G.P. Hancke and K. Markantonakis (Eds.): RFIDSec 2016, LNCS 10155, pp. 137–150, 2017.
DOI: 10.1007/978-3-319-62024-4_10

cryptographic protocol in order to ensure the authenticity of the receiver and
the integrity of the distance calculation. Such a cryptographic protocol is called
a *distance bounding protocol* [4], that is, an authentication protocol that also
determines an upper bound on the distance between the protocol's participants.
In this setting, the transmitter is called *verifier* and the receiver is called *prover*.

Like most cryptographic protocols, a distance bounding protocol consists of
a series of challenge-response rounds, with the peculiarity that some of these
rounds are used to compute round-trip times. Replying to such a round-trip
challenge should be a computationally inexpensive task, because otherwise the
round-trip time will become tainted by the prover's computation time as illustrated in Fig. 1.

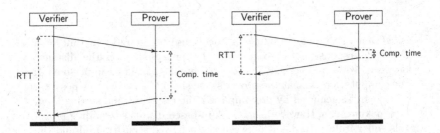

Fig. 1. The impact of the prover's computation time on the round-trip-time (RTT)
measurement.

A fundamental approach to computational efficiency is precomputation. In
distance bounding, this technique was first proposed by Hancke and Kuhn [8] in
2005, and later improved in [2,7,9,10,12–14]. These protocols, named lookup-
based protocols in [12], contain an initial precomputation phase in which the verifier and the prover secretly agree on a lookup table. This phase is followed by n
round-trip-time measurements realized by an n-fold challenge-response process.
For each challenge, the prover determines his response by looking it up in the
table. The protocol finishes successfully if all responses are correct with respect
to the precomputed lookup table and all round-trip-times are below a given
time threshold. Simplicity and efficiency make this type of protocols appealing
for battery-less or constrained devices, such as RFID tags. Moreover, their security can be arbitrarily improved by increasing n, with little or no computational
overhead [8].

Despite the simplicity of lookup-based protocols, none of them have been
proven optimal in terms of security, given a practical threshold on the size of
the lookup table. This is a security-memory trade-off problem which resem-
bles the classical time-memory trade-off problem occurring in other application
domains, such as cryptanalysis, rainbow tables, and dynamic programming. A
recent work [12] shows that if an exponential number of values (in terms of n)
can be precomputed, then the tree-based protocol proposed in [3] is optimal.
However, an exponentially large lookup table is unattainable in practice.

Contributions. In this article, we study the security-memory trade-off problem for a large class of lookup-based protocols; called *layered protocols*. The class of layered protocols is not trivial, as it contains all lookup-based distance bounding protocols proposed to date, except for the Poulidor protocol [14]. Our findings can be listed as follows.

- First, we rely on the automata-based model proposed in [12] (Sect. 3) to provide mathematical definitions of common design decisions used in lookup-based protocols (Sect. 4). For example, many lookup-based protocols use a fixed and known data access structure for the lookup table. Others, such as the Poulidor protocol [14], use a randomized indexing technique. We formalize both techniques by exploiting equivalence relations between automata, and perform general security analyses for those layered protocols using either of the two techniques (Sect. 4).
- Second, we formalize an interpretation of the security-memory trade-off problem for layered protocols, and provide a non-trivial protocol transformation approach towards optimality (Sect. 5). In more detail, for every protocol P with size s (a measure of memory), we show how to obtain another protocol P' of the same size and with equal or higher resistance to pre-ask attacks. We also prove that the proposed transformation has the full class of layered protocols as domain. We can thus conclude that an optimal layered protocol is within the image set of our transformation.

2   Related Work

The earliest distance bounding protocol based on RTT measurements was proposed by Brands and Chaum [4] in 1993 (see Fig. 2a). Their protocol (BC) assumes a verifier and a prover, each armed with a public/private key pair. By considering n to be the number of RTT measurements, the prover commits to a random sequence of bits $m_1 \cdots m_n$, after which the fast phase or RTT measurement phase starts. The fast phase consists of n rounds of a single bit-exchange. At the ith round, the verifier sends a random bit-challenge c_i and the prover instantly replies with $c_i \oplus m_i$. Proximity checking fails if the computed RTT at any round is above a given threshold. Authentication, on the other hand, is verified during a final phase where the prover opens the commit and signs all exchanges during the fast phase.

In 2005, Hancke and Kuhn (HK) proposed a different design for distance bounding protocols [8], where proximity checking and authentication are performed together during the fast phase. Because each round during the fast phase is quick and inexpensive, this makes it possible to improve the security with very-low computational overhead by simply increasing n. Hancke and Kuhn's protocol, depicted in Fig. 2b, works as follows. First, the parties exchange one nonce each (n_v and n_p). The two nonces and a shared secret key x are used by both parties as input to a pseudo-random function f, whose output is a sequence of $2n$ bits $H_1 \cdots H_{2n}$. As usual, the fast phase consists of n rounds. At the i-th

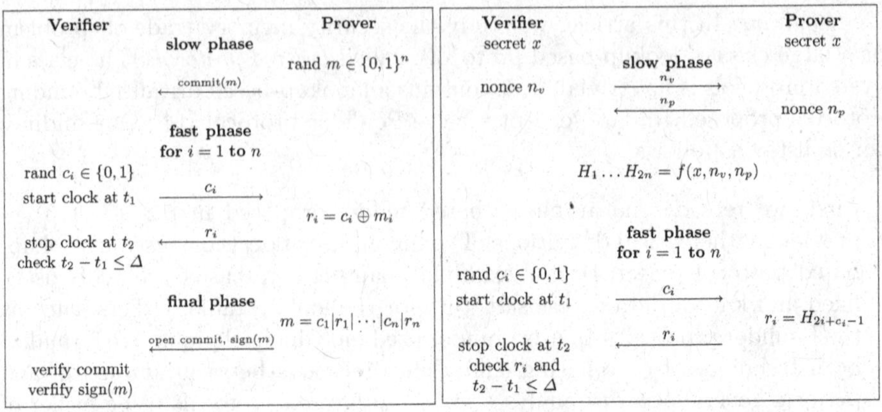

(a) Brands and Chaum's protocol   (b) Hancke and Kuhn's protocol

Fig. 2. Two distance bounding protocols.

round, the verifier generates a random bit-challenge c_i. If the bit-challenge is 0, the prover replies H_{2i-1}, otherwise H_{2i}. The protocol succeeds if all responses are correct and all round-trip times are below a predefined threshold.

The difference between HK and BC approaches becomes apparent if we consider the role of the sequences $m = m_1 \ldots m_n$ and $H = H_1 \ldots H_{2n}$ in their corresponding protocols. Revealing m allows an adversary to successfully pass the proximity checking phase in Brands and Chaum's protocol, yet the adversary cannot impersonate the prover as the prover's signature is required after the fast phase.

Hancke and Kuhn's protocol, instead, fails to provide proximity checking and authentication if H is revealed, as the two properties rely on the secrecy of H. Both approaches have their merits and shortcomings, resulting in the publication of two different types of distance bounding protocols: those based on Brands and Chaum's approach (e.g., [3–5,11]) and those based on Hancke and Kuhn's approach (e.g., [2,7,9,10,14]).

A common feature of HK-based protocols is that, during the fast phase, the prover uses a simple lookup operation to compute the correct reply to the verifier's challenge; hence their name *lookup-based protocols*. The drawback of lookup-based protocols, as shown in [1,12], is its low resistance to *pre-ask attacks*. A pre-ask attack is a sophisticated version of the so-called *mafia-fraud attack*, introduced by Desmedt, Goutier, and Bengio in 1987 [6].

For example, a pre-ask attack against Hancke and Kuhn's proposal might be the following. The adversary queries the legitimate prover with all-zero challenges to learn half of the sequence H. If the adversary then moves sufficiently close to the verifier, he can use this knowledge to impersonate the prover. By using his knowledge of half of H, the adversary will provide the correct response for the verifier's challenges that are equal to 0. For the challenges equal to 1, the adversary simply replies with random bits. With this strategy, the adversary will pass Hancke and Kuhn's protocol with probability $(3/4)^n$. In contrast, a pre-ask attack against Brands and Chaum's protocol succeeds with probability $(1/2)^n$.

Resisting pre-ask attacks and reducing the size of the lookup table has been the aim of many lookup-based protocols proposed in the last ten years [2,7,9–14]. However, these two goals, namely improving security and reducing size, seem to be in conflict in lookup-based protocols. This is a security-memory trade-off problem which has not been formally addressed yet. In the remainder of this article we study this problem for a subclass of lookup-based protocols.

3 Preliminaries

In this section we present the MTT security model introduced in [12] to study lookup-based distance bounding protocols.

3.1 The MTT Model

The security model is based on state-labeled Deterministic Finite Automata (DFAs) of the form $(\Sigma, \Gamma, Q, q_0, \delta, \ell)$, where Σ is a set of input symbols, Γ is a set of output symbols, Q is a set of states, $q_0 \in Q$ is the initial state, $\delta \colon Q \times \Sigma \to Q$ is a transition function, and $\ell \colon Q \to \Gamma$ is a labeling function. Given input and output symbol sets Σ and Γ, respectively, we use $\mathbf{U}_{\Sigma,\Gamma}$ to denote the universe of all DFAs over Σ and Γ.

Definition 1 (Lookup-based protocol). *A lookup-based distance bounding protocol, lookup-based protocol for short, with input set Σ and output set Γ is a finite non-empty subset of $\mathbf{U}_{\Sigma,\Gamma}$.*

A restriction imposed by Definition 1 on a lookup-based protocol is that it must be formed by automata with the same input and output sets. The reason is that Σ and Γ define the alphabets of the verifier's challenges and prover's responses, respectively.

Given an automaton $A = (\Sigma, \Gamma, Q, q_0, \delta, \ell)$ and a current state $q \in Q$, a lookup operation is regarded as a transition to a new state $q' = \delta(q, c)$ where $c \in \Sigma$ is a verifier's challenge. The corresponding response for such challenge is the output symbol attached to the new state q', i.e., $\ell(q')$. Successive lookup operations form a path in the automaton. We thus introduce additional notation for a sequence of input symbols $c = c_1 \cdots c_i \in \Sigma^i$:

- $\hat{\delta}(c) = q_0$ if $i = 0$, i.e., c is an empty string, otherwise $\hat{\delta}(c) = \delta(\hat{\delta}(c_1 \ldots c_{i-1}), c_i)$. In a nutshell, $\hat{\delta}(c)$ returns the state reached by the input sequence c.
- $\hat{\ell}(c) = \ell(\hat{\delta}(c))$, which is the output symbol attached to the state reached by the sequence c.
- $\Omega_A(c)$ is used to represent the sequence of labels attached to the states $\hat{\delta}(c_1), \hat{\delta}(c_1 c_2), \ldots, \hat{\delta}(c_1 c_2 \cdots c_i)$ in that order, i.e., $\Omega_A(c) = r_1 \cdots r_i \in \Gamma^i$, where $r_j = \hat{\ell}(c_1 \cdots c_j), \forall j \in \{1, \ldots, i\}$.

The model in [12] abstracts away from the precomputation phase in lookup-based protocols by considering the following execution model.

Definition 2 (Execution model). *A correct execution of a lookup-based protocol P with $n > 0$ rounds is a triple (A, C, R), where A is an automaton randomly selected from P, C is an input sequence randomly selected from Σ^n and R is an output sequence from Γ^n such that $R = \Omega_A(C)$.*

The outcome of the precomputation phase is considered to be a random automaton $A \in_R P$ within the set of automata defining the lookup-based protocol P. The input sequence $C = c_1 \cdots c_n$ corresponds to the verifier's challenges, and the correct replies $R = r_1 \cdots r_n$ must satisfy that $\hat{\ell}(c_1) = r_1, \hat{\ell}(c_1 c_2) = r_2, \cdots, \hat{\ell}(c_1 \cdots c_n) = r_n$.

3.2 Layered Protocols

The set-of-automata representation of many existing lookup-based protocols, e.g., [2,8,9,11,12], satisfies that, given an automaton $A = (\Sigma, \Gamma, Q, q_0, \delta, \ell)$ and two input sequences x and y, $\hat{\delta}(x) = \hat{\delta}(y)$ implies that the sizes of x and y are equal. Formulated differently, given any of the automata defining a protocol, two sequences of different size do not end in the same state. Protocols satisfying this property are called *layered protocols* [12].

Definition 3 (Layered protocol). *A lookup-based protocol P is layered if, for every $(\Sigma, \Gamma, Q, q_0, \delta, \ell) \in P$ and every $x, y \in \Sigma^*$, $\hat{\delta}(x) = \hat{\delta}(y) \implies |x| = |y|$.*

Layered protocols guarantee that the prover's answers at different rounds rely on different states regardless of the verifier's challenges. Given an automaton $(\Sigma, \Gamma, Q, q_0, \delta, \ell)$ in a layered protocol, we thus consider Q to be partitioned in $Q_0 \cup Q_1 \cup Q_2 \cdots$ where $Q_i = \{\hat{\delta}(x) \mid x \in \Sigma^i\}$.

For the sake of simplicity, and because most distance bounding protocols consider bit exchanges during the fast phase, we assume that the input and output symbol sets are binary, i.e., $\Sigma = \Gamma = \{0, 1\}$. Consequently, unless otherwise specified, all DFAs considered in the remainder of this article belong to the universe $\mathbf{U}_{\Sigma,\Gamma}$ with $\Sigma = \Gamma = \{0, 1\}$.

4 Security Analysis Through Equivalence Relations

While modeling lookup-based protocols by a set of automata, we have found that most lookup-based protocols defined in literature share some structural properties. For instance, the automata for the HK protocol all have a similar layered structure with two nodes in each layer [12]. We will exploit such similarities when reasoning about protocols. In this section, we will introduce two equivalence relations on automata that express relevant similarities and we will define closure and consistency with respect to these equivalences. Based on these relations, we provide a general security analysis of layered protocols.

4.1 Equivalence Relations Between Automata

A common feature of many lookup-based protocols is that all their automata have the same *shape* and differ only in the symbols attached to the states. This property, which we name *state-label-insensitive*, is satisfied by HK [8], KA [10], Tree-based [2], PUF [9], and Uniform [12], amongst others. The design decision represented by the state-label-insensitive property makes it easy for participants in a protocol to agree on the shape or structure of the lookup table, while only requiring randomness on the precomputed values.

Definition 4 (State-label-insensitive). *The* state-label-insensitive *relation* $\sim_S$ *is a symmetric binary relation on* $\mathbf{U}_{\Sigma,\Gamma}$, *defined by* $(\Sigma, \Gamma, Q, q_0, \delta, \ell) \sim_S$ $(\Sigma, \Gamma, Q', q_0', \delta', \ell')$ *if and only if* $Q = Q'$, $q_0 = q_0'$ *and* $\delta = \delta'$.

A few lookup-based protocols contain automata that are not related according to $\sim_S$, e.g., the Poulidor protocol [14]. In this protocol, the authors designed a mechanism to prevent (to some extent) an adversary from knowing which state is being used by the prover at any round of the fast phase. The idea is simple, the probability of two automata sharing the same transition function must be negligible. Such a mechanism seems to improve the resistance to pre-ask attacks as the adversary cannot easily use knowledge acquired in previous rounds to succeed in the current round of the fast phase.

Even though two automata in the Poulidor protocol can have different transition functions, they still preserve a slightly weaker structural property than the above mentioned state-label-insensitive property. If we ignore the edge labels of the automata, i.e., if we only look at the structure of the underlying graph of the automata, the transition functions of the automata in the Poulidor protocol are identical. We provide a formal definition for this structural relation next.

Definition 5 (Label-insensitive). *The* label-insensitive *relation* $\sim_L$ *is a symmetric binary relation on* $\mathbf{U}_{\Sigma,\Gamma}$, *defined by* $(\Sigma, \Gamma, Q, q_0, \delta, \ell)$ $\sim_L$ $(\Sigma, \Gamma, Q', q_0', \delta', \ell')$ *if and only if* $Q = Q'$, $q_0 = q_0'$ *and* $\{\delta(q,c) \mid c \in \Sigma\} = \{\delta'(q,c) \mid c \in \Sigma\}$ *for every* $q \in Q$.

A fundamental operator in binary relations is the *closure* with respect to a given property.

Definition 6 (Closure). *Let* P *be a lookup-based protocol and* $\sim_R \subseteq \mathbf{U}_{\Sigma,\Gamma} \times \mathbf{U}_{\Sigma,\Gamma}$ *be a binary relation. The* closure *of* P *with respect to* $\sim_R$, *denoted by* $\overline{P}^R$, *is the minimal superset of* P *such that* $\forall (A, A') \in \sim_R \colon A \in \overline{P}^R \implies A' \in \overline{P}^R$.

We observe that most existing lookup-based protocols can be easily defined by using the closure operator. As an example, we show next a representation of the Poulidor protocol by using the closure w.r.t. the label-insensitive relation.

Example 1 (Poulidor protocol). Consider the automaton $A = (\Sigma, \Gamma, Q, q_0, \delta, \ell)$ with $\Sigma = \Gamma = \{0, 1\}$, where $Q = \{0, 1, \ldots, 2n - 1\}$, $q_0 = 0$, $\delta(q, c) = (q + c + 1) \pmod{2n}$ and $\ell(q) = 0$, $\forall q \in Q$. The Poulidor protocol, up to n rounds, can be defined as a set of automata that is the closure of $\{A\}$ with respect to $\sim_L$, i.e., $\overline{\{A\}}^L$.

We say that a protocol P is *closed under* $\sim_R$ if $P = \overline{P}^R$. Moreover, if $\forall A, A' \in P\colon A \sim_R A'$, then P is said to be *consistent with respect to* $\sim_R$. The Poulidor protocol, for example, is closed with respect to $\sim_S$ and $\sim_L$, and it is consistent with respect to $\sim_L$. However, it is not consistent with respect to $\sim_S$.

4.2   Resistance to Pre-ask Attacks of Layered Protocols

Avoine et al. concluded in [1] that in the context of DB protocols without a final authentication phase, the most efficient adversarial strategy when conducting a mafia-fraud attack is the pre-ask strategy.

In a recent work [12], it was proven that, if a protocol is layered and closed under $\sim_S$ (called random-labeled in [12]), then there exists a deterministic optimal strategy to execute a pre-ask attack against the protocol. This strategy consists in replying to the verifier's challenges with exactly the same sequence of responses obtained from the prover in the pre-ask session. The next proposition is based on this result.

Proposition 1 (Mafia success probability). *Let P be a layered protocol with $n > 0$ rounds. For every $x \in \{0,1\}^n$, let E^x be the event that $\Omega_A(x) = \Omega_A(c)$ for a random automaton $A \in P$ and a random input sequence $c \in \{0,1\}^n$. If P is closed under $\sim_S$, then the probability of success of an optimal pre-ask attack against P, denoted by $\mathcal{M}(P)$, can be computed as follows:*

$$\mathcal{M}(P) = \max_{x \in \{0,1\}^n} \{\Pr(E^x)\}.$$

Proof. The proposition easily follows from the definition of optimal strategy, and the underlying assumption that the adversary can find out $x \in \{0,1\}^n$ such that $\Pr(E^x) \geq \Pr(E^y)$ for every $y \in \{0,1\}^n$.   □

In Lemmas 1 and 2 below, we make Proposition 1 more precise by providing formulas to compute $\Pr(E^x)$ in protocols that are consistent and closed with respect to $\sim_S$ and $\sim_L$, respectively. We do so by considering, for a given automaton, the meeting points between the input sequence used by the adversary during the pre-ask session and the challenges sent by the verifier.

Definition 7 (Meeting points set). *Given an automaton $A = (\Sigma, \Gamma, Q, q_0, \delta, \ell)$ and two input sequences $x, y \in \Sigma^n$, the meeting points set $\mathcal{I}(A, x, y)$ is the set $\left\{ i \in \{1, \dots, n\} \mid \hat{\delta}(x_1 \cdots x_i) = \hat{\delta}(y_1 \cdots y_i) \right\}$.*

Lemma 1. *Let P be a layered protocol with $n > 0$ rounds and A any automaton in P. If P is consistent and closed with respect to $\sim_S$, then:*

$$\mathcal{M}(P) = \max_{x \in \{0,1\}^n} \left\{ \frac{1}{4^n} \sum_{y \in \{0,1\}^n} 2^{|\mathcal{I}(A,x,y)|} \right\}.$$

Proof. Let $x, y \in \{0,1\}^n$ be two random input sequences. As P is consistent with respect to $\sim_S$, we have that $\mathcal{I}(A, x, y) = \mathcal{I}(A', x, y)$ for every $A' \in P$. In addition, given that P is closed under $\sim_S$, there are $2^{|Q| - (n - |\mathcal{I}(A,x,y)|)}$ automata A' in P such that $\Omega_{A'}(x) = \Omega_{A'}(y)$. Therefore, for a random automaton $A' \in P$, we have:

$$\Pr\left(\Omega_{A'}(x) = \Omega_{A'}(y)\right) = \frac{2^{|Q| - (n - |\mathcal{I}(A,x,y)|)}}{2^{|Q|}} = \frac{2^{|\mathcal{I}(A,x,y)|}}{2^n}. \tag{1}$$

Now, define the event E^x that $\Omega_{A'}(x) = \Omega_{A'}(c)$ for a random input sequence $c \in \{0,1\}^n$ and a random automaton $A' \in P$ (as in Proposition 1). Hence, by the law of total probability we have:

$$\Pr(E^x) = \sum_{y \in \{0,1\}^n} \Pr(E^x \mid c = y) \Pr(c = y). \tag{2}$$

But, $\Pr(c = y) = \frac{1}{2^n}$ and $\Pr(E^x \mid c = y) = 2^{|\mathcal{I}(A,x,y)|} / 2^n$ (see Eq. 1). Therefore, by applying these results in Eq. 2 we obtain:

$$\Pr(E^x) = \frac{1}{4^n} \sum_{y \in \{0,1\}^n} 2^{|\mathcal{I}(A,x,y)|}. \tag{3}$$

Finally, by using Eq. 3 in Proposition 1 we obtain the expected result. $\qquad\square$

Lemma 2. *Let P be a layered protocol with $n > 0$ rounds and A any automaton in P. If P is consistent and closed with respect to $\sim_L$, then:*

$$\mathcal{M}(P) = \frac{1}{8^n} \sum_{x,y \in \{0,1\}^n} 2^{|\mathcal{I}(A,x,y)|}.$$

Proof. For every $x \in \{0,1\}^n$, we define the event E^x that $\Omega_{A'}(x) = \Omega_{A'}(c)$ for a random automaton $A' \in P$ and a random input sequence $c \in \{0,1\}^n$. Let $\{P_1, P_2, \ldots, P_k\}$ be the equivalence classes of P with respect to $\sim_S$, i.e., $\forall B, B' \in P: B \sim_S B' \implies \exists i \in \{1, \ldots, k\}: B \in P_i \wedge B' \in P_i$. Since P is consistent and closed with respect to $\sim_L$ we derive that $\forall i, j \in \{1, \ldots, k\}: |P_i| = |P_j|$. Moreover, for every $i \in \{1, \ldots, k\}$ the protocol defined by the set of automata P_i is consistent and closed with respect to $\sim_S$.

Let x be a sequence in $\{0,1\}^n$ and $r \in \{1, \ldots, k\}$ such that $A \in P_r$ and let A' be a random automaton in P. According to the law of total probability we have:

$$\Pr(E^x) = \sum_{i=1}^k \Pr(E^x | A' \in P_i) \Pr(A' \in P_i) = \frac{1}{k} \sum_{i=1}^k \Pr(E^x | A' \in P_i). \tag{4}$$

Consider the sets $R_i = \left\{ y \in \{0,1\}^n \mid \forall j \leq n: \hat{\delta}_r(x_1 \cdots x_j) = \hat{\delta}_i(y_1 \cdots y_j) \right\}$, for every $i \in \{1, \ldots, k\}$, where δ_i is the common transition function of the automata in P_i; remark that P_i is consistent and closed with respect to $\sim_S$. Thus, for every $i \in \{1, \ldots, k\}$ and every $y \in R_i$, we have:

$$\Pr(E^x | A' \in P_i) = \Pr(E^y | A' \in P_r). \tag{5}$$

Therefore, by iterating i over $\{1, \ldots, k\}$ and y on the corresponding R_i, we get:

$$\sum_{i=1}^{k} \sum_{y \in R_i} \Pr(E^x | A' \in P_i) = \sum_{i=1}^{k} \sum_{y \in R_i} \Pr(E^y | A' \in P_r). \tag{6}$$

Let $C_y = \{i \in \{1, \ldots, k\} \mid y \in R_i\}$ for every $y \in \{0,1\}^n$. By symmetry, $|R_i| = |R_j|, \forall i, j \in \{1, \ldots, k\}$ and $|C_y| = |C_z|, \forall y, z \in \{0,1\}^n$. Let $t = |R_i|$ and $c = |C_y|$. The left-hand and right-hand sides of Eq. 6 are respectively equivalent to:

$$\sum_{i=1}^{k} \sum_{y \in R_i} \Pr(E^x | A' \in P_i) = t \sum_{i=1}^{k} \Pr(E^x | A' \in P_i), \text{ and} \tag{7}$$

$$\sum_{i=1}^{k} \sum_{y \in R_i} \Pr(E^y | A' \in P_r) = c \sum_{y \in \{0,1\}^n} \Pr(E^y | A' \in P_r). \tag{8}$$

Thus, from Eqs. 4, 6, 7 and 8 we obtain $\Pr(E^x) = \frac{c}{tk} \sum_{y \in \{0,1\}^n} \Pr(E^y | A' \in P_r)$. But, given that P_r is consistent and closed with respect to $\sim_S$ we derive that $\Pr(E^y | A' \in P_r) = \frac{1}{4^n} \sum_{z \in \{0,1\}^n} 2^{|\mathcal{I}(A,y,z)|}$ (see Eq. 3). Therefore:

$$\Pr(E^x) = \frac{c}{4^n tk} \sum_{y,z \in \{0,1\}^n} 2^{|\mathcal{I}(A,y,z)|}. \tag{9}$$

Observe that the right-hand side of Eq. 9 does not depend on x, therefore $\mathcal{M}(P) = \Pr(E^x), \forall x \in \{0,1\}^n$. On the other hand, $\sum_{i=1}^{k} |R_i| = \sum_{y \in \{0,1\}^n} |C_y|$ which gives $tk = 2^n c$. By using this in Eq. 9 we complete the proof. □

The closed formulas from the two lemmas above will be used in the next section to prove that, for every layered protocol P, there exists a protocol $P' \subseteq P$ (i.e. a protocol formed by a subset of the automata in P) such that its closure under $\sim_L$ results in a protocol with equal or better resistance to pre-ask attacks than the original protocol P.

5   A Protocol Transformation Towards Optimality

As pointed out in the previous section, all lookup-based protocols found in the literature are closed and consistent with respect to either $\sim_S$ or $\sim_L$. Both design principles have been shown effective by comparing different protocol designs, but it is not clear whether they must be applied in general. In this section, we give, to the best of our knowledge, the first formal proof that those design principles are indeed well-founded. We do so by providing a protocol transformation that uses the closure with respect to both $\sim_S$ and $\sim_L$, and results in a better or equal protocol with respect to the resistance to pre-ask attacks.

Theorem 1. *Let P be a layered protocol with $n > 0$ rounds, then:*

$$\mathcal{M}(P) \geq \mathcal{M}\left(\overline{P}^s\right).$$

Proof. Let $x \in \{0,1\}^n$ be the input sequence selected by the adversary to query the prover in the pre-ask session. Consider the following pre-ask strategy, for a given $z \in \{0,1\}^n$ and the responses from the prover $y \in \{0,1\}^n$: at the i-th round, the adversary will reply to the verifier's challenges c with the sequence $y \oplus \neg z$. In other words, the adversary will reply with $\Omega_A^z(c) = \Omega_A(x) \oplus \neg z$, where A is the selected automaton for the execution. Let $\mathcal{M}^z(P)$ be the probability that the adversary succeeds with z in P, i.e., $\mathcal{M}^z(P) = \Pr(\Omega_A(c) = \Omega_A^z(c))$, for a random $A \in P$ and a random $c \in \{0,1\}^n$. Therefore,

$$\mathcal{M}^z(P) = \frac{1}{2^n|P|} \sum_{A \in P} \sum_{c \in \{0,1\}^n} D\left(\Omega_A(c), \Omega_A^z(c)\right), \tag{10}$$

where $D(u,v)$ is 1, if $u = v$ or 0, otherwise. Let us assume that $\overline{P}^s \neq P$, otherwise the theorem holds straightforwardly. Hence, $\mathcal{M}^z\left(\overline{P}^s\right) = a \cdot \mathcal{M}^z(P) + b \cdot \mathcal{M}^z\left(\overline{P}^s - P\right)$, where $a = \frac{|P|}{|\overline{P}^s|}$ and $b = \frac{|\overline{P}^s - P|}{|\overline{P}^s|}$. Now, assume that P is more resistant than $\overline{P}^s$ to pre-ask attacks, i.e. $\forall z \in \{0,1\}^n : \mathcal{M}^z\left(\overline{P}^s\right) \geq \mathcal{M}^z(P)$ and there exists at least one value z such that the inequality is strict. Therefore, $\forall z \in \{0,1\}^n : \mathcal{M}^z\left(\overline{P}^s - P\right) \geq \mathcal{M}^z(P)$ (and at least for one z the inequality is strict). This gives us:

$$\sum_{z \in \{0,1\}^n} \mathcal{M}^z(\overline{P}^s - P) > \sum_{z \in \{0,1\}^n} \mathcal{M}^z(P). \tag{11}$$

Our goal is to reach a contradiction. To do so, consider the set $B^{c,z}$ of automata A in P such that $\Omega_A(c) = \Omega_A^z(c)$. Hence, from Eq. 10 we have:

$$\mathcal{M}^z(P) = \frac{1}{2^n|P|} \sum_{c \in \{0,1\}^n} |B^{c,z}|. \tag{12}$$

Now, observe that $\forall z, z' \in \{0,1\}^n : z \neq z' \implies B^{c,z} \cap B^{c,z'} = \emptyset$. Besides, $\forall (A,c) \in P \times \{0,1\}^n : \Omega_A(c) = \Omega_A^z(c)$ where $z = \Omega_A(x) \oplus \Omega_A(c)$. This gives that for every $c \in \{0,1\}^n$ it holds that $\{B^{c,z} \mid z \in \{0,1\}^n\}$ is a partition of P which gives $\forall c \in \{0,1\}^n : \sum_{z \in \{0,1\}^n} |B^{c,z}| = |P|$. Therefore, by applying this in Eq. 12 we derive $\sum_{z \in \{0,1\}^n} \mathcal{M}^z(P) = 1$. Analogously, we obtain that $\sum_{z \in \{0,1\}^n} \mathcal{M}^z(\overline{P}^s - P) = 1$, which is in contradiction with the inequality in Eq. 11. □

A consequence of Theorem 1 is the following. If P is optimal in terms of resistance to pre-ask attacks, then $\overline{P}^s$ is optimal as well. This result is relevant, as the closure $\overline{P}^s$ only differs from P on the distribution of the precomputed values, while it keeps the same structure of the lookup table.

The second design principle is defined as the property of the protocol to be consistent and closed with respect to $\sim_L$. In the case that P is already closed under $\sim_S$ (i.e., it satisfies the first principle), we prove, in Theorem 2 below, that there exists a subset of P whose closure w.r.t. $\sim_L$ is at least as resistant to pre-ask attacks as the former.

Theorem 2. *Let P be a layered protocol with $n > 0$ rounds and $\{P_1, \ldots, P_k\}$ be the equivalence classes of P with respect to $\sim_S$. Let $j \in \{1, \ldots, k\}$ such that $\forall i \in \{1, \ldots, k\}: \mathcal{M}\left(\overline{P_i}^L\right) \geq \mathcal{M}\left(\overline{P_j}^L\right)$. If P is closed under $\sim_S$, then:*

$$\mathcal{M}(P) \geq \mathcal{M}\left(\overline{P_j}^L\right).$$

Proof. Given that P is closed under $\sim_S$, P_i is consistent and closed with respect to $\sim_S$, for every $i \in \{1, \ldots, k\}$. Now, let A be a random automaton in P. As in Proposition 1, for every $x \in \{0,1\}^n$, we define the event E^x that $\Omega_A(x) = \Omega_A(c)$ for a random input sequence $c \in \{0,1\}^n$. By the law of total probability we have that for every $x \in \{0,1\}^n$:

$$\Pr(E^x) = \sum_{i=1}^{k} \Pr(E^x \mid A \in P_i) \Pr(A \in P_i). \tag{13}$$

From $\mathcal{M}(P) = \max_{x \in \{0,1\}^n} \Pr(E^x)$ we deduce that $\mathcal{M}(P) \geq \frac{1}{2^n} \sum_{x \in \{0,1\}^n} \Pr(E^x)$. By substituting Eq. 13 in such inequality, and inverting the order of the sums we obtain:

$$\mathcal{M}(P) \geq \sum_{i=1}^{k} \left(\frac{1}{2^n} \sum_{x \in \{0,1\}^n} \Pr\left(E^x \mid A \in P_i\right) \right) \Pr(A \in P_i). \tag{14}$$

On the other hand, we derive from Lemmas 1 and 2 that, for every $i \in \{1, \ldots, k\}$, $\frac{1}{2^n} \sum_{x \in \{0,1\}^n} \Pr\left(E^x \mid A \in P_i\right) = \mathcal{M}\left(\overline{P_i}^L\right) \geq \mathcal{M}\left(\overline{P_j}^L\right)$ as P_i is consistent and closed with respect to $\sim_S$. By applying this result in Eq. 14 and given that $\sum_{i=1}^{k} \Pr(A \in P_i) = 1$, we complete the proof. $\square$

Our protocol transformation towards optimality consists of successive applications of Theorems 1 and 2. We observe that, by only considering the structure of the underlying graph of the automata, both transformations either preserve or simplify a protocol. We capture this notion of structural complexity of a protocol by the following notion of *size*.

Definition 8 (Size). *The size of a lookup-based protocol P, denoted by $\mathcal{S}(P)$, is the number of states of the largest automaton in P.*

In a nutshell, the size of a protocol is determined by the largest automaton that can be used during a fast phase. Remark that the number of states is a standard measure of size in automata theory.

Corollary 1 (Optimal Trade-off). *Given a positive integer number s, consider the set S of layered lookup-based protocols with size less or equal than s, i.e., $S = \{P \subseteq \mathbf{U}_{\Sigma,\Gamma} \mid \mathcal{S}(P) \leq s\}$. Let $O \subseteq S$ be the set of protocols that are optimal in terms of resistance to pre-ask attacks, within the set S, i.e., $O = \{P \in S \mid \nexists P' \in S \colon \mathcal{M}(P') < \mathcal{M}(P)\}$. If S is not empty, then there exists a protocol P in O that is consistent and closed with respect to $\sim_L$.*

Proof. The proof comes straightforwardly from Theorems 1 and 2. Let $P \in O$, from Theorem 1 we have $\mathcal{M}(P) \geq \mathcal{M}(\overline{P}^s)$. Because $\mathcal{S}(P) = \mathcal{S}\left(\overline{P}^s\right)$, then $\overline{P}^s \in O$. On the other hand, because of Theorem 2, there exists P_1 consistent with respect to $\sim_S$ such that $P_1 \subseteq \overline{P}^s$ and $\mathcal{M}(\overline{P}^s) \geq \mathcal{M}(\overline{P_1}^L)$. Besides, $\mathcal{S}\left(\overline{P_1}^L\right) = \mathcal{S}(P_1) \leq \mathcal{S}\left(\overline{P}^s\right) = \mathcal{S}(P) \leq s$. Therefore $\overline{P_1}^L \in S$ and $\overline{P_1}^L \in O$.   □

Corollary 1 is a useful result towards finding an optimal layered protocol, as it reduces the search space to the subclass of protocols that are consistent and closed with respect to $\sim_L$. It is worth noticing that a consistent protocol with respect to $\sim_L$ imposes a rather strong structural property on a protocol, that is, all the automata in the protocol are equal if we ignore the edge and state labels. This rules out, for example, protocol composition as a technique to obtain an optimal protocol, where a protocol composition is simply the union of the sets of automata defining the two protocols, e.g. the union of Hancke and Kuhn's protocol [8] and the Uniform protocol [12].

We conclude by stressing that we have focused on non-trivial transformations in lookup-based protocols, while there exist others that can be easily included in our analyses. For example, the security-memory trade-off of every lookup-based protocol can be improved by simply removing all unreachable states in its automata representation. This consideration corresponds to a rather trivial design principle whereby states that are not reachable from the initial state can be removed, as they are not used in the protocol execution. Similarly, it can be easily proven that two equivalent protocols up to isomorphism are equal in size and resistance to pre-ask attacks.

6   Conclusions

We have studied layered protocols, a subclass of lookup-up based distance bounding protocols that contains most lookup-based protocols proposed to date. Relevant structural properties of this type of protocols that have been used in previous work in a rather intuitive way, have been formalized in this article. As a result, we developed a general security analysis that applies to all layered protocols. We have also addressed the security-memory trade-off problem in lookup-based protocols. Our results indicate that there exists an optimal layered protocol that is consistent and closed with respect to $\sim_L$, if an optimal protocol exists at all. Our future work will be oriented towards finding sufficient conditions for a layered protocol to be optimal. We plan to also extend this study to those lookup-based protocols that are not layered.

References

1. Avoine, G., Bingöl, M.A., Kardas, S., Lauradoux, C., Martin, B.: A framework for analyzing RFID distance bounding protocols. J. Comput. Secur. **19**(2), 289–317 (2011)
2. Avoine, G., Tchamkerten, A.: An efficient distance bounding rfid authentication protocol: balancing false-acceptance rate and memory requirement. In: Samarati, P., Yung, M., Martinelli, F., Ardagna, C.A. (eds.) ISC 2009. LNCS, vol. 5735, pp. 250–261. Springer, Heidelberg (2009). doi:10.1007/978-3-642-04474-8_21
3. Boureanu, I., Mitrokotsa, A., Vaudenay, S.: Secure and lightweight distance-bounding. In: Avoine, G., Kara, O. (eds.) LightSec 2013. LNCS, vol. 8162, pp. 97–113. Springer, Heidelberg (2013). doi:10.1007/978-3-642-40392-7_8
4. Brands, S., Chaum, D.: Distance-bounding protocols. In: Helleseth, T. (ed.) EUROCRYPT 1993. LNCS, vol. 765, pp. 344–359. Springer, Heidelberg (1994). doi:10.1007/3-540-48285-7_30
5. Bussard, L., Bagga, W.: Distance-bounding proof of knowledge to avoid realtime attacks. In: Sasaki, R., Qing, S., Okamoto, E., Yoshiura, H. (eds.) SEC 2005. IAICT, vol. 181, pp. 223–238. Springer, Boston, MA (2005). doi:10.1007/0-387-25660-1_15
6. Desmedt, Y., Goutier, C., Bengio, S.: Special uses and abuses of the fiatshamir passport protocol (extended abstract). In: Pomerance, C. (ed.) CRYPTO 1987. LNCS, vol. 293, pp. 21–39. Springer, Heidelberg (1988). doi:10.1007/3-540-48184-2_3
7. Özhan Gürel, A., Arslan, A., Akgün, M.: Non-uniform stepping approach to rfid distance bounding problem. In: Garcia-Alfaro, J., Navarro-Arribas, G., Cavalli, A., Leneutre, J. (eds.) DPM/SETOP -2010. LNCS, vol. 6514, pp. 64–78. Springer, Heidelberg (2011). doi:10.1007/978-3-642-19348-4_6
8. Hancke, G.P., Kuhn, M.G.: An RFID distance bounding protocol. In: Proceedings of the First International Conference on Security and Privacy for Emerging Areas in Communications Networks (SecureComm-2005), Athens, Greece, 5–9 September 2005, pp. 67–73. IEEE Computer Society, Washington, DC (2005)
9. Kardaş, S., Kiraz, M.S., Bingöl, M.A., Demirci, H.: A novel RFID distance bounding protocol based on physically unclonable functions. In: Juels, A., Paar, C. (eds.) RFIDSec 2011. LNCS, vol. 7055, pp. 78–93. Springer, Heidelberg (2012). doi:10.1007/978-3-642-25286-0_6
10. Kim, C.H., Avoine, G.: RFID distance bounding protocols with mixed challenges. IEEE Trans. Wireless Commun. **10**(5), 1618–1626 (2011)
11. Kim, C.H., Avoine, G., Koeune, F., Standaert, F.-X., Pereira, O.: The swissknife RFID distance bounding protocol. In: Lee, P.J., Cheon, J.H. (eds.) ICISC 2008. LNCS, vol. 5461, pp. 98–115. Springer, Heidelberg (2009). doi:10.1007/978-3-642-00730-9_7
12. Mauw, S., Toro-Pozo, J., Trujillo-Rasua, R.: A Class of precomputation-based distance-bounding protocols. In: Proceedings of the 1st IEEE European Symposium on Security and Privacy - EuroS&P'16. Saarbrücken, Germany (2016)
13. Munilla, J., Peinado, A.: Distance bounding protocols for RFID enhanced by using void-challenges and analysis in noisy channels. Wirel. Commun. Mob. Comput. **8**(9), 1227–1232 (2008)
14. Trujillo-Rasua, R., Martin, B., Avoine, G.: The poulidor distance-bounding protocol. In: Ors Yalcin, S.B. (ed.) RFIDSec 2010. LNCS, vol. 6370, pp. 239–257. Springer, Heidelberg (2010). doi:10.1007/978-3-642-16822-2_19

Towards Quantum Distance Bounding Protocols

Aysajan Abidin[(⊠)], Eduard Marin, Dave Singelée, and Bart Preneel

imec-COSIC KU Leuven, Leuven, Belgium
{aysajan.abidin,eduard.marin,dave.singelee,bart.preneel}@esat.kuleuven.be

Abstract. Distance Bounding (DB) is a security technique through which it is possible to determine an upper-bound on the physical distance between two parties (denoted as verifier and prover). These protocols typically combine physical properties of the communication channel with cryptographic challenge-response schemes. A key challenge to design secure DB protocols is to keep the time required by the prover to process the challenges and compute and transmit the responses as low as possible. For this purpose, different implementation approaches have been proposed in the literature, both in the analog as in the digital domain. Moreover, different types of communication channels have been proposed as well to find an optimal balance between security and implementation feasibility. This paper is the first to evaluate the feasibility of implementing DB protocols using quantum communication. Unlike conventional DB protocols, which execute the rapid-bit exchanges over a Radio Frequency (RF) or ultrasound channel, our quantum-based DB protocol makes use of quantum-bit (qubit) transmissions and detection during the challenge-response phase. Our protocol offers security against distance fraud, mafia fraud and terrorist attacks. We also discuss how to protect against some specific implementation attacks, such as double read-out and quantum attacks, and give an overview of the main implementation challenges as well as possible limitations.

Keywords: Distance bounding · Quantum transmission and measurement · Qubits

1 Introduction

Distance Bounding (DB) protocols allow to establish an upper-bound on the physical distance between two parties which are typically denoted as verifier and prover. For this, DB protocols rely on cryptography and physics. For example, RF-based DB protocols leverage on the fact that it is impossible for adversaries to transmit signals faster than the speed of light. Brands and Chaum [1] were the first to introduce a DB protocol to counter relay attacks in Automatic Teller Machines (ATM) systems. Subsequently, a number of articles [2–8] has contributed not only to improve or design new DB protocols, but also to implement these protocols. There are two main families of DB protocols: those that are derived from the protocol proposed by Brands and Chaum [1] and the ones that

© Springer International Publishing AG 2017
G.P. Hancke and K. Markantonakis (Eds.): RFIDSec 2016, LNCS 10155, pp. 151–162, 2017.
DOI: 10.1007/978-3-319-62024-4_11

are based on the protocol proposed by Hancke and Kuhn [2]. All DB protocols have a *setup* and a *rapid-bit exchange phase*. In the setup phase, the verifier and the prover agree or commit to some information that will be used in the next protocol phase(s). In the rapid-bit exchange phase, which is the most difficult phase to implement due to severe timing constraints, the verifier sends a series of single-bit challenges to which the prover replies with single-bit responses. The verifier can then obtain its distance to the prover by measuring the Round-Trip Time (RTT) between sending its challenge and receiving the response from the prover. In some DB protocols, there is also a *verification phase* for checking that all protocol steps were performed using the parameters previously agreed on.

The goal of DB protocols is typically to protect against the following attacks: (i) *distance fraud*, (ii) *mafia fraud* and (iii) *terrorist fraud*. In a distance fraud attack, a dishonest prover tries to convince a verifier that it is in the verifier's close proximity while in reality it is far away. Mafia fraud (or relay attacks) involve an honest prover, a verifier and a Man-In-The-Middle (MITM) adversary. More specifically, the adversary uses a proxy-prover close to the verifier and a proxy-verifier close to the legitimate prover to relay over a long distance the messages exchanged between both parties. In a terrorist fraud attack, a dishonest prover collaborates with the adversary to convince the verifier that he is in its close proximity, while actually it is the adversary who is close to the verifier. It is common to assume that the prover only wants to collude with the adversary without revealing any information about its long-term secret key. This would prevent any attempt by the adversary to use the long-term secret key to conduct attacks at a later stage.

Our contributions. This paper investigates the feasibility of implementing quantum-based distance bounding protocols. The main physical principle upon which our protocol is based, is that unlike bits sent over conventional channels, qubits cannot neither be measured without modifying their states nor be decoded before fully receiving them. Without knowing the basis of the qubits, which the prover and verifier agreed upon based on a shared secret key, adversaries can only guess the qubits that are being sent. Therefore, our proposal by itself is resistant to some of the well-known DB attacks. We also note that our proposal could be transformed into a post-quantum DB by just replacing the PseudoRandom Function (PRF), used in the initialisation phase, by a post-quantum PRF. Based on a theoretical analysis, we estimate the delay introduced by each of the hardware components at the prover, and conclude that our solution keeps this delay at a reasonable level compared to other implementation approaches. Finally, we also evaluate our scheme against some implementation-specific attacks, more in particular double read-out and quantum attacks, and then elaborate on the main implementation challenges and possible limitations.

Paper outline. Section 2 gives an overview of related work. Section 3 provides the necessary background on quantum communication and qubits. Next, Sect. 4 describes our quantum-based distance bounding protocol, whereas a detailed security analysis of our solution is given in Sect. 5. Section 6 discusses the feasibility of our proposed implementation approach. Section 7 gives concluding remarks.

2   Related Work

The security provided by DB protocols, which measure the RTT to estimate the distance between prover and verifier, relies on the fact that the prover is able to process the challenge and then compute and transmit the response in negligible time compared to the propagation time. If the verifier overestimates the prover's processing time (i.e., the prover can process the challenge faster), the prover can pretend to be closer than it actually is. On the contrary, if the verifier underestimates the prover's processing time, the prover may not be able to successfully execute the DB protocol with the verifier, even when it is in its close proximity. As the processing time depends only on the prover's hardware, which is not under the control of the verifier, for DB protocols to be resistant to attacks the processing time at the prover needs to be as close as possible to zero.

Intuitively, one possibility would be to send the response over an ultrasonic channel, provided that this channel is relatively slow compared to the processing time at the prover. However, ultrasonic-based DB protocols are vulnerable to worm-hole attacks [9]. This attack involves a MITM adversary who uses both a proxy-prover and a proxy-verifier to convert the audio signal to a radiofrequency (RF) signal (and vice versa) in order to accelerate the transmission time on the relay channel. This would allow adversaries to extend the maximum distance from which the verifier successfully authenticates the prover by several orders of magnitude.

For practical realisations of DB protocols over an RF channel, the main challenge for the prover is to compute the response using a function that can be executed significantly fast. We distinguish between two types of functions, depending on whether they are conducted in the analog or digital domain. Brands and Chaum [1] proposed that the response sent by the prover is the result of the XOR between the challenge and a value agreed upon between the verifier and the prover in the setup phase. Hancke and Kuhn [2] proposed to choose a value from two locally stored registers at the prover depending on the challenge sent by the verifier. Although both operations are relatively simple, they require the prover to convert the signal from the analog to the digital domain using an Analog-to-Digital Converter (ADC), demodulate the signal to obtain the challenge bit, compute and modulate the response bit and convert the signal from the digital to the analog domain using a Digital-to-Analog Converter (DAC). This process typically results in a processing time delay in the order of at least a few hundred nano seconds. This large delay allows adversaries with dedicated hardware to successfully execute the protocol with the verifier from several dozen meters away.

Another approach consists of computing the response by the prover based on a function that can be directly executed in the analog domain. Rasmussen and

Capkun proposed an analog function – which they call Challenge Reflection with Channel Selection (CRCS) – for which the prover reflects the challenges sent by the verifier in a specific way depending on the received challenge and the response (i.e. the value of the register) [4]. The prover demodulates the signal to recover the challenges only after finishing the rapid-bit exchange phase. This approach does not introduce any delay in the time-critical rapid-bit exchange phase, while still allows the prover to prove knowledge of the challenge bits in the last protocol phase. However, Ranganathan et al. found that the CRCS implementation is vulnerable to a double read-out attack, which allows an adversary to obtain the values of the prover's two registers simultaneously [6]. Ranganathan et al. proposed an hybrid solution – which they call Switched Challenge Reflector with Carrier Shifting (SCRCS) – that prevents the double read-out attack by introducing a new digital component that disables part of the analog circuitry after detecting the challenge [6]. However, both the analog and hybrid approaches require complex hardware and storage at the prover.

We are the first to investigate the feasibility of implementing DB protocols using quantum communication. The closest work to ours is the quantum-based positioning system proposed by Buhrman et al. [10]. In their paper, multiple verifiers interact with the prover to determine its position. In our paper, we apply quantum techniques to DB protocols.

3   Background on Quantum Communication

In the classical (non-quantum) domain, communication can always be eavesdropped or copied. This is in contrast to quantum communication where the transmitted information is encoded in non-orthogonal quantum states that cannot be reliably read or copied, due to the Heisenberg uncertainty principle in quantum physics. Any attempt by an adversary to eavesdrop the quantum communication will introduce random errors.

Qubits. A qubit is a unit of quantum information, just as a bit (0 or 1) is the classical unit of information. A qubit is a vector in a 2-dimensional Hilbert space (a vector space with inner product). The basis $\{|0\rangle = \begin{bmatrix} 1 \\ 0 \end{bmatrix}, \ |1\rangle = \begin{bmatrix} 0 \\ 1 \end{bmatrix}\}$ for a qubit is called the computational basis, while the basis $\{|+\rangle = (|0\rangle + |1\rangle)/\sqrt{2}, \ |-\rangle = (|0\rangle - |1\rangle)/\sqrt{2}\}$ is called the diagonal (or the Hadamard) basis. In general, a normalised quantum state can be expressed as a superposition of $|0\rangle$ and $|1\rangle$ as

$$a\,|0\rangle + b\,|1\rangle,$$

where $a, b \in \mathbb{C}$ satisfying $|a|^2 + |b|^2 = 1$.

If we measure a qubit in state $a\,|0\rangle + b\,|1\rangle$ in the computational basis (i.e., if the state is projected on the computational basis), then with probability $|a|^2$ we obtain $|0\rangle$ and with probability $|b|^2$ we obtain $|1\rangle$. If the state of a qubit is unknown, the values a and b cannot be determined with a single measurement.

And after a measurement, say in the $\{|0\rangle, |1\rangle\}$ basis, the qubit state collapses into $|0\rangle$ or $|1\rangle$, which is different from the original state.

Now let us take a closer look at the four states: $|0\rangle$, $|1\rangle$, $|+\rangle$, and $|-\rangle$. It is straightforward to see that:

$$|0\rangle = (|+\rangle + |-\rangle)/\sqrt{2}$$

and

$$|1\rangle = (|+\rangle - |-\rangle)/\sqrt{2}.$$

Therefore, if the qubits $|0\rangle$ and $|1\rangle$ are measured in the computational basis (i.e., projected onto the $\{|0\rangle, |1\rangle\}$ basis), then the states are not disturbed; whereas the measurement in the Hadamard basis destroys the state, since in this case $|+\rangle$ and $|-\rangle$ are obtained with equal probability. Similarly, if the qubits $|+\rangle$ and $|-\rangle$ are measured in the Hadamard basis, then the states are not disturbed; whereas the measurement in the computational basis destroys the state, since in this case $|0\rangle$ and $|1\rangle$ are obtained with equal probability. It is exactly this principle that we will use in our protocol.

More specifically, in our proposal we make use of these four states, which are usually called the BB84 states in quantum key distribution (QKD) [11]. Namely, we propose to implement the rapid challenge-response phase of a DB protocol by employing qubits, as opposed to the classical approach using RF signals or ultra-wide-band (UWB) pulses. These four states correspond to different polarisations of photons. These photons are sent from prover to verifier, or vice versa, via laser beams. The states $|0\rangle$ and $|1\rangle$ respectively correspond to horizontally $\rightarrow$ and vertically $\uparrow$ polarised photons, while the states $|+\rangle$ and $|-\rangle$ to $\nearrow$ and $\nwarrow$ polarised photons. The qubit $|0\rangle$ or $|+\rangle$ is used to encode the classical bit value 0 and $|1\rangle$ or $|-\rangle$ the value 1. The qubits are measured either in the computational or the Hadamard basis. In what follows, we let 0 to denote the computational (+) basis and 1 the Hadamard ($\times$) basis (Table 1).

Table 1. An encoding rule. In our proposal, the value 0 corresponds to the computational (or simply + basis), and 1 to the Hadamard (or simply $\times$) basis.

Data	Computational (or +) basis	Hadamard (or $\times$) basis
0	$|0\rangle$ (i.e., $\rightarrow$)	$|+\rangle$ (i.e., $\nearrow$)
1	$|1\rangle$ (i.e., $\uparrow$)	$|-\rangle$ (i.e., $\nwarrow$)

4   Our Quantum-Based Distance Bounding Protocol

Our approach is based on the exchange of polarised photons. Similarly as in the DB protocol of Hancke and Kuhn, the prover and verifier first execute a setup phase in which random nonces are exchanged. Based on these nonces and a shared secret, both parties compute the output a of a PseudoRandom Function (PRF). During the rapid-bit exchange phase, the verifier encodes randomly chosen challenge bits into polarisation states of photons in the bases determined by the bitstring a.

For example, if $a_i = 0$, then a challenge bit 0 would be encoded as the $\rightarrow$ photon, whereas a challenge bit 1 would be encoded as the $\uparrow$ photon. Similarly, if $a_i = 1$, then a challenge bit 0 would be encoded as the $\nearrow$ polarised photon, whereas a challenge bit 1 would be encoded as the $\nwarrow$ polarised photon. If $a = 01011$ and the challenge bits are 10010, then a series of photons polarised as $\uparrow, \nearrow, \rightarrow, \nwarrow, \nearrow$, respectively, will be sent by the verifier. The prover then decodes the photons in the bases determined by the PRF output (denoted as a) and sends its responses as photons that encode the decoded results in the bases determined by the bits of a. Since the encoding and decoding bases are the same, the verifier receives photons in the same polarisation states as the ones that were sent. From the RTT of the photons, the verifier calculates an upper-bound on the physical distance between itself and the prover.

This is similar to QKD, except that now the two communicating parties use the same bases as opposed to the randomly chosen bases in the case of QKD. An adversary would need to guess what encoding basis is used to successfully intercept and decode the verifier's signal and then send the result back to the verifier. Therefore, there is a 50% chance that the adversary guesses wrong. Thus, as a consequence of the quantum *uncertainty principle*, the adversary will destroy the information encoded by the verifier and render the received responses uncorrelated to the challenges that are sent.

A schematic description of a DB protocol employing the aforementioned technique, using polarised photons, is given in Fig. 1. As can be seen, during the challenge-response phase, instead of sending and receiving classical challenge-response pairs, the verifier sends and receives quantum challenge-response pairs. As long as the prover is the legitimate prover with whom the verifier computed $a = f_{x_p}(N_v, N_p)$, the verifier always receives photons that are in the same polarisation states as the ones that are sent, since the photons are encoded/decoded in the same bases determined by the bit values of a. The prover stores the decoded bits in a register c and uses them during the verification phase. In this third phase of the protocol, the prover computes a MAC on the ID of prover and verifier, the nonces exchanged in the setup phase, and the bitstring c. This last step is critical for security. Without the prover sending a MAC in the verification phase, an adversary could just reflect all the photons back to the verifier without actually performing any measurements at all.

To summarise, the main components needed for our solution are an encoder, a decoder, and a data processing unit. The encoder consists of a tuneable polariser which polarises incoming photons or laser pulses. The incoming pulses are polarised according to the previously mentioned encoding rule, e.g., $c = 0$ is encoded as $\nwarrow$ polarised photon if the corresponding register value is 1. The decoder consists of a detector and a data processing unit. The detector measures the photons in $+$ basis if the register value is 0 and in $\times$ basis if the register value is 1. The data processing unit analyses the measurement result and outputs 0/1.

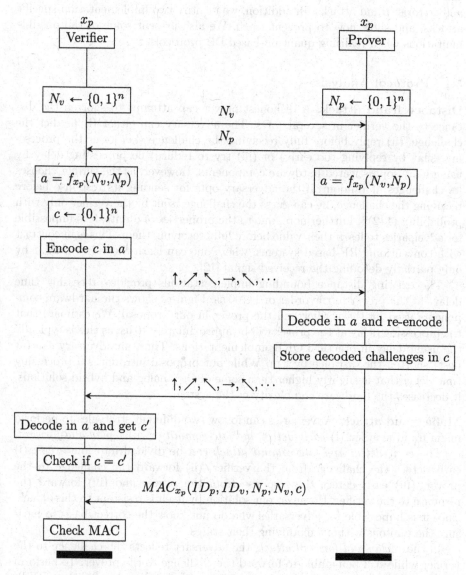

Fig. 1. Example of a quanutm-based DB protocol using polarised photons in the rapid-bit exchange phase. It should be noted that each challenge is sent only after the verifier received the response to the previous challenge.

5   Security Analysis

This section analyses the resistance of our protocol to distance fraud, mafia fraud and terrorist fraud attacks. In addition, we identify two implementation-specific attacks, and show how to prevent them. We also present some of the possible limitations when realising quantum-based DB protocols.

5.1   Protocol Analysis

Distance fraud attack. A dishonest prover can attempt to shorten the distance to the verifier in several ways. The adversary can either (i) predict the challenge, (ii) reply before fully receiving the challenge (i.e. lower the processing delay by replying too early) or (iii) try to reduce the processing delay by using more sophisticated hardware components. However, as the verifier chooses its challenges at random, if the adversary opts for sending its response before receiving the challenge, he can guess the challenges sent by the verifier only with probability $(1/2)^n$. Furthermore, due to the properties of qubits, it is impossible for adversaries to learn their value before fully receiving them. This is in contrast with conventional RF-based systems, where one can learn the value of a bit by only partially decoding the received signal [12].

The existing distance bounding implementations provide processing time delays at the prover in the order of 1–100 ns. Figure 2 shows the hardware components used by the verifier and the prover in our proposal. We estimate that the processing delay at the prover will be approximately 10 ns, as this is typically the usual delay in practical QKD implementations. Thus, an adversary can (at best) shorten the distance by 3 m. While our proposal introduces a processing time delay that is slightly higher than some of the analog and hybrid solutions, it decreases the hardware complexity of the system.

Mafia fraud attack. Adversaries can follow two different strategies to perform mafia fraud attacks: (i) *early-detect and late-commit* or (ii) *replay-and-forward*.

The *early-detect and late-commit attack* can be divided into four steps: (i) early-detect the challenge from the verifier, (ii) forward the challenge to the prover, (iii) early-detect the response from the prover and (iv) forward the response to the verifier. However, our solution by itself is resistant to this attack, since it is impossible for adversaries who do not know the correct basis to measure the photons without modifying their states.

In the *replay-and-forward attack*, the adversary reflects the challenge to the verifier while still being able to forward the challenge to the prover. To perform this attack, the adversary would have to use a Photon Number Splitter (PNS). It is important to point out that this attack, which is analogous to PNS attacks on QKD implementations, can only be conducted if the challenge contains more than one photon per pulse. In that case, the adversary could reflect one photon, and decode another photon in the same pulse. The goal of the adversary is to convince the verifer that the prover decoded and encoded the photon correctly. Since our protocol has a verification phase where the prover proves knowledge of

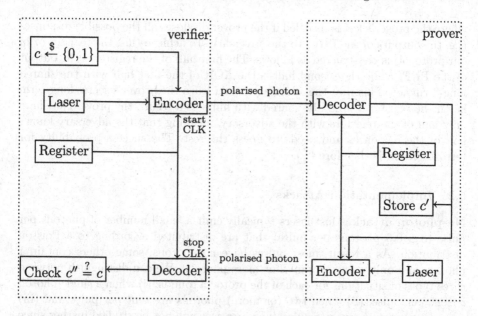

Fig. 2. High-level schematic description of our quantum-based approach during one challenge-response round. The verifier selects a random challenge bit c, encodes it into a polarisation of a photon emitted from the photon source (Laser) in the basis determined by the first bit of the Register, and starts the clock. The prover decodes the photon in the basis determined by the first bit of the Register and obtains c', which is then encoded into a polarisation of a photon emitted from the prover's photon source (Laser) in the same basis used for decoding. The prover also stores c', which will be used later in the verification phase. The verifier decodes the incoming photon in the basis previously used to encode the challenge bit and obtains c'', stops the clock, and checks whether $c'' = c$. This process is repeated as many times as the number of bits in the Register. If the number of rounds in which $c'' = c$ is above a threshold, then the verifier can use the maximum of all the RTT to compute the physical distance of the prover.

the challenges sent by the verifier, the adversary needs to forward the challenge to the prover as well. To prevent this attack, one has to avoid that photons in a pulse can be splitted. Therefore, it is necessary to use efficient single-photon sources in the design, and hence select the most appropriate laser source.

Assuming the photon splitting attack is prevented by the selection of the laser source, the mafia fraud attack succeeds with probability $\left(\frac{3}{4}\right)^n$, *i.e.* an adversary can pre-ask the prover for responses – if he guesses the pre-asked challenge correctly he always wins the round, otherwise he needs to guess the response with probability $\left(\frac{1}{2}\right)$.

Terrorist fraud attack. In the literature, protocols that are terrorist-fraud resistant are all based on a similar design approach [13]. Therefore to make our protocol terrorist-fraud resistant, one needs to implement a response function where the prover's key is revealed if the prover discloses all the possible responses (i.e. the outputs of the PRF) to the adversary. To achieve this, the register (a in our protocol) is constructed as follows. The first half of the register is the output of the PRF, while the second half is the XOR of the first half with the shared long-term key. This way, the adversary would learn the prover's secret long-term key if the register a would be shared with him. As a result, the prover can share only half of the registers with the adversary, meaning that the adversary knows half of the responses and needs to guess the rest. The success probability for terrorist fraud is therefore $\left(\frac{3}{4}\right)^n$.

5.2　Implementation Attacks

No-photon attack. Most lasers typically emit a small number of photons per pulse (e.g. 0.3 photons per pulse) that are distributed according to a Poisson distribution. As a result, most pulses have no photons, some others contain 1 photon, and only a few contain 2 or more photons. We can distinguish between three types of situations for each of the protocol rounds: (i) when a single photon is sent per pulse, (ii) when two (or more) photons are sent per pulse and (iii) when no photon is sent per pulse. The first case will not be studied further since it is the ideal case and does not introduce any security problems. The second case is relevant to perform mafia fraud attacks and is explained above. In the third case, the adversary does not need to send any response at all. This would drastically reduce the security level of the protocol, since the adversary wins in all rounds where no pulses are being sent. To overcome this limitation, one could increase the number of rounds of the protocol, to ensure that there are sufficient rounds with at least one photon being exchanged.

Double read-out attack. The goal of this attack is to exploit the specific implementation of the DB protocol to obtain the values of the two registers of the prover. A similar attack could be performed on our scheme to obtain the bases being used by the prover and the verifier. The adversary could recover the basis being used only if the prover would reuse a basis to measure different challenges and responds to each of these challenges. In practice, the attack would work as follows: the adversary first lets the prover and the verifier start executing the protocol and exchanging the nonces. The adversary then follows a pre-ask strategy, it first executes the rapid-bit exchange phase with the prover to obtain the basis being used and then executes the protocol with the verifier. For this, the adversary first encodes a photon using a basis (chosen at random) and sends it to the prover. The idea is that the adversary exploits the implementation of the protocol by sending multiple photons, using the same base, during one round of the protocol. We can distinguish between two situations depending on whether the adversary has guessed the basis used by the prover. If so, then all the challenges (i.e. photons) sent during the same round will be decoded correctly by the prover, and all the responses will be equal to the challenges. If the guess was wrong, the prover encodes the bits using the wrong basis, and will obtain random bits for each of these challenges. The adversary will notice that the responses are not equal, and hence the wrong basis was used.

The key aspect of this attack is that the adversary could send multiple challenges during a single round. To prevent this type of attack, the prover needs to have a reliable detector that updates its setting after measuring the challenges (i.e. switch to the basis of the next round) and hence avoids basis reuse in a single round.

6   Feasibility Analysis

Our proposal is similar to the quantum transmission and measurement phase of a BB84 type QKD protocol. The only difference is that in our case the preparation and measurement bases for the qubits are kept secret, while they are publicly announced in QKD. QKD has long been successfully implemented, and there are even commercially available QKD products. Since the QKD setup for the quantum transmission and measurement can be used as is to experimentally realise our proposal, the feasibility of our proposal is not an issue. However, we are interested in keeping the actual processing delay at the prover as low as possible. While the actual experimental demonstration is beyond the scope of this paper, based on the experimental results on QKD we estimate that the delay can be around 10 ns. In future work, we want to perform experiments using the QKD setup to validate the short processing delay of our proposed solution.

The three main components on both the prover and verifier sides are a single photon source, a single photon detector, and a data processing unit. All of these components are available on the market.

7   Conclusions

This paper has investigated the feasibility of implementing distance bounding protocols based on quantum communication. We proposed a quantum-based distance bounding protocol that uses a function to compute the prover's response based only on knowing the basis to measure the quantum bits. We analysed its security against various attacks and gave a theoretical analysis of the processing delay at the prover.

Acknowledgments. The authors would like to thank the anonymous reviewers for their helpful comments. This work was partially supported by the Research Council KU Leuven: C16/15/058 and by the European Commission through the SECURITY programme under FP7-SEC-2013-1-607049 EKSISTENZ.

References

1. Brands, S., Chaum, D.: Distance-bounding protocols. In: Helleseth, T. (ed.) EURO-CRYPT 1993. LNCS, vol. 765, pp. 344–359. Springer, Heidelberg (1994). doi:10.1007/3-540-48285-7_30

2. Hancke, G.P., Kuhn, M.G.: An rfid distance bounding protocol. In: Proceedings of the First International Conference on Security and Privacy for Emerging Areas in Communications Networks. SECURECOMM 2005, Computer Society, pp. 67–73. IEEE, Washington, DC (2005)

3. Tippenhauer, N.O., Čapkun, S.: ID-based secure distance bounding and localization. In: Backes, M., Ning, P. (eds.) ESORICS 2009. LNCS, vol. 5789, pp. 621–636. Springer, Heidelberg (2009). doi:10.1007/978-3-642-04444-1_38

4. Rasmussen, K.B., Čapkun, S.: Realization of rf distance bounding. In: Proceedings of the 19th USENIX Conference on Security. USENIX Security 2010, Berkeley, CA, USA, pp. 25–25. USENIX Association (2010)

5. Singelée, D., Preneel, B.: Distance bounding in noisy environments. In: Stajano, F., Meadows, C., Capkun, S., Moore, T. (eds.) ESAS 2007. LNCS, vol. 4572, pp. 101–115. Springer, Heidelberg (2007). doi:10.1007/978-3-540-73275-4_8

6. Ranganathan, A., Tippenhauer, N.O., Škorić, B., Singelée, D., Čapkun, S.: Design and implementation of a terrorist fraud resilient distance bounding system. In: Foresti, S., Yung, M., Martinelli, F. (eds.) ESORICS 2012. LNCS, vol. 7459, pp. 415–432. Springer, Heidelberg (2012). doi:10.1007/978-3-642-33167-1_24

7. Rasmussen, K.B., Castelluccia, C., Heydt-Benjamin, T.S., Capkun, S.: Proximity-based access control for implantable medical devices. In: Proceedings of the 16th ACM Conference on Computer and Communications Security. CCS 2009, pp. 410–419(2009)

8. Ranganathan, A., Danev, B., Capkun, S.: Proximity verification for contactless access control and authentication systems. In: Proceedings of the 31st Annual Computer Security Applications Conference. ACSAC 2015, pp. 271–280. ACM, New York (2015)

9. Sedighpour, S., Capkun, S., Ganeriwal, S., Srivastava, M.: Implementation of attacks on ultrasonic ranging systems, November 2005

10. Buhrman, H., Chandran, N., Fehr, S., Gelles, R., Goyal, V., Ostrovsky, R., Schaffner, C.: Position-based quantum cryptography: impossibility and constructions. SIAM J. Comput. 43(1), 150–178 (2014)

11. Bennett, C.H., Brassard, G.: Quantum cryptography: public key distribution and coin tossing. In: Proceedings of the IEEE International Conference on Computers, Systems, and Signal Processing, pp. 175–179, Bangalore, India. IEEE, New York (1984)

12. Clulow, J., Hancke, G.P., Kuhn, M.G., Moore, T.: So near and yet so far: distance-bounding attacks in wireless networks. In: Buttyán, L., Gligor, V.D., Westhoff, D. (eds.) ESAS 2006. LNCS, vol. 4357, pp. 83–97. Springer, Heidelberg (2006). doi:10.1007/11964254_9

13. Reid, J., Gonzalez Nieto, J.M., Tang, T., Senadji, B.: Detecting relay attacks with timing-based protocols. In: Proceedings of ASIACCS (2007)

Matching in Proximity Authentication and Mobile Payment EcoSystem: What Are We Missing?

Yunhui Zhuang[1,2(✉)], Alvin Chung Man Leung[1], and James Hughes[3]

[1] Department of Information Systems, City University of Hong Kong,
Kowloon Tong, Hong Kong
yhzhuang2-c@my.cityu.edu.hk, acmleung@cityu.edu.hk
[2] Department of Computer Science, City University of Hong Kong,
Kowloon Tong, Hong Kong
[3] Jack Baskin School of Engineering, University of California,
Santa Cruz, CA, USA
japhughe@ucsc.edu

Abstract. During the past decade, cybersecurity threats have drawn everyone's attention and it's becoming a national priority in many leading countries. With the development of sophisticated mobile technology, mobile (contactless) payment insecurity, which may cause huge financial losses, is now becoming a serious threat to our daily life. During the holiday season in 2013, China's most welcome mobile payment system provider - Alipay - lost over 20 GB worth of customer data in a security breach, which affected at least 15 million customers. Even though the company has promised to evaluate the security of the system and to take necessary measures to protect customer's data, are we still safe with the payment? In this paper, we investigate several security vulnerabilities for Alipay wallet, which may cause individual's personal data and financial losses. This is due to not only less regulation by authorities but also the failure of enabling secure proximity authentication during mobile payment. By going through these surprising vulnerabilities, we come up with some ideas on how to combat them and show how to enhance the mobile payment security by enabling proximity authentication before monetary transactions.

Keywords: Mobile payment · Alipay wallet · QR code · Security

1 Introduction

The recent burgeoning digital economy is changing how we work, interact, and live. Various practices that will impact the way of how people doing business and adapt in a world of profound digital transformation. In the meantime, the rapid growth of the on-demand economy, or sharing economy, has brought great attractions to individuals for collaborative consumption. Unlike traditional renting which measures mainly to transform a cash-flow stream in time, sharing

© Springer International Publishing AG 2017
G.P. Hancke and K. Markantonakis (Eds.): RFIDSec 2016, LNCS 10155, pp. 163–172, 2017.
DOI: 10.1007/978-3-319-62024-4_12

happens contingent on a realized need [1,2]. Likewise, the mobile ecosystem on which the sharing economy relies has been one of the most successful markets in recent years [3,4]. Tens of thousands of mobile apps have been developed in various app markets such as Google Play Store and Apple App Store. The demand for mobile apps keeps increasing in the sense that billions of people are adopting smartphones and tablets as their main Internet devices. This successful two-sided market is opening up a post-PC era in the IT industry [5].

Founded in 2010, Uber has enabled peer-to-peer sharing of riding seats, currently boasting over 300 cities in 58 countries and has a market capitalization of over 40 billion US dollars in 2015 [18]. In China, Uber extends its partnership with Alipay to provide one-stop cashless mobile payment services. Recently, two tech giants even expand the partnership to facilitate payment in RMB when using Uber outside China. However, while people enjoy these sharing services through the mobile ecosystem, the concerns for providing security and protecting personal privacy when conducting monetary transactions via mobile platform remain a big challenge.

In this paper, we investigate several security vulnerabilities for Alipay wallet, which may cause individual's personal data and financial losses. This is due to not only less regulation by authorities but also the failure of enabling secure proximity authentication during mobile payment. We also suggest some ideas on how to combat those vulnerabilities and show how to enhance the mobile payment security by enabling proximity authentication before monetary transactions. This paper sheds some light on the design and analysis of secure mobile payment solutions.

2   Mobile Payment Ecosystem

As per [16], a successful mobile payment ecosystem needs to have five components: (1) mobile payment at the POS (Point-of-Sale), (2) mobile payment as the POS, (3) mobile payment platform, (4) independent mobile payment system, and (5) direct carrier billing. In addition to five traditional payment entities (Cardholder, Merchant, Acquiring bank, Issuing bank, Card associations), two new entities are introduced (Mobile Network Operator and Mobile Payment Service Provider). According to Juniper Research report that global mobile payments to reach USD 3.6 trillion in 2016, up from USD 3 trillion on 2015, resulting in a 20% increase [17]. Figure 1 shows a modern process of mobile payment ecosystem for monetary transactions. There are total seven entities involved in the system. This ecosystem also allows one user to transfer money to another user within this mobile payment system, where the whole process only involves card and smartphone holders and the designated mobile payment service provider. The most famous example would be the red pocket of Alipay wallet.

2.1   QR Code

QR Code (Quick Response Code) has gained popularity in our daily life with a broad range of advantages for various applications, such as the venue booking,

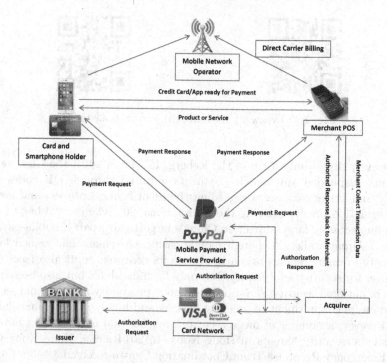

Fig. 1. Mobile payment process

polling, and classroom teaching. Recently, QR Code has been used in mobile payment in China. A QR Code is actually a 2-D machine-readable "codes" usually consisting of a matrix of various size black and white "square dots" as shown in Fig. 2a. It encodes simple-to-read data (e.g. a link to a website or a short alphanumeric text) that can be read and displayed by a mobile device and can hold more than 3 kb of data. It was invented by Denso Wave in Japan back to 1994 for supply chain purpose with the main focus on tracking automotive parts during the production process. The production and deployment of a QR Code are so cheap that many organizations use QR Codes as their medium of choice in advertising to attract potential customers. In Hong Kong, QR Codes have been adopted in classroom teaching, where instructors can get an instant feedback from students [21].

2.2 Security Challenges

Recently, QR codes have been misused as phishing attacks where attackers encode malicious links into the codes to redirect users to phishing websites [19]. Figure 2 shows an example of QR Code individual module modification (phishing) attack, where an attacker modifies the original QR code to a malicious City University of Hong Kong website.

Fig. 2. (a) www.cityu.edu.hk (b) www.c1tyu.edu.hk

However, this is only a tip of the iceberg. In March 2014, the Chinese central bank suspended any mobile payments initiated through QR codes amid security and privacy concerns regarding the identification process and government regulation involved during the transactions [20]. The central bank's edict has an immediately large impact on China's largest third-party mobile-payment provider: Alipay wallet. Although mobile cashless payment has gained lots of popularity in many regions primarily due to its convenience, it also faces many challenges for security and privacy. Not only for individuals but also becoming a matter of national security. A nation's economic prosperity and national security depend on its commitment to securing healthy and highly reliable financial system. However, a number of mega security breaches and cyberattacks have put serious cybersecurity threats in Hong Kong. In 2014 alone, Hong Kong Computer Emergency Response Team Coordination Centre received 3,443 reports of security incidents, with a sharp increase of 103% over 2013 [6].

To curb mobile and cybersecurity threats to the financial system, Hong Kong Monetary Authority (HKMA) has mandated every bank to incorporate two-factor authentication for online transactions in 2005 to tackle identity theft [9]. Recently HKMA also initiated a new payment method –e-Cheque– to replace old-fashioned paper-based cheque and has already rolled out in the first quarter of 2016 [8]. e-Cheque is facing a challenge similar to Bitcoin on double spending, and thus its digital signature is verified by a centralized presentment entity. Almost at the same time, China's tech giant, Alipay, has infiltrated into Hong Kong's mobile payment market. With a large number of customers in mainland China, Alipay has partnered with many sharing services to provide easy-to-use mobile payment solutions, e.g., Uber, DiDi Taxi, group buying services. The concept and practice of mobile sharing economy have been fast becoming a mainstream phenomenon across China. Meanwhile, researchers are now beginning to weigh in with the deeper analysis in terms of security and privacy, which turn out to be one critical area of argument when conducting mobile-based monetary transactions.

3   The Alipay Wallet

In this section, we first give a brief introduction of how the Alipay wallet works in Sect. 3.1 and some security vulnerabilities when using Alipay wallet QR Code payment in Sect. 3.2.

Unlike Apple Pay, which implemented the new EMVCo tokenization specification [15], Alipay wallet is using QR Code to conduct the payment, as shown in Fig. 3. By linking bank cards to the Alipay wallet, a user can top up the wallet balance by transfer money from the linked bank cards. The payment can be done by generating a one-time QR Code and scanned by merchant's EFTPOS.

A certain number of mobile payment apps across different countries in various app stores are certainly innovating the way of new payment philosophy. Besides Alipay, there exist some mobile payment applications are also using QR codes, such as WeChat[1], PayCash[2], LevelUp[3], and GO4Q[4], which all apply the QR code in traditional commercial settings. The QR Code payment is gaining popularity fast in mainland China due to its low entry barrier and convenient for consumers as compared to the traditional on-the-go payment methods.

(a)   (b)   (c)   (d)

Fig. 3. Alipay wallet

3.1   Payment Process for Alipay Wallet

The layout of Alipay wallet is shown in Fig. 3a–d. The users can check their balance and top-up money to the wallet by linking one or more debit/credit cards (Fig. 3b–c), or authorize Alipay wallet to direct deduct money from the debit/credit cards (Fig. 3c).

To make a payment at the merchant, simply tap the "Pay" button in Fig. 3a to generate a one-time 1-D barcode and a 2-D QR Code (in Fig. 3d), both of which are associated with an 18-digit number that is the identification number for this particular transaction. After merchant's EFTPOS scans the QR Code, the payment can be made instantly.

The payment is designed in such a way that users do not have to input any password or enable NFC on their smartphone. Alipay claims that once the

---

[1] https://pay.weixin.qq.com, accessed at: 10/15/2016.
[2] http://www.paycash.eu/, accessed at: 10/15/2016.
[3] https://www.thelevelup.com/, accessed at: 10/15/2016.
[4] http://go4q.mobi/, accessed at: 10/15/2016.

QR code is scanned, the Alipay wallet will verify its source before carrying out payment instructions and sensitive user's information is stripped. Moreover, the QR code that was scanned by the EFTPOS will be encrypted and signed by RSA signature. The final payment process can only be made through Alipay's backend servers. The developer platform for any interested party who wants to incorporate Alipay API to their payment interface does not disclose further information on how this payment process actually proceeds. However, we will show in next section that the aforementioned claim is actually too strong to provide minimum security protection against customers' security and privacy concerns.

3.2   Security Vulnerabilities with Alipay Wallet

At the beginning of 2014, the high profile of clampdown of QR code payment by China's central bank amid security and privacy concerns has spark controversy on the design of this new technology, which may lead to security issues. In order to speed up the payment process, many apps allow a small amount of payment to bypass authentication so that anyone with possession of a smartphone can make the payment without proving he/she is the true owner or the account holder.

Online QR code Fraud Case. There has been an online fraud case in China during the holiday season in 2014 that exhibits the weakness of QR code payment. The attack is described as below:

1. A user with an Alipay wallet account goes online shopping via smartphone and gets ready to pay for an item.
2. The online shop shows a QR Code next to the payment screen claiming it's like some kind of cash rebate (e.g., the customer can claim back a certain amount of money after scanning this QR Code).
3. The user snaps the QR code without any suspicious and the data embedded within the QR code redirects the user to quietly download a piece of malware even without asking for user's permission.
4. The malware abuse the "Password Reset" feature of the user's Alipay account and reset his/her password by forwarding the password reset SMS to the attacker's phone instead.
5. As a result, the attacker got user's Alipay account and stole RMB 39,000 (approx USD 6,000).

Although this attack is not directly to the QR code payment, it shows the potential risk of using any uncertified QR code which could lead to unexpected threats. This type of attack on a smartphone is known as "attagging", where the victim even does not know his money was stolen from the Alipay wallet.

Some Takeaways for Alipay Wallet

1. Alipay wallet supports offline QR code payment, which means a smartphone without Internet connection can make payment by showing the QR code to the merchant EFTPOS for scanning. The user may receive an SMS showing how much money was deducted after this transaction.

2. Each generated QR code is acting like a "one-time pad" and its "TTL" is 60 s. The QR code cannot be used more than once, regardless the payment is successful or not.
3. Enforced from Version 9.2 onwards, the payment screen which shows generated QR code cannot take screenshot due to a "FLAG_SECURE" method by Android.

No Authentication before/after Scanning QR Code. We have successfully conducted an attack by taking a photo of newly generated QR code from phone A installed with Alipay wallet (Fig. 4), and use the photo stored in phone B without Alipay wallet (Fig. 3d) to make the payment. This attack demonstrates the contradiction claims made by Alipay that it will first verify the source of QR code and its integrity before carrying out payment instructions.

Fig. 4. Photo taken from another phone

Attack on Rooted Android Phone. Since Alipay 9.2, it blocks the screenshot in the payment screen due to a "FLAG_SECURE" method in onCreate() and before setContentView as shown in Listing 1.1. According to Android, this window flag will treat the content of current window as secure, preventing it from appearing in screenshots or from being viewed on non-secure displays. However, Listing 1.1 shows how to remove FLAG_SECURE to enable screenshot.

Listing 1.1. Set/Clear Window Flag.

```
Window win = getWindow();
win.addFlags(WindowManager.LayoutParams.FLAG_SECURE); //Set Flag_Secure

win.clearFlags(WindowManager.LayoutParams.FLAG_SECURE); //Remove Flag_Secure
```

Without a rooted phone, it is almost impossible for anyone to remove this flag. However, according to a report by Tencent in 2014, the rooted Android phones in China comprised of 27.44% of all Android phones [7]. With a rooted phone, it is possible to remove this flag by installing a Xposed framework and a DisableFlagSecure module to disable "FLAG_SECURE" on Android system-wide (Fig. 5 shows an unrooted phone installed with the framework and module). This

(a)   (b)

Fig. 5. Xposed framework and DisableFlagSecure module

lets the user take screenshots and do screen capture even without notifying the user. Therefore, by launching a similar attack above, but instead first try to detect whether victim's phone is rooted or not, and then install the framework and module on victim's phone without victim's consent. Now the attacker has unlimited access to victim's Alipay wallet and takes screenshots without the knowledge of the victim. As we demonstrated above, anyone can bring the newly generated QR code within one minute to make the payment.

4   Ideas on Possible Solutions

We believe above mentioned vulnerabilities are very serious design flaws in terms of security and privacy concerns. We hereby present some ideas on possible solutions to combat these vulnerabilities.

4.1   Visual Distance Bounding with QR Code

This idea is inspired by a set of state-of-the-art proximity-based authentication protocols proposed by prominent researchers [10–14]. A distance bounding protocol is the combination of distance checking and authentication. It would be perfect to be executed before monetary transaction initiated by QR code. Our idea goes as follows:

1. Each Alipay wallet user is in possession of a secret key x but, for the purpose of forward security, the secret key is updated each time a new one-time 18-digit random number (this random number, r) is generated and securely stored in the wallet, e.g., $x = \mathsf{Enc}(x, r)$.
2. The user taps to generate this random number ready for the payment.
3. The Alipay wallet uses this random number as a session key sk to hash the user's secret key x by a one-way collision-resistant hash function and generate a fixed n-bit output for distance bounding.

4. The payment terminal runs the distance bounding protocol with user's Alipay wallet via a designated wireless channel.
5. If both user's distance and authenticity are verified by the payment terminal, the payment can be done instantly.

Steps 1–5 can effectively prevent the attack described in Sect. 3.2, while there still exist several challenges with this approach. In a real-life implementation, the communication between the payment terminal and the smartphone would be challenging. In the current setting, the communication is limited to capturing a QR code since no authentication or distance checking is performed. However, a stable and reliable network connectivity is essential for executing a distance bounding protocol.

4.2 One-Time Password

When a user makes a transaction with Alipay wallet, a one-time password via an SMS will be sent to user's registered mobile phone. The user is then required to verify transaction details and input this unique password to complete the transaction. The drawback of this approach would be slowing down the payment process in the sense that an SMS may be delayed/lost because of the traffic of the mobile network.

5 Concluding Remarks

In this paper, we investigated several security vulnerabilities for Alipay wallet and suggest some possible solutions to fix them. We believe that these vulnerabilities are mainly due to the failure of enabling proximity authentication during mobile payment with Alipay wallet. We also showed how to enhance the mobile payment security by enabling proximity authentication before the monetary transactions.

Acknowledgment. This work was supported by a research grant (Project Number: 2015.A1.030.16A) from the Public Policy Research Funding Scheme of the Central Policy Unit of the Hong Kong Special Administrative Region Government. We also thank anonymous reviewers' valuable comments and PC Chairs' shepherding.

References

1. Weber, T.A.: The question of ownership in a sharing economy. In: 2015 48th Hawaii International Conference on System Sciences (HICSS), Kauai, HI, pp. 4874–4883 (2015)
2. Weber, T.A.: Intermediation in a Sharing Economy: Insurance, Moral Hazard, and Rent Extraction. Journal of Management Information Systems. SSRN: http://ssrn.com/abstract=2439110. Accessed 15 Nov 2016
3. Petsas, T., Papadogiannakis, A., Polychronakis, M., Markatos, E.P., Karagiannis, T.: Rise of the planet of the apps: a systematic study of the mobile app ecosystem. In: Proceedings of the Internet Measurement Conference, pp. 277–290 (2013)

4. Breshahan, T., Greenstein, S.: Economics of the internet and mobile computing: the next platform rivalry. Am. Econ. Rev. Pap. Proc. **104**(5), 475–480 (2014)
5. Lee, G.M., Lee, J., Whinston, A.B.: Matching mobile applications for cross promotion. In: Proceedings of the Workshop on e-Business (2014)
6. HKPC Warns of Intensive Cyber Attacks in 2015. https://www.hkpc.org/en/corporate-info/media-centre/press-releases/2015/5668-hkpc-warns-of-intensive-cyber-attacks-in-2015. Accessed 15 Nov 2016
7. Tencent Mobile Security Labs: 2014 First Series Security Report of Rooted Phone. Chinese Only http://m.qq.com/security_lab/news_detail_278.html. Accessed 15 Nov 2016
8. Electronic Cheque (e-Cheque) E-Brochure. http://www.hkma.gov.hk/media/eng/doc/key-functions/finanical-infrastructure/infrastructure/retail-payment-initiatives/e-Cheque_e-brochure_Plaictrext_eng.pdf. Accessed 15 Nov 2016
9. Ryback, W.: Launch of Two-Factor Authentication for Internet Banking. Hong Kong Monetary Authority (2005)
10. Hancke, G., Kuhn, M.: An RFID distance bounding protocol. In: SecureComm 2005, pp. 67–73. IEEE Computer Society (2005)
11. Kim, C.H., Avoine, G., Koeune, F., Standaert, F.-X., Pereira, O.: The swissknife RFID distance bounding protocol. In: Lee, P.J., Cheon, J.H. (eds.) ICISC 2008. LNCS, vol. 5461, pp. 98–115. Springer, Heidelberg (2009). doi:10.1007/978-3-642-00730-9_7
12. Avoine, G., Lauradoux, C., Marin, B.: How secret-sharing can defeat terrorist fraud. In: ACM Wisec 2011, pp. 145–156. ACM SIGSAC (2011)
13. Yang, A., Zhuang, Y., Wong, D.S.: An efficient single-slow-phase mutually authenticated RFID distance bounding protocol with tag privacy. In: Chim, T.W., Yuen, T.H. (eds.) ICICS 2012. LNCS, vol. 7618, pp. 285–292. Springer, Heidelberg (2012). doi:10.1007/978-3-642-34129-8_25
14. Zhuang, Y., Yang, A., Wong, D.S., Yang, G., Xie, Q.: A highly efficient rfid distance bounding protocol without real-time PRF evaluation. In: Lopez, J., Huang, X., Sandhu, R. (eds.) NSS 2013. LNCS, vol. 7873, pp. 451–464. Springer, Heidelberg (2013). doi:10.1007/978-3-642-38631-2_33
15. EMVCo Specifications. https://www.emvco.com/specifications.aspx. Accessed 15 Nov 2016
16. Wang, Y., Hahn, C., Sutrave, K.: Mobile payment security, threats, and challenges. In: Second International Conference on Mobile and Secure Services (MobiSecServ 2016), Gainesville, FL, pp. 1–5 (2016)
17. Research, J.: Global digital payments to reach USD 3.6 trillion in 2016. http://www.juniperresearch.com/press/press-releases/global-digital-payments-to-reach-$3-6-trillion. Accessed 15 Nov 2016
18. Zhuang, Y., Hancke, G.P., Wong, D.S.: How to demonstrate our presence without disclosing identity? Evidence from a grouping-proof protocol. In: Kim, H., Choi, D. (eds.) WISA 2015. LNCS, vol. 9503, pp. 423–435. Springer, Cham (2016). doi:10.1007/978-3-319-31875-2_35
19. Vidas, T., Owusu, E., Wang, S., Zeng, C., Cranor, L.F., Christin, N.: QRishing: the susceptibility of smartphone users to QR code phishing attacks. In: Adams, A.A., Brenner, M., Smith, M. (eds.) FC 2013. LNCS, vol. 7862, pp. 52–69. Springer, Heidelberg (2013). doi:10.1007/978-3-642-41320-9_4
20. China's central bank halts Tencent, Alibaba mobile payment process. http://www.reuters.com/article/us-china-cbank-payments-idUSBREA2D06420140314. Accessed 15 Nov 2016
21. e-Learning in HSMC. http://ctl.hsmc.edu.hk/en/e-learning. Accessed 15 Nov 2016

Communication

μProxy: A Hardware Relay for Anonymous and Secure Internet Access

David Cox and David Oswald[(✉)]

School of Computer Science, The University of Birmingham, Birmingham, UK
davidcoxcontact@gmail.com, d.f.oswald@bham.ac.uk

Abstract. Privacy and anonymity on the Internet have become a serious concern. Even when anonymity tools like Tor or VPNs are used, the IP and therefore the approximate geolocation from which the user connects to such a service is still visible to an adversary who controls the network. Our proposal μProxy aims to mitigate this problem by providing a relay of user-controlled hardware proxies that allows to connect to a (potentially public) network over a large physical distance. One endpoint is connected to a public Wifi hotspot, while the other end connects (over a chain of relay nodes) to the user's computer. μProxy uses a lightweight protocol to create a secure channel between two endpoint nodes, whereas the communication can be routed over an arbitrary amount of relay nodes. The employed cryptography is based on NaCl, using Curve25519 for the key exchange as well as Salsa20 and Poly1305 for authenticated payload encryption. μProxy tunnels TCP/IP connections and can therefore be used to secure and anonymize existing, unprotected protocols. We implemented μProxy on the ESP8266, a popular Wifi microcontroller, and show that μProxy incurs a latency of 20.4 ms per hop under normal operating conditions.

Keywords: Privacy · Anonymity · ESP8266 · Secure channel · Protocol implementation · Wireless networks

1 Introduction

In recent years, anonymity and privacy on the Internet has gained increasing attention. In a "post-Snowden" world, many seek to avoid ever growing government observation, be they political dissidents or simply concerned citizens. An important privacy leak is that a user's geolocation can be associated with their public IP address, giving the adversary an approximate real-time location. Often, this information is enough for an adversary to begin closing in, employing traditional methods to improve this approximation and eventually locate the user.

Current anonymity technologies, such as The Onion Routing Project (Tor) [5] or Virtual Private Network (VPNs) aim to address this by relaying traffic through one or multiple third party nodes. This prevents an adversary from knowing both the true source and destination of a packet. This method is effective in separating a user from the sites they are browsing, however does little to

© Springer International Publishing AG 2017
G.P. Hancke and K. Markantonakis (Eds.): RFIDSec 2016, LNCS 10155, pp. 175–187, 2017.
DOI: 10.1007/978-3-319-62024-4_13

guard their location—an adversary still sees Tor or VPN traffic originating from the user's Internet connection, and can still pinpoint the respective person.

Therefore, a system is required that severs this association between public IP and actual location. In this paper, we present µProxy as a low-cost solution to this problem. µProxy achieves the goal of location anonymity using an arbitrary number of interconnected Wifi nodes that form a relay. The relay spans between the user and the network to which they wish to anonymously connect, e.g., a public Wifi hotspot. Traffic appears to stem from the final device in the relay, rather than the user. Attempts to trace the user's IP address will only lead to the relay endpoint. Further tracking requires locating an arbitrary number of (potentially covert) nodes, thus yielding an exponentially expanding search radius. Such a search is beyond the capability of all but the most well equipped and dedicated adversary and, in can case, cannot be conducted quickly.

1.1 Related Work

In the research area of unlinking a user's IP from his geolocation, two notable efforts have been made: The first is ProxyHam [4], a project that attempted to do so by providing a device forwarding Wifi connections over a 900 MHz Radio Frequency (RF) link. The unit (with an approximate cost of USD 200) could operate up to a maximum range of 2.5 km, which the developers stated would be sufficient to disrupt any physical search, should the IP be traced. The project was unexpectedly discontinued shortly before its debut at Defcon 2015 [10].

ProxyGambit is a reincarnation of ProxyHam. The project seeks to improve upon its predecessor by providing greater range and potentially global availability [13]. This is achieved via the addition of a 2G Global System for Mobile Communications (GSM) connection as a low-speed alternative when the 900 MHz link is unavailable. The project itself is in the prototype stages, and is not yet a single unit. The cost for building the device totals USD 234. ProxyGambit is, by the creators own admission, "an insecure, bare bones proof of concept", that is not in active development [13].

Tor [5] and VPN services represent the current defacto anonymity mechanisms on the Internet. As described, they effectively prevent an attacker from knowing both the source and destination of a given connection. Tor or VPNs allow a user to access online material without revealing that they have done so. Such tools are critical when the remote resources being accessed by a user are sensitive or censored. However it does little to hide that the user has connected to Tor itself, as the produced traffic is identifiable. In cases where the use of such privacy tools are grounds for suspicion or even prosecution, this is a serious problem. This, combined with the lack of location privacy are weakness in the Tor project.

1.2 Contribution and Outline

µProxy attempts to improve on the existing relay solutions (ProxyHam and ProxyGambit) outlined above by prioritizing size and affordability at the expense of range per module. We use a widely available, low-cost Wifi microcontroller, the ESP8266 (ESP) [8,9], for which ready-made modules (cf. Fig. 1) can be bought for less than USD 3 per unit. Both relay and endpoint connections are then established over Wifi, which removes the need for a second band support (e.g. GSM or 900 MHz RF). This vastly reduces unit cost and form factor, and hence potentially allows covert deployment. For example, an ESP module could be hidden inside a phone charger or power outlet, which also solves the problem that the module needs a power supply. Furthermore, the reduction in unit cost increases the economic viability of multiple unit relays, where all previous solutions having been limited to a single pair of conspicuous devices. When used in combination with Tor or a VPN, the separation of IP address and user location prevents Tor/VPN traffic from being associated with an individual. If a Tor or VPN session, running through μProxy, is successfully reconstructed, the adversary is still unaware of the user's true location. As such, μProxy and other anonymity tools complement each other and are expected to be used in tandem. The code for μProxy is placed in the public domain.

Fig. 1. Different ESP modules, Euro coin for scale.

The remainder of this paper is structured as follows: In Sect. 2, we describe the general design decisions behind μProxy and introduce the utilized implementation platform, the ESP. Section 3 provides details on the employed cryptographic functionality to secure the relay traffic based on the Networking and Cryptographic Library (NaCl) [1] and evaluates the system's security. In Sect. 4, we present the underlying protocol and evaluate the overhead of our prototypical implementation, before concluding in Sect. 5.

2   System Design

At its core, μProxy is formed by a Wifi *relay* (a series of nodes) with a "daisy chain" topology, as shown in Fig. 2. The relay has two *endpoints*: the local endpoint to which the user connects, and the remote endpoint, which connects to the Internet, e.g., through a public Wifi hotspot. Between the endpoints, a series of *relay nodes* forwards the traffic. Note that in general, there can be N relay nodes, rather than the single one shown in Fig. 2. Hidden Wifi networks are broadcast by the individual relay nodes, realized with ESP modules. These modules are placed along a physical path between the two endpoint locations. A tunnel between these two endpoints is created that seamlessly forwards all traffic. Each module connects to the Wifi of the module ahead of it in the chain, while accepting a connection from the previous module. The ability of the ESP to act both as Wifi client and access point at the same time forms the backbone of the μProxy relay.

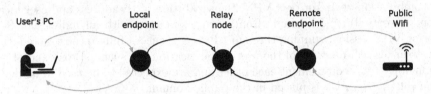

Fig. 2. μProxy topology with a single relay node. Dark arrows represent hidden Wifi connections, green arrows normal Wifi connections. (Color figure online)

Requirements and Protocol Design. The design and development of a protocol to manage the Wifi relay was required, and represented one of main undertakings of the μProxy project. The protocol has to control the set-up of the relay (with an arbitrary number of devices), provide external endpoint interfaces, support required cryptography, and perform data transmission over the relay. This protocol has to run within the restrictive embedded system environment of the ESP. As such, runtime resource usage as well as complied code size had to be minimized. The protocol also has to be sufficiently lightweight as not not monopolize the ESPs 80 MHz processor core, as doing so would prevent the Wifi from functioning correctly.

Robustness and Reliability. We require that the μProxy control protocol must be expected to run, without failure, for an indefinite period. Manually resetting relay nodes after a firmware crash would be a serious problem, as doing so might expose the existence of the relay. In order to remain covert, the individual devices must be as robust and autonomous as possible. Also, reaching devices installed in remote locations may be impractical once deployed. μProxy does not guarantee that the end-to-end link it creates is reliable, i.e., the relay does not ensure that every packet will reach its destination. Like other hardware solutions that provide a physical networking layer link, it is assumed that transmission reliability is a responsibility of the transport layer. In the vast majority of cases this will be the TCP session underpinning the network application. This TCP session will itself ensure reliability by resending all lost packets. Reimplementing this functionality on the μProxy level would be redundant, and mandate that intra-relay communications be constructed via TCP sessions between every node. The additional complexity would increase packet processing time and thus reduce overall throughput while proving no tangible benefit to users. Therefore, the μProxy protocol does not guarantee transmission reliability.

Endpoints. The endpoint nodes form a connection to the outside world; be it to the user or the remote network the relay is tunneling to. A user connects to the relay simply by connecting to the access point opened by his local endpoint. Similarly, data leaves the relay by having the remote endpoint connect to the far-off Wifi hotspot. The relay should then transparently tunnel TCP/IP connections transparently on both sides. However, this proved impossible to achieve on the ESP modules. In both cases doing so required an interface that could send or receive arbitrary packets from the device's Wifi stack. In the case of the local endpoint, all packets from the user needed to be intercepted before they were routed by the Wifi stack, and instead diverted into the relay. In the case of the remote endpoint, the ability to send arbitrary packets onto a remote network was required. These packets would be relay traffic, whose source IP had been changed to match the IP of the remote endpoint. Yet, the necessary hooks into the ESP Wifi stack do not exist in the available API. Therefore, rather than forwarding arbitrary traffic, μProxy creates TCP sockets at each end of the relay. It is the data from these connections that is then tunneled. For a user this requires to connect to a listener at the local endpoint IP. At the remote endpoint, the module connects to a preconfigured address.

This creates an end-to-end connection between the user and the server while still proving the required features of μProxy. To improve the usability of this approach, the local endpoint could provide a (automatic) proxy configuration (e.g., for HTTP(S)). An alternative solution would be to integrate the information on remote IP to connect to into the protocol and have a software component on the user's side that provides a transparent network adapter locally. Finally, the remote endpoint could also connect to a VPN server to realize transparent forwarding through the relay: the user the connects to the VPN port on the local endpoint, while the remote endpoint connects to the VPN server (with the IP pre-programmed into the endpoint's firmware).

3   Cryptography and System Security

Secure and correctly implemented cryptography is essential to μProxy, but the algorithms offered by the ESP are poorly documented and not easily accessible to a developer. The encryption for the Wifi and TCP/IP stacks (WPA2, TLS, etc.), are, to the knowledge of the author, correct implementations of standard specifications. However this functionality is private to the OS, and is not accessible through the provided Application Programming Interface (API). Therefore, it can only be used as part of a larger API call, such as connecting to a WPA2 access point. The "ESPnow" functionality [7] also provides encryption, however no documentation exists as to what scheme is employed.

NaCl Implementation. Therefore, we opted to use a pure software implementation for securing the transmission channel. We selected NaCl, a cryptographic library initially presented in [1]. NaCl supports Elliptic Curve Cryptography (ECC) based key exchange using Curve25519 [2], as well as authenticated encryption using Salsa20 and Poly1305. Since it avoids any secret-dependent load addresses and branches, it is inherently protected against timing attacks.

As a starting point for porting the NaCl library to a 32-bit microcontroller such as the ESP, two variations exist: μNaCl and TweetNaCl. Rather than being optimised for desktop environments, μNaCl is a project that aims at providing optimized implementations for specific embedded microprocessors [12]. Currently, μNaCl is available for Atmel Atmega, TI MSP430 and ARM Cortex-M0. The second variation is TweetNaCl, a reimplementation of NaCl [3] that fits into 100 tweets.

We chose TweetNaCl as the foundation of the ESP NaCl implementation. Due to the code simplicity of TweetNaCl, the complexity of any modifications and implementation changes is drastically reduced. When producing an ESP compatible version of TweetNaCl, a major challenge is compiled code size. The compiled μProxy firmware is stored on the external flash of the module. The default boot behavior is to load the entire code segment of this flash image into the instruction RAM (IRAM). The unmodified TweetNaCl binaries were too large to be loaded into the ESP's limited IRAM. However, it is possible to prevent specific functions from being loading into IRAM; instead they are read from flash at runtime [14]. This allowed for the majority of the TweetNaCl binary to remain in flash, reducing IRAM usage. Rarely used functions, such as key pre-computation, remain in flash with only negligible impact on performance. However, "high traffic" areas, such as the Salsa20 stream cipher, were kept in IRAM in order to improve performance. Furthermore, we made use of the fact that the asymmetric keys of the nodes change never or infrequently. NaCl allow for pre-computation of the ECC key exchange [1], effectively reducing the computation overhead to symmetric crypto only during normal operation.

3.1 Key Distribution and Random Number Generation

Unlike typical desktop computers, the ESP does not have inbuilt support to generate cryptographically secure randomness. In fact, the device API gives no means of generating random bytes. This limits the cryptography capabilities of the device, most notably, on-device key generation. Therefore, we did not use dynamically keys entirely and opted for static key information. These key are generated by a secure source at compile time, therefore bypassing the ESP's inherent entropy problems. Being based on public key cryptography, NaCl has the advantage that the public keys can be exchanged in the setup phase. However, as mentioned, in the implementation created for the purposes of this paper, the public key of the respective communication partner is hardcoded into the firmware of the module.

In cascade systems like Tor, re-encryption is used to hide previous header information and provide forward secrecy. Since all data takes a single path in μProxy, we did not use re-encryption: all cryptographic operations are performed on the endpoints, while the intermediary relay nodes only forward already encrypted packets. This ensures that *(i)* a compromise of a relay node does not leak any key material and *(ii)* reduces the computational load on relay nodes.

3.2   Security Considerations

For evaluating the system security of μProxy, we use the following *adversary model*: It is assumed that the adversary knows the μProxy system and can passively eavesdrop on Wifi traffic as well as actively inject packets. Furthermore, if he has physical access to an ESP module, he is able to extract the contents of the flash memory and can also replace the firmware with a modified version. Finally, we assume that the adversary cannot break the used cryptographic primitives provided by NaCl.

We do not consider the case of an adversary controlling the network beyond the remote endpoint or (parts of) the Internet. As stated, the goal of μProxy is to decouple the user's physical location from his entry point to the Internet, not to anonymize the network traffic itself. Hence, as mentioned in Sect. 1.2, μProxy should be combined with anonymity tools like Tor or VPN.

Relay Nodes. In μProxy, packets sent across the relay are encrypted on one endpoint and decrypted on the other. All intermediary nodes do not re-encrypt data, but simply forward it to the neighboring node. Data is transmitted across the relay using local IP addresses (within the separate network between each pair of nodes), therefore, no information is leaked if an IP or MAC address is seen. When observing a packet of traffic between two relay nodes, the attacker can assume that its destination is the next relay node and its source the previous one. Besides, since hidden Wifi networks are used to connect between the relay nodes, the SSIDs do not reveal information, e.g., the location within the relay.

Successful impersonation of an intermediate node does not compromise the relay, as doing so does not yield any cryptographic keys. However, it allows an attacker to disrupt relay communications without physically locating and destroying a node. An attacker can be in the vicinity of a node and subsequently impersonate it to disrupt the relay by "black-holing" all incoming relay traffic. μProxy is not designed to protect against Denial of Service (DoS) attacks

Local Endpoint and Remote Endpoint. With key information only contained within the two endpoints, they represent the main vulnerable nodes of the relay. We assume that the local endpoint is inherently secure, as it is under direct user control, and a compromise of the local endpoint also implies that the user's location has been discovered. The connection between the user's PC and the local endpoint is secured using WPA2, hence, this connection has identical security guarantees as a standard Wifi network.

For the remote endpoint, if an adversary can overcome the obstacles of tracing and subsequently locating the external edge of the relay, then it would be possible for them to read key information from the ESP flash and decrypt the μProxy session. Alternatively, the adversary could change the ESP firmware to forward a copy of the complete traffic to his own host, or perform arbitrary modifications to the relay traffic. However, this does not substantially reduce security because once the endpoint has been located, the attacker could in any case eavesdrop or modify the decrypted traffic on the (public) hotspot network that the remote endpoint is connected to. This vulnerability is inherent to any connection across a network not in the user's control.

Furthermore, a compromise of the remote endpoint does not imply that the user's location can be instantly revealed: the adversary still only obtains information on the relay node adjacent to the remote endpoint. He then would have to discover this relay node and trace the path back to the local endpoint step-by-step.

4   Prototypical Implementation

In this section, we describe the central aspects of our μProxy implementation, and evaluate the overhead of μProxy in terms of latency added per relay node.

4.1   Relay Protocol

ESPnow. As the underlying transfer protocol between relay nodes, we used ESP-now, an API functionality that provides an interface that allows ESP modules to communicate with each other below the IP layer. It allows to register a number of MAC addresses as known ESP modules. A role flag indicates the Wifi mode that the given module is currently in. Once a pair of modules have been paired, data can be sent between them in a single API call, independent of higher layers like TCP/IP. This API is used for all μProxy intra-relay communication for two reasons:

First, ESPnow allows for data transfer without the management requirements of establishing TCP sockets and subsequent sessions for each node, i.e., is simple to employ. Secondly, the payload of these messages is easily and directly accessible. This is crucial as it allows manipulation of packet data, giving the means to encrypt and decrypt traffic sent via this API using our NaCl implementation. Without ESPnow, much of the complexity and runtime computation of μProxy would be spent managing a series of TCP sessions.

A μProxy packet is composed of an 8-byte counter `ctr`, followed by an arbitrary amount of authenticated ciphertext generated by the NaCl function `crypto_box_afternm()`. The counter is incremented for each transmitted and received packet, and taken as the lower eight byte of the 24-byte nonce used by NaCl. The upper 16-byte of the nonce are set to a fixed value, which can be specific to a μProxy instance. Having an eight byte counter allows to exchange at most 2^{64} bytes over the relay, a value that should be sufficient for practical use cases.

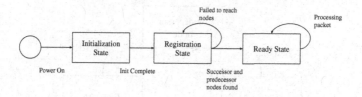

Fig. 3. Overview of the μProxy protocol.

State Machines. As shown in Fig. 3, the protocol begins by initializing the node. Various API calls initialize all OS functionality, and configure the access point and Wifi station. This initialization runs in a method that is automatically called after the firmware has been loaded into IRAM. Once initialization has been completed, the node enters a registration phase. In this phase, the node repeatedly attempts to confirm the existence of its successor and predecessor nodes, only exiting from this state once it has found these nodes. It achieves this by first establishing the respective Wifi connection. In the case of the predecessor, the node waits for a matching MAC address to connect to its access point, while in the case of successor, the node attempts to connect to the access point of its successor. Once these connections have been made, the MAC addresses are registered with the ESPnow API.

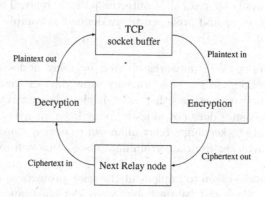

Fig. 4. Data processing loop for μProxy endpoints.

After being registered, the node is operational and ready to receive data. Callback functions are established for the receipt of data from another relay node, and if required, an external TCP source. The device remains in this state, processing all incoming data, until loss of power. Details on how intermediary nodes and endpoint nodes process data are shown in Figs. 5 and 4, respectively.

Static Routing. All routing between μProxy nodes is statically defined. Each module has routing information for its two neighbor nodes. This removes the

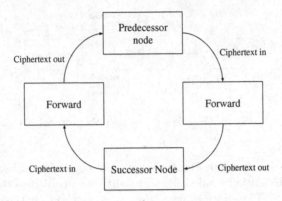

Fig. 5. Data forwarding loop for μProxy intermediary relay nodes.

need for any active routing protocol within the relay. Dynamic routing using modified variants of interior routing protocols such as Routing Information Protocol (RIP) [11] and Open Shortest Path First (OSPF) [15] were considered, allowing the relay to reconfigure after initial deployment. This would open up the possibility of adding or removing nodes within the relay and potentially allow for arbitrary network topologies. However, for reasons of security (to prevent the addition of malicious nodes) and to minimize overhead in our prototype, the decision was made to statically route the μProxy relay. The MAC address of each node's successor and predecessor are defined at compile time as part of the node's firmware.

Relay Wifi Networks. Wifi networks created by relay nodes are hidden, i.e., do not broadcast their SSID. This prevents some devices from displaying the existence of the network, while other may display the generic SSID: "Hidden Network". This measure does not hide the relay from an adversary completely, however it may help to keeping a relay unknown to nearby smartphone users. It also prevents an attacker from ascertaining a node's function from the SSID.

Robustness. Care was taken to implement the relay protocol in a way that maximizes robustness. Potential failure points were identified, and fail-safes implemented that allow the relay to remain operational. Nodes will automatically attempt to reconnect to its successor if the connection was lost. All memory management exceptions, such as heap allocation failures, are caught and handled in a non-fatal way. In such situations, μProxy opts to potentially discard relay packets that cannot be allocated in order to maintain the overall operation of the relay. As discussed previously, μProxy, by design, does not provide transmission reliability, so potential packet loss is not a serious concern. Memory failures remain rare, and are only experienced when the relay is attempting to perform a transmission with throughput beyond its capacity. In these cases, the TCP session will adjust its transfer rate to match the maximum throughput of the relay, meaning that packet loss will be temporary.

Successor and predecessor nodes may be registered even if those nodes are in the active state. This allows a node to re-establish itself within the relay if it experienced power loss. This is of special importance, as continuous power availability cannot be guaranteed if devices are placed at a location outside the user's control. As a last resort, nodes are able to re-establish the relay after a kernel exception. Devices then reboot and follow the protocol steps as normal. The static design of the protocol and much of the node configuration information allows the node to reach the registration phase using only information stored in the device memory.

The result of these implementation decisions is a relay that can operate indefinitely (given power supply), allowing μProxy to provide a secure link that is available to the user without the need for post-deployment maintenance.

4.2   Performance Evaluation

Unlike other solutions, μProxy supports a relay of an arbitrary number of hops a opposed to a single pair of devices. Hence, relay scalability and the impact of length on performance become an important consideration.

To evaluate this aspect, we estimated how the number of nodes N affects the round trip time T. We define the end of the relay to be the point at which data is pushed out to the TCP socket buffer, rather than the time of receipt on an external machine. This is to remove the impact of non-relay hardware from any performance evaluation, as this hardware is outside the control of μProxy. We can define T as:

$$T = 2\,x\,N = 2\left((N-1)\,W + E + D + NK\right)$$

where x is the sum of all latency incurred by using the relay. This latency has three sources: (i) the series of Wifi connections that are used to transmit data between relay nodes (W), (ii) the cost of cryptography at both the of the endpoints (E, D), and (iii) the latency incurred by other internal computations such as passing the message between internal functions (K). The term K turned out to be negligible and therefore is absorbed into W, yielding:

$$T = (2N - 2)\,W + 2E + 2D$$

From this formula, it is clear that μProxy latency scales linearly with the number of nodes. To quantify this further, data was collected on the time taken to encrypt and decrypt data as well as the overall round trip time of a packet. These values are then substituted into the formula to provide an estimate of W.

Although the cryptographic term is represented as constants E, D, this is not strictly true: The value is highly dependent of the length of the message. This relation is linear, as can be seen in the test data. Hereafter it is assumed that the relay is only transporting packets of a size of 225 bytes. This is the ESPnow Maximum Transmission Unit (MTU), and represents the worst case scenario for relay performance. Other user applications such as Telnet [16], which send exclusively single byte packets, will produce significantly better results for the cryptographic variable. At maximum packet length, average encrypt and decrypt times were $E = 1.9$ ms and $D = 2.3$ ms, respectively.

It was not possible to accurately measure the time taken to transmit over a single Wifi connection, as this would require the synchronization of separate device clocks. Therefore, the packet round trip time T was measured and interpolated to represent a single Wifi connection. Testing was conducted with a relay of $N = 3$ devices, yielding $T = 90$ ms.

With the above data, we have $W = \frac{T}{4} - 2.1$ ms $= 20.4$ ms. This value represents the latency incurred per node beyond the two endpoints. For example, a relay of $N = 11$ nodes would have an expected round trip time of $T = 416.4$ ms. The cost for the ESP modules to form such a relay would be USD 35 at most.

Regarding the range, the manufacturer Espressif report the module of have a maximum open-air range of 360 m [6]. This is possibly an overstatement and likely only accounts for an access point being visible on a specialized Wifi receiver. μProxy requires an access point to be visible to other ESP modules, and have a signal strength sufficient for data transmission. Our testing has shown that a value closer to 200 m is appropriate, with 100 m being an estimate with safety margin. Hence, an 11-node relay could stretch over 1 km. The latency of round trip time of $T = 416.4$ ms is high compared to typical connections (cables, long-range RF) over the same distance. Still, in our tests, this latency does not prevent μProxy from delivering a usable browsing experience. Furthermore, testing showed that round trip times were more than halved when sending smaller packets, e.g., representative of an SSH connection.

5   Conclusion and Future Work

In this paper we presented μProxy, a relay solution to anonymously connect to the Internet through a remote Wifi, e.g., a public hotspot. Due to the low-cost nature of the ESP, long relays can be established at minimal cost. The measured delay per relay hop of approximately 20 ms is sufficiently low to allow for practical use of this relay in cases where geolocation privacy is crucial. To secure the relay channel, NaCl is ported to the ESP and used to encrypt and authenticate the tunneled traffic.

With respect to future work, there are several open problems in μProxy: First, it would be desirable to establish a fully transparent relay, either through potentially available functions on the side of the ESP or by providing a custom network driver for the user's OS. Secondly, a more dynamic approach of key management should be investigated, for example, exchanging long-term keys during the setup phase by placing the respective endpoints in a shielded environment and transmitting the public keys to the other partner. The necessary extensions to the protocol would be minimal and facilitate the actual use of the devices. An additional aspect would be to provide forward security by integrating re-keying into the protocol, e.g., by exchanging ephemeral keys at certain intervals, authenticated with the long-term keys.

To facilitate such modifications and improvements as well as security reviews, we placed the source code of μProxy in the public domain and published it online at: https://github.com/david-oswald/microproxy.

References

1. Bernstein, D.J., Lange, T., Schwabe, P.: The security impact of a new cryptographic library. In: Hevia, A., Neven, G. (eds.) LATINCRYPT 2012. LNCS, vol. 7533, pp. 159–176. Springer, Heidelberg (2012). doi:10.1007/978-3-642-33481-8_9
2. Bernstein, D.J.: Curve25519: new Diffie-Hellman speed records. In: Yung, M., Dodis, Y., Kiayias, A., Malkin, T. (eds.) PKC 2006. LNCS, vol. 3958, pp. 207–228. Springer, Heidelberg (2006). doi:10.1007/11745853_14
3. Bernstein, D.J., Gastel, B., Janssen, W., Lange, T., Schwabe, P., Smetsers, S.: TweetNaCl: a crypto library in 100 tweets. In: Aranha, D.F., Menezes, A. (eds.) LATINCRYPT 2014. LNCS, vol. 8895, pp. 64–83. Springer, Cham (2015). doi:10.1007/978-3-319-16295-9_4
4. Caudill, B., Paranoia, P.: High-stakes anonymity on the internet (2015). https://www.defcon.org/html/defcon-23/dc-23-speakers.html
5. Dingledine, R., Mathewson, N., Syverson, P.: Tor: the second-generation onion router. In: Proceedings of the 13th USENIX Security Symposium (SSYM 2004). USENIX Association (2004)
6. Espressif. Espressif smart connectivity platform: ESP8266 (2013). https://nurdspace.nl/images/e/e0/ESP8266_Specifications_English.pdf
7. Espressif. ESP-NOW User Guide (2016). https://espressif.com/sites/default/files/documentation/esp-now_user_guide_en.pdf
8. Espressif. ESP8266 Datasheet (2016). https://espressif.com/sites/default/files/documentation/0a-esp8266ex_datasheet_en.pdf
9. Espressif. ESP8266EX (2016). http://espressif.com/products/hardware/esp8266ex/overview/
10. Greenberg, A.: Online anonymity project proxyham mysteriously vanishes (2015). http://www.wired.com/2015/07/online-anonymity-project-proxyham-mysteriously-vanishes/
11. Hedrick, C.: Routing Information Protocol. RFC 1058, RFC Editor (1988)
12. Hutter, M., Schwabe, P.: μNaCl–the networking and cryptography library for microcontrollers (2015). http://munacl.cryptojedi.org/index.shtml
13. Kamkar, S.: ProxyGambit (2015). http://samy.pl/proxygambit/
14. Lohr, C.: How to directly program an inexpensive ESP8266 Wifi module (2015). http://hackaday.com/2015/03/18/how-to-directly-program-an-inexpensive-esp8266-wifi-module/
15. Moy, J.: OSPF Version 2. RFC 2178, RFC Editor (1997). https://www.rfc-editor.org/info/rfc2178
16. O'Sullivan, T.: Telnet Protocol: A Proposed Document. RFC 0495, RFC Editor (1971)

Self-jamming Audio Channels: Investigating the Feasibility of Perceiving Overshadowing Attacks

Qiao Hu[✉] and Gerhard Hancke

Department of Computer Science, City University of Hong Kong,
Kowloon Tong, Hong Kong
qiaohu2-c@my.cityu.edu.hk

Abstract. Recently there has been interesting in short-range communication using audio channels for device pairing and as a self-jamming communication medium. Given that such channels are audible to participants they are considered more resistant to active attacks, i.e. the attack could be distinguished by the participants. In this paper, we investigate the validity of this assumption in the only two practical acoustic self-jamming systems using different modulation schemes. We show that basic overshadowing is possible in these systems using an audio channel and that the attack cannot be effectively detected by the participants.

Keywords: Self-jamming · Active attack · Audio channel communication

1 Introduction

Devices are increasingly becoming smart and interconnected in part due to technology initiatives related to machine-to-machine communication and the Internet-of-Things [1,9,15,20]. The large number of devices that potentially need to make ad-hoc connections offers challenges in terms of security [10], especially when devices have no prior shared cryptographic key. In this regard, researchers are looking to the physical layer of wireless communication to enable keyless secure communication. Self-jamming is a widely proposed method for providing confidential communication between devices that have no prior secure relationship. The basic idea is that the jamming noise transmitted by the receiver can hide the data signal of the sender from passive adversaries. This builds on the initial theory of Wyner's wiretap model [27], where a channel is shown to allow secure communication of the noise affecting the attacker's signal is greater than that affecting the receiver's channel. To ensure that this is the case additional noise, which can later be removed by the legitimate receiver, is intentionally added to the system [17]. This can be done by either a third party (friendly-jamming) or the receiver himself (self-jamming). There are numerous works on self-jamming schemes to create confidential channels, e.g. [6,7,22], and the effectiveness of such schemes, e.g. [13,24,26]. Short-range ad-hoc connectivity is useful for mobile devices, with near field communication [5,18] or audio channels [3] being possible with off-the-shelf devices. Self-jamming has been proposed

G.P. Hancke and K. Markantonakis (Eds.): RFIDSec 2016, LNCS 10155, pp. 188–203, 2017.
DOI: 10.1007/978-3-319-62024-4_14

for both RFID-type channels [2,4,11,12,14,21] and audio channels [16,28]. The majority of these schemes rigorously evaluate their effectiveness against single and/or multiple passive attackers.

In this paper we focus on the self-jamming. Self-jamming keeps the confidentiality of communication by the jamming signal which will arrive at the attacker at the same time with or before the confidential message signal to make the attacker hard to demodulate the message signal correctly. Due to the fact that mobile devices lack special hardware for radio jamming, researchers adopt sound to achieve self-jamming. Acoustic communication is a conventional communication channel which has already been used in underwater wireless communications for years and almost all widely used mobile devices, such as smartphones and tablets, have a speaker and a microphone to transmit and receive the acoustic signal. By far, only two practical acoustic self-jamming methods [16,28] have been proposed to improve the security. We focus our analyze on these two schemes.

Confidentiality against passive attackers is a core requirement of secure communication, but a reasonable question to ask is whether such systems could also withstand active attacks. This is especially relevant given that overshadowing attacks, whereby an attacker could modify data between two parties during transmission, have been successfully demonstrated [19]. Depending on the application, the ability to modify the hidden data could compromise the overarching secure application. Ensuring the integrity of the data and detecting attempts at active attacks is therefore an important next step to consider in self-jamming systems. At first glance it would indeed appear sensible to suggest that audio channels have an advantage in this regard as any attempt from an attacker to interfere should be audible to the legitimate participants [8,23]. However, this assumption that an attack could be audibly detected, especially in the presence of jamming has not been investigated.

In this paper, we test the assumption that overshadowing attacks can be audibly detected when used against self-jammed audio communication. In doing so we implement the attack against two well-known schemes [16,28]. We fully accept that these two schemes are not designed to protect against active attacks. The purpose of this paper in not to comment on the security of these two schemes against active attacks but simply to use these as representative test systems of audio communication to evaluate the effectiveness of audibility as a countermeasure to overshadowing. Our contribution is as follows:

1. We show that an active attack cannot be reliably discerned from the self-jammed data exchange. We hope this initial work on the topic further encourages work on physical-layer integrity mechanisms to complement confidentiality mechanisms.
2. A secondary finding is that the jamming scheme does not inhibit the overshadowing. This is confirmation of an expected result, but still useful as previous overshadowing attacks have only been demonstrated on standard channels.

2 Background

2.1 Self-Jamming Audio Schemes

To test attack audibility we apply our overshadowing attack to two secure audio channel designs. Dhwani [16] uses pseudo-random noise sequence as jamming signal and combines Orthogonal Frequency Division Multiplexing (OFDM) with Phase-shift Keying (PSK) to transmit data. PriWhisper [28] uses bandpass filtered additive white Gaussian noise, bandpass filtered to cover the data spectrum, with Frequency-shift Keying (FSK) to transmit data. Dhwani and PriWhisper share the same basic idea, but the protocol sequence differs as shown in Fig. 1. Black arrows in figures mean that the signal is transmitted by audio and red arrow refers to radio communication. Blocks represent the duration period of all actions represented by arrows.

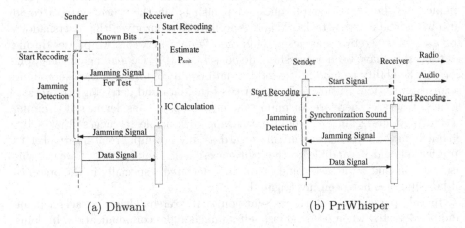

(a) Dhwani   (b) PriWhisper

Fig. 1. Basic concepts of RFID tag response and Power Varying.

Dhwani starts by transmitting known bits to the receiver to estimate the power of signal P_{xmit} coming from the sender. Next, the receiver will transmit a jamming signal to calculate the interference cancellation (IC) it can achieve. SNR_{min} is a set threshold for the Signal-to-Noise Ratio (SNR) of the data signal for which the bit-error rate at the receiver is acceptable. The receiver then calculates the power of jamming signal as Eq. 1. Finally, the receiver transmits the jamming signal and the sender starts transmitting data as soon as it detects the jamming.

$$P_{jam} = P_{xmit} - SNR_{min} + IC \qquad (1)$$

For PriWhisper the sender first transmits a start signal to the receiver to indicate its intention to communicate. Then the sender waits to detect the jamming signal. The receiver begins to record and then transmits a synchronization signal followed by the jamming noise. The power of the jamming signal is simply specified as the maximum power that the receiver can achieve. The sender starts to transmit the data once it detects the jamming signal.

2.2 Overshadowing and Auditory Masking Threshold

Overshadowing is conceptually a simple attack where an adversary transmits his message at the same time as the legitimate sender in such a way that the receiver believes this is the intended message from the sender [19]. It is not simply a case of 'overpowering' the original message, with overshadowing requiring a combination of power and receiver synchronization to succeed.

Since the self-jamming systems we talk about communicate by the acoustic signal which can be heard by human, we also need to consider whether our attack signal would be perceived by users. The phenomenon that the perceivable of an audio signal is affected by co-existed another audio signal is called auditory masking. There are two kinds of auditory masking: the jamming signal masking the attack signal or the attack signal masking the jamming signal. But in normal communication case, users can only hear the jamming signal. The jamming signal and the attack signal sounds different due to their different frequencies. This means that when we transmitting a powerful attack signal to masking the jamming signal, users always can perceive the attack as they hear a different sound. Only the first kind of auditory masking can make the attack signal unperceivable as users will hear their familiar jamming noise.

Researchers have established the perceiving auditory masking threshold of human hearing [25]. This power ratio threshold is what we called auditory masking threshold in this paper. Researchers have demonstrated that if the SNR of the single-frequency audio signal is above $-13\,\mathrm{dB}$ an average human can distinguish this audio from background noise, while for multi-frequency audio the SNR should be larger than 0 dB. The auditory masking threshold of these two cases are $-13\,\mathrm{dB}$ and 0 dB separately.

3 Inaudible Overshadowing Attacks

In this section we test the audibility of an adversary's message in the context of the Dhwani and PriWhisper secure audio channel schemes [16,28]. It is generally accepted that injecting messages through overshadowing is feasible. However, for us to succeed in our attack we need to modify the message while at the same time remaining below the auditory masking threshold. In practice, there are some technical challenges to achieving this goal.

The first challenge is to synchronize with the receiver in such a way that it is more likely to accept our message. The attack strategy depends on whether the receiver's demodulation is coherent (Dhwani) or non-coherent (PriWhisper). For coherent demodulation, any transmission is preceded by synchronization between the sender and receiver. In Dhwani this is accomplished by means of a known preamble preceding the message signal. An attacker would therefore attempt to make the receiver synchronize with his version of the preamble as it will lead to its message being the more likely accepted message. PriWhisper adopts a non-coherent demodulation method, which means there is no definite signal synchronization stage. In this is the attacker's signal should arrive earlier than the data signal. The second challenge is to transmit the attack message at a power level that makes the receiver accept it as the intended message but remain inaudible. In each experiment we attempt to transmit the attack signal at the power level needed to overshadow the data signal successfully, while remaining at a power ratio between the attack and jamming noise that falls below the auditory masking of human hearing. This might require adapting to the jamming noise as it is sent.

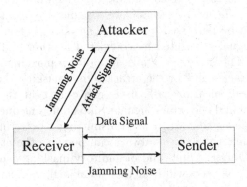

Fig. 2. Basic Attack model.

We follow an experimental approach to illustrate that overshadowing succeeds without being audible. Our experiment consists of a sender, a receiver and an attacker as shown on Fig. 2. We use SONY Xperia e3 mobile phones as the sender and the receiver, with the attack signal generated from a stationary PC with an external loudspeaker. The legitimate sender and receiver are physically close, i.e. held against another as recommended in [28]. We assume that the attacker can listen to messages in the protocol and detect when the jamming noise is sent. The attacker knows the protocol flow and the parameters of the scheme's channel, e.g. modulation scheme, nature of the jamming noise and preamble, but does not know parts of or the whole message or the jamming noise signal. The preamble is not part of the message and if it was secret this would need to have been agreed between the two devices previously, which is unlikely since one of the main benefits of self-jamming is to provide a secure channel without participants sharing a secret.

3.1 Experiment 1: Dhwani

The workflow of the overshadowing attack on Dhwani is shown in Fig. 3. After detecting the known bits transmitted by the sender, the attacker knows the

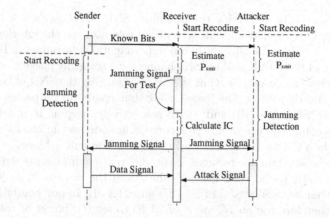

Fig. 3. Workflow of unperceivable overshadowing attack on Dhwani.

scheme is about to start and waits to detect the start of the jamming noise hiding the data. Once the jamming signal is detected the attack transmits the preamble following by his message. Also sending the preamble is an important aspect of the attack. An attacker could in theory try to estimate when the sender's preamble will end and try to overshadow the following message but given the coherent nature of the receiver, this estimation would need to be very accurate given this synchronizes the coherent receiver to the incoming data. The receiver utilizes correlation to search for the position of the preamble, looked for the first significant correlation peak, and uses this to set the expected start of the data. A similar preamble with higher power will yield a larger correlation result so sending a stronger preamble causes the receiver to synchronizes the start time of data recovery to the attack signal. This also reduces the influence of the legitimate message. As such, the attacker's signal could actually arrive a while after the sender's message has started.

Channel Parameters: We use the channel parameters as specified in [16]. Dhwani could use binary phase-shift keying (BPSK) or quadrature phase-shift keying (QPSK) modulation methods and we implement channels with both. Due to the use of orthogonal frequency-division multiplexing (OFDM) technology, the carrier frequencies of PSK and QPSK are between 6 kHz to 7 kHz with an interval of 171 Hz. The sampling rate in our experiment is 44 kHz. The preamble used is a two-fold chirp signal and it lasts 256 sample points, which equal to about 5.81 ms. An OFDM symbol also lasts 5.81 ms or 256 sample points. We choose $M = 1000$ and $K = 5$ to generate the jamming signal. Finally, Dhwani prescribes the use of error correcting code but does not specify a specific scheme so we choose to implement a Bose, Chaudhuri, and Hocquenghem (BCH) error correcting code with parameters set as $n = 255$ and $k = 131$.

Then we need to determine the power of the jamming signal and the data signal. The power of the data signal is determined by the sender. As mentioned in Sect. 2.1, the power of the jamming signal is calculated by the receiver as Eq. 1.

We therefore need to determine the minimum SNR SNR_{min}, which means the largest power of noise that Dhwani system can tolerate, and the interference cancellation IC variables for Dhwani in our experimental environment. To measure the SNR_{min} of the BPSK and QPSK channels, we transmit packets of data and measure packet error rate (PER) at the receiver varying the SNR of transmitted message to additive noise. The lowest SNR that results in no packet errors for QPSK and BPSK are $-2\,$dB and $-6\,$dB respectively, keeping in mind that this takes into account the use of an error correction code on the channel. Next we determine the IC that our reference implementation can achieve. We conduct 10 trails where we train the receiver in two different environments, an office and an outside location, and then measure the IC of the devices in each location. In each location we achieve IC of 20.4 dB and 21.1 dB. In our audibility consideration we therefore use an IC value of 20 dB to set the power of the jamming signal.

Synchronization: The first aspect of the attack we discuss is the feasibility of making the receiver synchronize to the attacker's preamble PRE_{att} instead of the legitimate preamble PRE_{mess}. Figure 4(a) shows the effect on the synchronized time point chosen by the receiver PRE_{syn} relative to PRE_{att} and PRE_{mess}. The power ratio of PRE_{att} and PRE_{mes} kept constant at 1.2 dB (chosen low to also illustrate the result if the attacker's synchronization manipulation fails). We represent the delay as the number of sample points, keeping in mind that the sampling rate is 44 kHz and the preamble is 256 samples long. The values of the x-axis represent the time delay between the arrival time at the receiver of PRE_{mes} and PRE_{att}. The arrival time of PRE_{mes} is considered to be 0, with the value indicating how much later PRE_{att} arrives. The values of the y-axis represent the time difference between the arrival of PRE_{mes} and the time the receiver believes the message starts PRE_{syn}. If the attacker succeeds in manipulating the receiver's synchronized start time the y-axis is equal to the x-axis value,

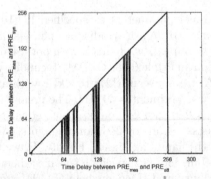
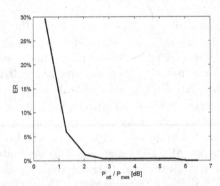

(a) PRE_{att} shifting receiver sync PRE_{syn} relative to real message start PRE_{mes}

(b) Effect of the Power Ratio of Preambles

Fig. 4. Synchronization results.

and when he fails the y-axis value should be 0, i.e. the received has synchronized to PRE_{mes}. We can observe from these results that the attacker could be successful in manipulating the receiver, although he must ensure that his preamble starts to arrive before the legitimate preamble is completely received.

Figure 4(a) does also show that this manipulation sometimes fails. This is as a result of the relationship between the power of the attacker's and the sender's signals. Figure 4(b) shows the error rate (ER) of synchronization manipulation when the power of the attacker's preamble signal P_{att} is 0 dB to 6.5 dB larger than the power of the preamble of the sender's signal P_{mes}. An 'error' in this case is from the attacker's perspective and indicates a case where the receiver does not synchronize with the attacker's preamble signals. From this figure we can observe that the error in our test system drops when the power ratio increases of the power ratio, with negligible errors as the ratio approach 3 dB and no errors once the ratio exceeds 6 dB.

Overshadowing: Once the attacker has made the receiver synchronize to his preamble he then needs to send his new message. The synchronization of the receiver will give the attacker's signal an advantage but for overshadowing to succeed the attacker's transmitted message should still be more powerful than the sender's legitimate message at the location of the receiver. This requirement is challenging given that the sender is right at the receiver and the attacker is most likely located further away, which attenuates the power of his transmission. It is expected that overshadowing could be successful but at which distance between the attacker and the receiver? In this section we evaluate how much more power the attacker needs to transmit to succeed in overshadowing the message.

In Dhwani et al. [16] it is stated that the receiver's jamming signal decreases to the level of background noise at a distance of 1.5 m. Since the attacker needs to detect the jamming signal to enable his attack it makes sense for the attacker to be located within this distance. In the previous section it was shown that the attacker's preamble should arrive before or during the sender's preamble for the synchronization manipulation to succeed. As both the sender and the attacker waits to detect the jamming signal before transmitting so we set a further requirement that attacker's preamble must arrive within 5.81 ms, the length of the preamble, after the jamming signal starts. From Fig. 3 we can see that the time delay for the attacker consists of two parts: the propagation of the jamming signal from the receiver to the attacker and the propagation time of the attack signal from the attacker to the receiver. We assume that the propagation time between the receiver and legitimate sender is negligible. The maximum distance between the attacker and the receiver D_{max} can therefore be calculated by: $D_{max} = T_{pre} * V_{sound}/2 \approx 1 \, \text{m}$

This derives from the requirement that the round trip propagation time must be less than the duration of the preamble T_{pre}, with V_{sound} being the speed of sound. We therefore investigate the success of overshadowing up to this distance.

Figure 5(a) shows the power ratio needed for the attack to succeed in overshadowing the message as observed when the attack distance varies from 0 to

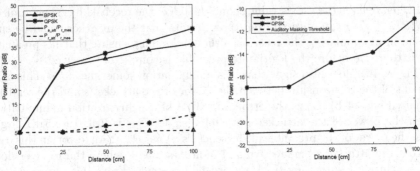

(a) Lowest Power Ratio for Successful Overs- (b) Auditory masking threshold and overshadowing at Various Distances   hadowing attack SNR ($P_{r\ att}$ vs P_{jam})

Fig. 5. Overshadowing results for Dhwani.

100 cm (in 25 cm intervals). The red plot lines (solid and dashed) indicates results from system adopting QPSK modulation scheme while black plot lines refer to BPSK modulation. P_{a_att} and P_{r_att} represents the power level of the attack signal as transmitted by the attacker and then as received by the receiver, i.e. it shows the signal attenuation over the distance. P_{r_mes} represents the power level of the sender's signal when it arrives at the receiver. The solid lines show us the lowest power ratio between P_{a_att} and P_{r_mes} which is needed to force the receiver to demodulate the attack message with no bit error. The dashed lines shows the power ratio of both signals P_{r_att} and P_{r_mes} at the receiver. The succeed from 25–100 cm away the attack signal transmitted needs 30 to 40 dB more power than the legitimate sender. However, at the location of the receiver, and sender, the arriving attack signal only needs to be 5 to 11 dB higher to overshadow the sender's message. This would indicate that the attack is feasible, especially since the attacker can estimate the transmitting power of the sender P_{xmit} during the initial test message and adjust its transmitted power accordingly.

Audibility: The final part of our experiment it to determine if the attack signal is audible to the attacker given the presence of jamming noise. In this case we are arguably dealing with the audibility of a near single-frequency signal, given that the channel is using phase-shift modulation on carriers spread between 6 kHz and 7 kHz. From Sect. 2.2, we know that when the jamming signal is a wide-band signal and the attack signal single frequency the auditory masking threshold is −13 dB. It could just as well be argued that the signal is multi-frequency, e.g. if the orthogonal channels happen to be multi-tonal as in close to 6 kHz and close to 7 kHz. However, −13 dB presents a more stringent requirement for the attacker so we use this value. As mentioned in Sect. 2.1, the power of the jamming signal is calculated by the receiver as Eq. 1.

We therefore need to determine the minimum SNR SNR_{min}, which is the SNR at which an attacker can no longer correctly recover the data, and the interference cancellation IC variables for Dhwani in our experimental environment.

To measure the SNR_{min} of the BPSK and QPSK channels, we transmit packets of data and measure packet error rate (PER) at the receiver varying the SNR of transmitted message to additive noise. The lowest SNR that results in no packet errors for QPSK and BPSK are $-2\,dB$ and $-6\,dB$ respectively, keeping in mind that this takes into account the use of an error correction code on the channel. Next we determine the IC that our reference implementation can achieve. We conduct 10 trails where we train the receiver in two different environments, an office and an outside location, and then measure the IC of the devices in each location. In each location we achieve IC of $20.4\,dB$ and $21.1\,dB$. In our audibility consideration we therefore use an IC value of $20\,dB$ to set the power of the jamming signal.

Considering that the receiver and sender are located in immediate proximity the jamming signal transmitted is assumed that the attenuation to the receiver is negligible. The auditory masking threshold for a human participant relative to the attack SNR, the ratio between the power of the attack signal at the receiver P_{r_att} and the power of the jamming signal P_{jam}, is shown in Fig. 5(b) for both QPSK and BPSK channels. To succeed the attack SNR is considerable less than the auditory masking threshold. We conclude that the attack signal can be unperceivable for BPSK modulation scheme, but for QPSK the attack signal always can be perceived by the participants above 80 cm.

3.2   Experiment 2: PriWhisper

The workflow of our attack on PriWhisper is shown in Fig. 6. After detecting the start signal by the sender, the attacker knows the scheme is about to start and waits for the start of the jamming noise, which includes the synchronization preamble indicating the start of the noise transmission. Once the jamming noise is detected the attacker transmit the overshadowing message. In PriWhisper the receiver uses a non-coherent receiver, which means that there is not a synchronization method that the attacker can manipulate as in Dhwani. The implication is that the attacker's message needs to start arriving before the sender's message for the overshadowing to succeed. If the attacker is late the received message would be partly the legitimate message followed by the attacker's message.

Channel Parameters: We use the channel parameters as specified in [28]. PriWhisper uses M-ary frequency-shift keying (MFSK) modulation methods with M equals to 2, 4 and 8. The carrier frequencies for the different M are shown in Table 1. The sampling rate in our experiment is 44 kHz, with each MFSK symbol lasting 88 sample points or 2 ms. The jamming noise used is different from that in Dhwani, with PriWhisper using bandpass filtered additive white Gaussian noise (AWGN) covering the band of the channel carrier frequencies. The channel allows for error correction using a narrow-sense Bose, Chaudhuri, and Hocquenghem (BCH) error correcting code with $n = 255$ and $k = 131$ (Table 2).

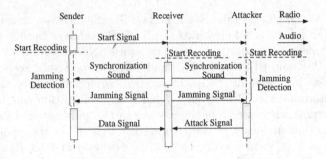

Fig. 6. Workflow of unperceivable overshadowing attack on PriWhisper.

Table 1. Carrier frequencies for different M.

M	Carrier Frequencies
2	9 kHz, 10 kHz
4	9 kHz, 10 kHz, 11 kHz, 12 kHz
8	9 kHz, 10 kHz, 11 kHz, 12 kHz, 13 kHz, 14 kHz, 15 kHz, 16 kHz

Table 2. IC Obtained at various locations.

Location	L1	L2
L1	20.4	7.3
L2	6.9	21.1

Early Arrival of Attack Signal: As the attacker's message needs to arrive before the sender's message, we first investigate the feasibility of the attacker detecting the jamming signal and then transmitting a signal to the receiver before the sender. In PriWhisper, the sender records 10 ms of background audio and calculates the root mean square of the sample amplitudes. If the result is larger than a set threshold the jamming signal is detected the sender transmits. After the detection of the jamming signal, the sender transmits the message.

For the attacker to succeed he would need to reliably detect the start of the jamming signal faster than the sender. Also the attacker needs to transmit the attack message earlier enough for the attack message arriving at the receiver earlier than the sender's message. Compared to the sender, extra time cost for the attacker consists of two parts: propagation time of the jamming signal from the receiver to the attacker and propagation time of the attack message from the attacker to the receiver. As the sender and the receiver against each other, we ignore the propagation time of the communication between them. The extra time cost is calculated by: $T_{ext} = D * 2/V_{sound}$. D is the distance between the attacker and the receiver. V_{sound} is the speed of sound. T_{ext} is the extra cost time.

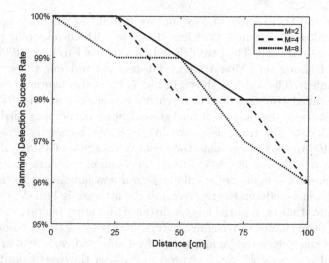

Fig. 7. Success rate of jamming detection at various distances on PriWhisper.

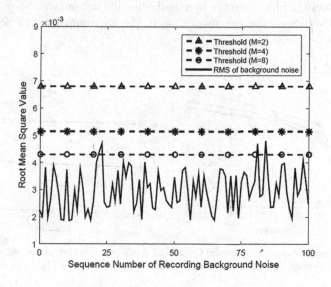

Fig. 8. Result of background noise impact experiment on PriWhisper.

Now we know the extra cost time. Where can we find time to fill in this gap? The answer is jamming detection period. The normal jamming detection time in the sender is 10 ms. We cut it by the sum of the extra cost time and 0.5 ms in our attacker to make sure that the attacker's message can arrive earlier than the sender's message, at most 0.5 ms earlier. But you may have doubt about the success rate of jamming detection due to the decreasing of the detection time. To make our modified jamming detection scheme more reliable, we train our attacker before we use it. We choose 1 m because this is the largest distance between the attacker and the receiver in Dhwani. We record the jamming signal of the receiver at different distances that less than 1 m with corresponding jamming detection duration time. Then we calculate a threshold to make 100% success rate in our training set. After training finished, we test our threshold in the real environment. The result is shown in Fig. 7. From this figure we can observe that our modified jamming detection scheme can achieve at least 97% success rate. Then we test the impact of background noise on our modified jamming detection scheme. The result is shown in Fig. 8. We record background noise outside for 100 times and calculate their root mean square (RMS) values which utilizing the way used in [28] to calculate the value of recording sound sample. The thresholds in the figure are calculated by our new jamming detection scheme when the distance between the receiver and the attacker is 1 m. We can observe from the figure that even in the largest distance and noisy background, our new scheme has little chance to recognize background noise as the jamming signal.

Since we can detect the jamming signal reliably and early, earlier arrival of attack signal is impossible. Next we need to consider the overshadowing.

Overshadowing: Similar to the overshadowing in Dhwani, we also measure the impact of distance on the overshadowing in the environment with SNR equals to SNR_{min}.

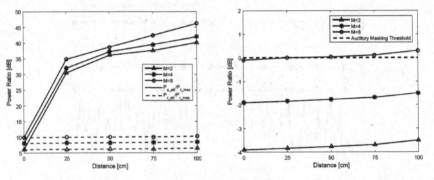

(a) Lowest Power Ratio for Successful Overshadowing at Various Distances

(b) Auditory masking threshold and overshadowing attack SNR ($P_{r\ att}$ vs P_{jam})

Fig. 9. Overshadowing Results for PriWhisper.

Figure 9(a) shows the power ratio needed for the attack to succeed in overshadowing the message as observed when the attack distance varies from 0 to 100 cm (in 25 cm intervals). The red lines (solid and dashed) represents the power ratio when the M of MFSK equals to 2, with the blue and black lines referring to M = 4 and M = 8. P_{a_att} and P_{r_att} represents the power level of the attack signal as transmitted by the attacker and then as received by the receiver, i.e. it shows the signal attenuation over the distance. P_{r_mes} represents the power level of the sender's signal when it arrives at the receiver. The solid lines show us the lowest power ratio between P_{a_att} and P_{r_mes} which is needed to force the receiver to demodulate the attack message with no bit error. The dashed lines shows the power ratio of both signals P_{r_att} and P_{r_mes} at the receiver. The succeed from 25–100 cm away the attack signal transmitted needs approximately 30 to 50 dB more power than the legitimate sender. However, at the location of the receiver, and sender, the arriving attack signal only needs to be 6 to 11 dB higher to overshadow the sender's message.

Audibility of Our Attack: The final part of our experiment it to determine if the attack signal is audible to the attacker given the presence of jamming noise. In this case we are arguably dealing with the audibility of a multi-frequency signal, given that the channel is using frequency-shift modulation on at least two distinct carriers, i.e. 2 to 8 distinct tones within the human hearing range. From Sect. 2.2, we know that when the jamming signal is a wide-band signal and the attack signal is a multi-frequency signal the audible threshold is 0 dB. For PriWhisper the sender adapts his transmission power to the jamming power detected, with the stated requirements that the message signal must be at least 10 dB less than the jamming signal. This is also the worse case for the attacker as he would only be able to exceed the sender signal by 10 dB in his overshadowing without being audible. We therefore consider audibility at this ratio between jamming signal and the message.

Considering that the receiver and sender are located in immediate proximity the jamming signal transmitted is assumed that the attenuation to the receiver is negligible. The audibility threshold for a human participant relative to the attack SNR, the ratio between the power of the attack signal at the receiver P_{r_att} and the power of the jamming signal P_{jam}, is shown in Fig. 9(b) for M equal to 2, 4 and 8. To succeed the attack SNR for M equal to 2 and 4 is considerable less than the audible threshold, but for M = 8 the attack is above the audible threshold above 25 cm.

4   Conclusion

We have shown that overshadowing attacks on audio channels are not always audible to human participants. We successfully executed practical overshadowing against two self-jamming schemes without the injected signals exceeding the accepted receiving power ratio threshold of human hearing for each case. Our experimental results therefore show that the audibility of attack signals to human participants is not an effective countermeasure and that self-jamming signals require further mechanisms to ensure the integrity of exchanged data. Future work would be to look at physical-layer integrity mechanisms.

References

1. Abu-Mahfouz, A.M., Hancke, G.P.: An efficient distributed localisation algorithm for wireless sensor networks: based on smart reference-selection method. Int. J. Sen. Netw. **13**(2), 94–111 (2013)

2. Achard, F., Savry, O.: A cross layer approach to preserve privacy in RFID ISO/IEC 15693 systems. In: RFID-TA, pp. 85–90. IEEE (2012)
3. Chung, M., Ilju Ko, I.: Data-sharing method for multi-smart devices at close range. In: Mobile Information Systems (2015)
4. Fei, H., Chouchang, Y., Guang, G., Radha, P.: A framework to securing RFID transmissions by varying transmitted reader's power. In: Radio Frequency Identification System Security: RFIDsec 2013 Asia Workshop Proceedings, vol. 11, pp. 57–68. IOS Press (2013)
5. Francis, L., Hancke, G., Mayes, K., Markantonakis, K.: Potential misuse of NFC enabled mobile phones with embedded security elements as contactless attack platforms. In: International Conference for Internet Technology and Secured Transactions, ICITST 2009, pp. 1–8 (2009)
6. Goel, S., Negi, R.: Guaranteeing secrecy using artificial noise. IEEE Trans. Wirel. Commun. **7**(6), 2180–2189 (2008)
7. Gollakota, S., Hassanieh, H., Ransford, B., Katabi, D., Fu, K.: They can hear your heartbeats noninvasive security for implantable medical devices. ACM SIGCOMM Comput. Commun. Rev. **41**(4), 2–13 (2011)
8. Goodrich, M.T., Sirivianos, M., Solis, J., Soriente, C., Tsudik, G., Uzun, E.: Using audio in secure device pairing. Int. J. Secure. Network. **4**(1–2), 57–68 (2009)
9. Han, G., Liu, L., Jiang, J., Shu, L., Hancke, G.: Analysis of energy-efficient connected target coverage algorithms for industrial wireless sensor networks. IEEE Trans. Industr. Inf. **13**(1), 135–143 (2017)
10. Hancke, G.P.: Distance-bounding for RFID: effectiveness of 'terrorist fraud' in the presence of bit errors. In: IEEE International Conference on RFID-Technologies and Applications (RFID-TA), pp. 91–96 (2012)
11. Hassanieh, H., Wang, J., Katabi, D., Kohno, T.: Securing RFIDs by randomizing the modulation and channel. In: 12th USENIX Symposium on Networked Systems Design and Implementation (NSDI 2015), pp. 235–249 (2015)
12. Hu, Q., Dinca, L.M., Hancke, G.: Device synchronisation: a practical limitation on reader assisted jamming methods for RFID confidentiality. In: Akram, R.N., Jajodia, S. (eds.) WISTP 2015. LNCS, vol. 9311, pp. 219–234. Springer, Cham (2015). doi:10.1007/978-3-319-24018-3_14
13. Hu, Q., Dinca, L.M., Yang, A., Hancke, G.: Practical limitation of co-operative RFID jamming methods in environments without accurate signal synchronization. Comput. Netw. **105**, 224–236 (2016)
14. Jin, R., Zeng, K.: SecNFC: securing inductively-coupled near field communication at physical layer. In: IEEE Conference on Communications and Network Security (CNS), pp. 149–157. IEEE (2015)
15. Kumar, A., Hancke, G.P.: A zigbee-based animal health monitoring system. IEEE Sens. J. **15**(1), 610–617 (2015)
16. Nandakumar, R., Chintalapudi, K.K., Padmanabhan, V., Venkatesan, R.: Dhwani Secure peer-to-peer acoustic NFC. SIGCOMM Comput. Commun. Rev. **43**(4), 63–74 (2013)
17. Negi, R., Goel, S. Secret communication using artificial noise. In: IEEE 62nd Vehicular Technology Conference, VTC-2005-Fall, vol. 3, pp. 1906–1910 (2005)
18. Opperman, C.A., Hancke, G.P.: Using NFC-enabled phones for remote data acquisition and digital control. AFRICON **2011**, 1–6 (2011)
19. Pöpper, C., Tippenhauer, N.O., Danev, B., Capkun, S.: Investigation of signal and message manipulations on the wireless channel. In: Atluri, V., Diaz, C. (eds.) ESORICS 2011. LNCS, vol. 6879, pp. 40–59. Springer, Heidelberg (2011). doi:10.1007/978-3-642-23822-2_3

20. Potter, C.H., Hancke, G.P., Silva, B.J.: Machine-to-machine: possible applications in industrial networks. In: IEEE International Conference on Industrial Technology (ICIT), pp. 1321–1326 (2013)
21. Savry, O., Pebay-Peyroula, F., Dehmas, F., Robert, G., Reverdy, J.: RFID noisy reader how to prevent from eavesdropping on the communication? In: Paillier, P., Verbauwhede, I. (eds.) CHES 2007. LNCS, vol. 4727, pp. 334–345. Springer, Heidelberg (2007). doi:10.1007/978-3-540-74735-2_23
22. Shen, W., Liu, Y., He, X., Dai, H., Ning, P.: No time to demodulate-fast physical layer verification of friendly jamming. In: Military Communications Conference, MILCOM 2015–2015 IEEE, pp. 653–658. IEEE (2015)
23. Soriente, C., Tsudik, G., Uzun, E.: HAPADEP: human-assisted pure audio device pairing. In: Wu, T.-C., Lei, C.-L., Rijmen, V., Lee, D.-T. (eds.) ISC 2008. LNCS, vol. 5222, pp. 385–400. Springer, Heidelberg (2008). doi:10.1007/ 978-3-540-85886-7_27
24. Steinmetzer, D., Schulz, M., Hollick, M.: Lockpicking physical layer key exchange weak adversary models invite the thief. In: Proceedings of the 8th ACM Conference on Security & Privacy in Wireless and Mobile Networks, p. 1. ACM (2015)
25. Stuart, J.R.: Noise methods for estimating detectability and threshold. J. Audio Eng. Soc. 42(3), 124–140 (1994)
26. Tippenhauer, N.O., Malisa, L., Ranganathan, A., Capkun, S.: On limitations of friendly jamming for confidentiality. In: IEEE Symposium on Security and Privacy, pp. 160–173. IEEE Computer Society (2013)
27. Wyner, A.D.: The wire-tap channel. Bell System Technical Journal, The 54(8), 1355–1387 (1975)
28. Zhang, B., Zhan, Q., Chen, S., Li, M., Ren, K., Wang, C., Ma, D.: Enabling keyless secure acoustic communication for smartphones. Internet of Things Journal, IEEE 1(1), 33–45 (2014)

Author Index

Printed in the United States
By Bookmasters